Canterbury Studies in Spir

A Following Holy Life

Jeremy Taylor and his Writings

Edited and introduced by
Kenneth Stevenson

Canterbury
Press
Norwich

First published in 2011 by the Canterbury Press Norwich
Editorial office
13–17 Long Lane,
London, SC1A 9PN, UK

Canterbury Press is an imprint of Hymns Ancient & Modern Ltd
(a registered charity)
13A Hellesdon Park Road
Norwich, Norfolk, NR6 5DR, UK

www.scm-canterburypress.co.uk

British Library Cataloguing in Publication data

A catalogue record for this book is available from the British Library

978 1 85311 982 8

Typeset by The Manila Typesetting Company
Printed and bound in Great Britain by
Lightning Source UK

Contents

Preface

When I was a theological student, a visiting lecturer tried to put us all off Jeremy Taylor. In time, I was able to adjust such a view considerably. His name kept coming up in conversations and in some of the readings in the various anthologies that have appeared since then. But it was when I became a parish priest that I really began to appreciate both the depth and the scope of his writing, not just 'Holy Living' – perhaps his best-known work – but other aspects of his theology.

Dated as his florid language and penitential tone appear to a culture that prefers the epigrammatic and suspects certain kinds of self-examination, Taylor's continues to resound across the centuries. In an age of polarized religious views, he held out for a thoughtful liberality that didn't avoid difficult questions. It was an age to which he brought his own distinct approach to sacramental theology; an age of both bawdiness and repression that could benefit from what he wrote about sex as something to be enjoyed responsibly; an age that had its fair share of economic exploitation, in which he took pains to warn against profiteering. And he had the courage to challenge what he saw as the overly negative view of original sin prevalent in his time.

In putting this collection together, I want to thank Christine Smith and Natalie Watson of Canterbury Press for their kindness and cooperation. And among the many people who have nurtured my appreciation of Taylor over the years, I must mention Henry McAdoo, who devoted so much of his retirement to the study of Taylor's many works, and Jessica Martin for her assistance as well.

Kenneth Stevenson
Chichester, December 2010

Introduction

Jeremy Taylor – Life, Writings and Theology

Taylor's life – a snapshot[1]

Jeremy Taylor was born in Cambridge in 1613 and died in Lisburn, Northern Ireland, in 1667. Into those fifty-four years he managed to pack a great deal, and not just in all his writings, which are contained in no fewer than ten volumes. He was a Cambridge scholar, an Oxford don, a parish priest in Rutland and then in Northamptonshire. Coming into prominence as a young preacher, he became a chaplain to the King and served later as a chaplain in the Royalist army. The victory of Oliver Cromwell (1599–1658) over King Charles I (1600–49) cost Taylor his career in the Church, and he lived a kind of internal exile from 1655 as a personal chaplain to an aristocrat in Carmarthenshire which was from a literary point of view the most prolific of his life. Imprisoned on three occasions for his views, another chaplaincy was eventually found for him in 1658, this time in Lisburn, not far from Belfast. At the Restoration in 1660, when Charles II came home as King, Taylor probably hoped he would be given an English bishopric, but he was made Bishop of Down and Connor, and Vice-Chancellor of Trinity College, Dublin.

1 Based on various sources, principally: C. J. Stranks, *The Life and Writings of Jeremy Taylor*, Church Historical Society, London: SPCK, 1952; P. G. Stanwood (ed.), *Jeremy Taylor: Holy Living and Holy Dying*, vol. I: *Holy Living*, Oxford: Clarendon Press, 1989; Thomas Carroll, *Wisdom and Waterland: Jeremy Taylor in his Prose and Preaching Today*, Dublin: Four Courts Press, 2001; H. Boone Porter, *Jeremy Taylor – Liturgist*, Alcuin Club Collections 61, London: SPCK, 1979; and the 'Life', in Reginald Heber and Charles Eden (eds), *The Whole Works of Jeremy Taylor*, vol. I, London: Longmans, 1847, pp. ix–ccl.

His life and writings in context[2]

Cambridge, London, Oxford, rural parish ministry, Civil War, imprisonments, domestic chaplaincy in Wales, parish chaplaincy in Ulster and a rural Irish bishopric: in some ways, this is a story of achievement nipped in the bud, and triumph prevailing over tragedy. But Taylor's voice and personality keep coming through, and they explain why he emerges from the turbulent mid-seventeenth century as one of the most formative Anglicans of his time. Before we look at the main aspects of his theological works, we need to see his life and writings in a wider context. The published works of any author have an 'occasional' quality to them, for the obvious reason that they emerge at a particular time, arising from circumstances as much to do with the development of the author's thinking as the era in which they live. Taylor's writings all have something that responds to a particular context while reflecting an overall maturing theology that is practical rather than systematic.

Taylor's background was neither impoverished nor well-to-do. His father, Nathaniel, was a Cambridge barber, who sent him to the Perse Grammar School, when he was six years old. Stephen Perse was a Fellow of Gonville and Caius College, and Taylor went there at the age of fifteen in 1628. We do not know the details of his course of studies, but we can be sure that they involved being steeped in the classics, an experience from which Taylor would have emerged fully accomplished in Latin and Greek. In many respects, a mind-frame shaped by the Renaissance in this way suited him well. In 1633 he was appointed to a Fellowship. Such a move required him to be ordained, in his case at the tender and technically uncanonical age of twenty (he should have been twenty-three).

In the following year, Taylor had what would nowadays be called a lucky break, when he had to stand in for a friend who was supposed to preach in St Paul's Cathedral. Someone with his talents in language and communication was bound to attract notice. It began with William Laud (1573–1644), Archbishop of Canterbury, who appointed him as one of his chaplains, and it led to being noticed by the King as well, and a move to Oxford, where Laud engineered a Fellowship for him at

2 See Reginald Heber and Charles Eden (eds), *The Whole Works of Jeremy Taylor*, vols I–X, London: Longmans, 1847–54; which should be read with Robert Gathorne-Hardy and William Proctor Williams, *A Bibliography of the Writings of Jeremy Taylor*, Dakelib IL: Northern Illinois University Press, 1971.

All Souls. There was some opposition to this, which may have been as much about Laud's way of working as about Taylor himself. One of the more influential Fellows was Gilbert Sheldon (1598–1677), who was to develop a somewhat cautious attitude towards Taylor, which probably explained why as Archbishop of Canterbury after the Restoration he did nothing to secure him an English diocese.

Among other contacts in Oxford, Taylor met William Chillingworth (1602–44) and the 'Great Tew Circle', whose theological views were for more 'latitude' in dealing with religious controversy, a recurrent theme in Taylor's later writings. Chillingworth did not doubt Taylor's ability but observed an unfortunate opinionated streak: 'he slights too much many times the arguments of those he discourses with'.[3] This may have been another cause for reserve in some quarters about him, perhaps added to by his suave style and good looks. But in that remark can be seen something else in Taylor: the makings of a man who sometimes needed to clear his mind while speaking and then express it primarily by writing.

The next stage in Taylor's life saw him appointed to the livings of Uppingham, Rutland (1638), and then Overstone, near Wellingborough (1643). Uppingham, according to John Evelyn (1620–1706) the diarist, whom Taylor was soon to befriend, was a poverty-stricken parish where he put into practice the liturgical customs of the 'Laudian' school, with a fully appointed chancel, altar-table, an organ, and more frequent (probably monthly) celebrations of the Eucharist; and he will have relished its elegant Elizabethan pulpit. He married his first wife Phoebe Landisdale there in 1639. He does not seem to have spent much time at Overstone, where he was presented after being extruded from Uppingham as the Civil War gathered momentum and his association with the Royalist cause made him unacceptable.

His Gunpowder Day Sermon delivered in Oxford in 1638, a workmanlike performance but no more, had allied him to the King; and this was even more the case with 'Episcopacy Asserted' (1642), written at a time when Presbyterians and Independents were renewing their attacks on the office of bishop, so that figures like Taylor and Henry Hammond (1605–60), another staunch and open defender of the episcopal office, whose influential 'Practical Catechism' first appeared in 1644, were bound to meet with decisive opposition. 'Episcopacy Asserted' is

3 Quoted, for example, in Gathorne-Hardy and Proctor Williams, *A Bibliography of the Writings of Jeremy Taylor*, p. 17.

a notable, thorough work. While lacking some of the inspiring qualities of Taylor's later output, it expounds the biblical and patristic evidence for episcopacy, in succession to the apostles, and separate from the presbyterate; he also makes a strong link between king and bishop – and Charles I is supposed to have encouraged his being made an Oxford DD for it.

When the Parliamentary forces took Cardigan Castle on the Pembrokeshire coast in 1645, Taylor was among those taken prisoner. This was probably because he was a Royalist army chaplain, but it may have been that he was in Wales already, seeking a livelihood away from Oxford, where he no longer felt welcome. Taylor was now to all intents and purposes about to enter a spell of living as an internal exile, not far from Cardigan. Initially, he helped run a school at Newton Hall in Llanfihangel-Aberbythych, to the west of Carmarthen in the Tywi valley. In the vicinity was Golden Grove, the large residence of Richard Vaughan (?1600–86), Earl of Carbery, Royalist commander in Pembrokeshire, in whose household Taylor soon went to serve as chaplain. In the comparative peace and tranquillity of this base, and with the friendship of Lady Frances Carbery, Taylor embarked on the most fruitful phase of his writing career. Had history turned out otherwise, he might have been given higher office in the Church at this stage in his life. So the works – and they are many and varied – kept flowing from his pen. It was a case of turning adversity into creativity, and it made his reputation for future generations.

Confined from the outer world, but aided by his teeming brain and amazing memory for facts and quotations, Taylor set to work in a way that could not be interpreted as trying to curry favour with his oppressors. In 1646, 'Prayer Ex Tempore' appeared, intended as a counterblast to the official 'Westminster Directory' (1644/45), which both outlawed and superseded the Book of Common Prayer in a Reformed direction. With quiet but firm courtesy, Taylor rehearses the arguments against 'free prayer' in public and those in favour of a set liturgy, as the possession of the whole Church; he expanded it into a much larger work three years later, 'Apology for Authorised and Set Forms of Liturgy' (1649), the year of the King's execution. But his first really major work was 'The Liberty of Prophesying' (1647), in which he argued against any kind of persecution for religious reasons, a liberal approach that may well have owed something to his friendship with Chillingworth and his circle. It is Taylor at his most judicious and fair, setting out the views of Anabaptists and Roman Catholics, refuting them where necessary, but pressing for generosity and liberality in an age that on the whole did not find such an approach congenial. The King was said not to be over-impressed by it. It was but one example among others where Taylor was ahead of his time.

Taylor was also working on a major project that had a less 'occasional' flavour, which embodies Taylor's whole theology – 'The Great Exemplar of Sanctity and Holy Life' (1649). The 'exemplar' in the title is, of course, Christ himself. It was a bold venture; while devotional books of various kinds were frequent best-sellers in the seventeenth century, this one was far more lengthy and complex. In genre, it is a kind of extended variation of the late mediaeval tradition, well-known through the 'Imitation of Christ' of Thomas à Kempis (c. 1380–1471). It does, however, have the unique distinction of being the very first of its kind to appear in English that is based throughout on a narrative of the life of Christ, and Taylor leaves his own stamp on it. The starting-point is not where it might have been for the time: the human condition, our sinfulness, our need for salvation, and the ways to deal with that through faith and forgiveness, or rather (to use more theological language) justification and sanctification. Taylor instead places us within the narrative that the Gospels provide, and he enfolds it with discussions on baptism, Eucharist, repentance, hints of his view on original sin, and much else, including the practical application of the faith to daily life. 'Great Exemplar', partly because of its subject, scope and length, contains the main features of Taylor's theology, which re-appear and become developed in his later works.

Unwieldy as the book is, it succeeds through the constant sequence of narratives, reflections (which he calls 'considerations'), and discourses – these last probably based on sermons preached from his time in Uppingham, and possibly even earlier. According to Jessica Martin, this threefold, almost Trinitarian pattern is derived from Bernard of Clairvaux's 'Memory' (Father), 'Understanding' (Son) and 'Will' or 'Love' (Holy Spirit), and is intended to give shape to the reader's approach to the work as a whole, helping to make Christ's life accessible to us. She sees the same three processes appear in the 'Discourse' on Meditation, where memory is about instruction, understanding directed to consideration, and will concerns reception. There are also copious prayers, christologically focused, which are appropriate for this kind of work, and a feature of Taylor's liturgical compositions to come. McAdoo likes to summarize Taylor's description of the work near the opening dedication as 'practical divinity'. It ran into several editions, the eighth in 1694. Taylor's free use of all four Gospels as a basis for his theological and devotional reflections obviously pre-dates biblical criticism, so that a book of this genre in our time would be difficult to write.[4] But it is still a remarkable achievement. What holds it together is its threefold structure: from the Annunciation to the Temptation; from Cana to the second year of Christ's preaching (reflecting here the shape of John's Gospel); and from then onwards to the crucifixion, death and resurrection. He has so much to say, but there is no 'slowing down' at the conclusion, with the result that the Ascension is not perhaps milked for its full meaning and significance.

Although Taylor incorporated a lot of his teaching about baptism elsewhere in this work, such as at the baptism of Christ, and in the lengthy 'Discourse' on Repentance, he took the opportunity to insert an additional 'Discourse on Baptism' (1653), and, a few years later, an early Syriac prayer which in those days was attributed to Christ at his own baptism (1657). This has the effect of placing Baptism more prominently in his theological scheme, with a starting-point of an almost iconographical kind based on the Jordan scene (Matt. 3.13–17) as a manifestation of the Trinity; this is a patristic motif that first appears in one of Augustine's earliest sermons, and also used by Lancelot Andrewes (1555–1624) earlier in the century.

'Great Exemplar' was overshadowed by the death of Lady Carbery, which launched Taylor in another new direction, the funeral sermon crafted along the conventional lines of such preaching, first on the Gospel text, and then giving reflections on the deceased – a tendency that could be followed in our own time. Around 1650 Taylor lost his wife Phoebe, a tragedy which merely added to his deprivations. Hemmed in as Taylor may have been by life's difficulties, he kept his pen in his hand and wrote copiously, perhaps even as a kind of therapy from it all. In 1650 came what is probably his best-known book of all – 'the Rule and Exercises of Holy Living', which was followed in 1651 by 'the Rule and Exercises of Holy Dying'. Both works were dedicated to Carbery, for it was Lady Carbery who apparently had encouraged him to write them. Both reflect the troubled times in which they were written – the 'epistle dedicatory' to the first work hits the nail on the head when near the start Taylor observes that 'men are apt to prefer a prosperous error to an afflicted truth'. Both books were best-sellers and reached their seventeenth editions in 1695. Although written separately, and (under-

4 H. R. McAdoo, *First of Its Kind: Jeremy Taylor's Life of Christ*, Norwich: Canterbury Press, 1994; see also Ian Green, *Print and Protestantism in Early Modern England*, Oxford: University Press, 2000, pp. 173–4; I am particularly grateful to Jessica Martin for the analysis in her paper, 'Jeremy Taylor's *Life of Christ*'.

standably for their subject-matter) in different styles, they were often bound together. The first proper combined edition appeared in 1700.

In the period since, they have frequently been reprinted and sometimes adapted and abbreviated. Although not as popular in our time as they once were, they probably remain Taylor's most lasting legacy to the Catholic Church. Both books take the reader on a journey which is interspersed with reflections and prayers, a medium in which Taylor excelled. In contrast to 'Great Exemplar', which starts with the life of Christ, Taylor now reaches more directly (and more accessibly) to the human soul. For example, 'Holy Living' begins with our use of time, and ends with teaching about the Eucharist and prayers in preparation for communion; there is even a prayer for the anniversary of one's baptism. He seems to cover everything in a 'holy life', including the physical side of marriage. He was the first devotional writer to do so, without any of the Augustinian baggage in that regard that has hampered Western Christianity for so long. For Taylor, sex could be a good thing, and therefore was to be enjoyed. Perhaps this was another area where he upset the more conventional minds of his time.

The next few years saw the appearance of some smaller works. These included collections of his sermons (1651 and 1653), with the two issued together as 'Eniautos', for the whole year. Surprisingly for someone of his Prayer Book views, these were not arranged in a strictly liturgical way to correspond with the Church Year. Among them were two on marriage, which have a strongly lyrical as well as practical quality, as well as one condemning death-bed confession, a recurring theme in Taylor, already explored in 'Great Exemplar', which rings a somewhat sour note for modern Christians, as it may well have done then. These sermons were probably preached at Golden Grove, though opinions differ on whether they were delivered in exactly the same form as they were printed.

There are hints that at this stage he spent time on visits to London. John Evelyn notes in his diary that he travelled there to hear Taylor preach on 15 April 1654 at St Gregory's Church, near St Paul's Cathedral, a small building, one of the few places where Oliver Cromwell permitted the Prayer Book services to be used. What a contrast from twenty years earlier, when he preached as an aspiring twenty-two year-old in the Cathedral itself! In that year appeared 'Real Presence', a serious exposition of eucharistic theology, directed against Transubstantiation (named in the characteristically lengthy title), as well as some of the Reformed views of the sacrament. It goes without saying that one of the challenges facing Anglicans (often more accurately described nowadays as 'Prayer Book Conformists'), particularly in the first part of the seventeenth century was along these lines. Transubstantiation was anathema for them and all the churches of the Reformation. Taylor was by no means alone in refuting it at the time. John Cosin (1594–1672), Restoration Bishop of Durham, was doing the same from the vantage-point of his self-imposed exile in Paris. We shall look at this question in more detail later. Taylor comes through this tricky exercise, backed up as it is with copious quotations from the patristic, mediaeval, Reformation and Counter-Reformation writers, with his stress on mystery and sacramentality – the devotional rather than the systematic writer.

Whatever people thought of 'Real Presence', Taylor's next publication irritated the authorities sufficiently to have him imprisoned again, at Chepstow. 'Golden Grove' (1655) is a small book of prayers and devotions, with a preface openly bemoaning the barren character of the Church in his time, and going so far as to say that 'the people have fallen under the harrows and saws of impertinent and ignorant preachers'. It reached its twentieth edition in 1700, which speaks for itself. On release from prison, Taylor went to Mandinam, not far from Golden Grove, where Joanna Bridges lived, whom he married around this time. There doesn't seem to have been a formal break with Carbery, but Cromwell had just decreed that Royalists were not allowed to keep private chaplains.

The real bombshell of his career, however, came in a book also published in 1655 on which he had obviously been working for some time, 'Unum Necessarium, or the Doctrine and Practice of Repentance'. Taylor wrote it as a general but probing devotional work, and most of it passed without comment. The one exception was chapter six, on original sin. He must have known that he was walking on theological egg-shells, since he had tested some of it out on Brian Duppa, Bishop of Salisbury (1588–1662). The book nonetheless unleashed a storm that made Taylor suspect in many peoples' minds for the rest of his life. What he said about original sin conflicted with the traditional tough Augustinian approach that held sway, with some variation, throughout the Catholic and Protestant world. It elicited from Taylor a 'Further Explication' (1656), which became chapter seven in subsequent editions, as well as correspondence with interlocutors after that.

To put it at its briefest, Taylor believed that we do not inherit Adam's guilt, but only the consequences of Adam's fall, which leaves us naturally sinful, but left us with the choice of 'holy living'. It was perhaps not the best time in the Church's history to propound a less pessimistic view about human nature. But although this debate rumbled on, it is clearly an area where Taylor was too far from public religious opinion. He was not undermining the reality of sin, the need for repentance, or, for that matter, the pastoral strength of private confession. But he was enough of a scholar of the Reformation to know that Article IX of the Thirty-Nine was not hard-line Calvinism, but was couched in carefully nuanced language. Taylor's approach would nowadays be called 'ecclesial', with sin and forgiveness placed in the sacramental context of baptism and Eucharist, something earlier Anglican divines such as Andrewes propounded. But the emphasis on free will that he taught and which may be regarded as a consequence of his emphasis on human freedom, left him stigmatized by his detractors with Semi-Pelagianism. The controversy emboldened him, and strained a number of friendships in consequence.

* * *

Then, in 1657, Taylor published a 'Discourse on Friendship', which was a letter to Katharine Phillips, a prominent young playwright married to an aged Roundhead. On the face of it, all Taylor is doing is defining the nature of Christian friendship, with its pitfalls and possibilities, as well as drawing out the particular characteristics of the female gender in this regard. And that is how successive writers in the period since have interpreted it. But Katharine Phillips, known in her literary circle as 'the matchless Orinda', had a very strong relationship with another woman, Anne Owen, about which she wrote a poem that – certainly to modern eyes – could (some would say should) be interpreted in lesbian terms, as Reginald Askew has shown.[5] Taylor's prose can be delightfully elusive at the best of times, but it is hard not to agree with such a fresh reading of Taylor's line. Homosexuality had been part of the court life of King James I, so that it was not a subject that could be avoided altogether. Writers like the Puritan leader Richard Baxter (1615–91) condemn it. Taylor on the other hand takes what would nowadays be called a 'pastoral' approach. We shall return to this later. But it is yet another area where Taylor, if the more – encoded – specific interpretation is accepted, was ahead of his time, and could therefore have been the subject of muted controversy.

Taylor's London trips seem to have been on the increase at this stage. John Evelyn, one of the few to stand by him in the furore over original sin, used him as what we would nowadays call a spiritual director.

---

5 Reginald Askew, *Muskets and Altars: Jeremy Taylor and the Last of the Anglicans*, London: Mowbrays, 1997, pp. 182–90.

Indeed, Evelyn's diary refers to services conducted by Taylor, including a Eucharist on 7 February 1658. At some stage, Taylor was imprisoned in the Tower of London, either in 1657 or, more likely, 1658. He had just published his 'Collection of Offices', the first Anglican to write his own liturgy. It is a rich series of services for all the occasions (and more as well) which are covered by the officially outlawed Book of Common Prayer, the only exception being the marriage service, which would have been excluded for legal reasons; Taylor defended the view that marriage was a sacrament. In these liturgies, Taylor's prose can at times be lavish, the prayers frequently more Trinitarian in scope than Cranmer's, and the sources often from the Greek liturgies of St Basil and St James. Consistent with his stress in 'Great Exemplar' on Christ's baptism as the prototype of ours, he has Jesus at the River Jordan as one of the lections in his baptismal office, unique in his time, but more familiar now in our day. Although Taylor could – just! – defend his book as within the flexible, anti-specific bounds of the Westminster Directory (1644), it may not have done him many favours with the authorities, and, on a wider front, may well have been the cause of his time in the Tower.

It probably became clear to his supporters that Taylor needed to be got out of the way, and a solution came through another aristocratic friendship, this time with Edward Conway, a strong Royalist who owned estates in Ulster. It took the form of a parish lectureship, to be shared with a Presbyterian. Taylor at first turned it down, but was persuaded to accept. He thus came to Lisnagarvey (from 1662 referred to as Lisburn) south-west of Belfast, a small town built around the castle where the Conways resided. He soon settled at Portmore, nor far away, and his main work was looking after the Conway household. It provided him with some respite, but hardly total seclusion from religious troubles, as the local population was divided between Scots Presbyterians colonized there and the Irish community who were Roman Catholics, and who had no desire to embrace Anglicanism.

In these last days, months, and years of the Commonwealth, Taylor completed his largest book of all. He had been working on it for some time. He used to refer to as his 'cases of conscience', and it appeared in 1660 as 'Ductor Dubitantium or the Rule of Conscience'. Twice as long as 'Great Exemplar', it represents a considerable amount of learning, and Taylor would have been justified in hoping that it would establish his reputation as a really major writer in his time. Casuistry as a field of what we would nowadays call social and pastoral theology was at its apogee in the Roman Catholic Church, partly as an aid to priests in the confessional, but it also figured among some Protestant theologians as well. It is long, thorough, and at times repetitive, but it shows Taylor as the pastoral theologian that he always was, responding to dilemmas that people might have over their faith, how they were to live the Christian life, and how society should be ordered in the best possible way for all this to happen.

With Oliver Cromwell dead in 1658, the hopes for a new régime had arisen. Taylor travelled to London in 1660 for the return of Charles II, to whom he wrote the dedication of his 'magnum opus'. Although others before him like Lancelot Andrewes had written on casuistry, it was the sheer length, scrupulous detail, and exhaustive breadth that marked it out but also limited its readership (a fourth edition appeared in 1698). It comes in four books, which deal with conscience and its definitions, divine laws, human laws, and the nature of good and evil. Book III has some observations about Church and State that are now dated, but what he has to say about free will in Book IV can be seen as a necessary corrective to popular piety at the time. A key throughout this complex work is the relationship between the givenness of revelation and the working of human rationality; for Taylor, faith and reason have to go hand in hand, not just in making sense of belief, but in applying it to everyday life.

In the same year he brought out 'Worthy Communicant', which was the last of his devotional works and which he dedicated to Princess Mary of Orange. Set in a wider context, it forms part of the Restoration drive towards proper teaching about the Eucharist and more frequent celebrations of the sacrament, of which the 'Mensa Mystica' of Simon Patrick (1625–1707) is another example, published in the same year.[6] There is a directness and a solemnity about the work, which sums up Taylor's theology in a readable and deep manner, and one of my treasured possessions is a first edition.

All this might well have given Taylor the hope of an English bishopric in the newly restored Established Church, with Prayer Book and episcopacy re-established alongside the monarchy. But perhaps Taylor's reputation among those in power in the Church was still tarnished by his plea for toleration in 'Liberty of Prophesying', the disputes over original sin in the aftermath of 'Unum Necessarium', and one might hazard a guess over other matters as well, including his liturgical project, the 'Collection of Offices'. Sheldon was now Bishop of London, a

6 Kenneth W. Stevenson, *Covenant of Grace Renewed: A Vision of the Eucharist in the Seventeenth Century*, London: Darton, Longman and Todd, 1994, pp. 111–27.

key player soon to move to Canterbury as the successor of the ailing William Juxon (1582–1663).

So it was back to Ulster that he went, but this time as Bishop of Down and Connor, the diocese in which he had lived as chaplain to the Conways, and to which Dromore was subsequently added as a responsibility. His consecration was a great occasion, the re-establishment of Anglicanism in Ireland. He was consecrated alongside two archbishops and nine other bishops in St Patrick's Cathedral, Dublin, on 27 January 1661, and he himself was chosen as the preacher, a mark of the confidence placed in him by the Restoration Church in Ireland. The sermon, subsequently published along with some others – including that preached at Lady Carbery's funeral – in 1663 as a supplement to the 'Eniautos' collection ten years earlier, is predictably a strong defence of episcopacy. Taylor was enough of a realist to know that he himself was not going to have an easy time in a diocese where the majority of the clergy were Presbyterians. It was already a country where the religious ethos was more Calvinist in leanings than England, doubtless partly due to the need to define itself more clearly over against the preponderantly Roman Catholic population.

Denied preferment in England, Taylor became the main theological driving force of the new Irish Bench, along with William Bramhall (1594–1663), Archbishop of Dublin, at whose funeral he preached in 1663. His largely Presbyterian clergy did not take kindly to the ways of their new bishop, perhaps hoping for a policy inspired by 'Liberty of Prophesying' that had been shaped by the needs of a different era. He was appointed Vice-Chancellor of the University of Dublin in 1661. This entailed a certain amount of time in residence there and it was a task that involved him in a great deal of financial and administrative work, at which he was well-skilled. A small university, it was nevertheless an important post, where he said he 'found all things in a perfect disorder'. But Taylor had a strange knack of seeing things whole, and it is interesting to observe that the sermon he preached before the University in 1661 (published as 'Via Intelligentiae') was based largely on a Visitation Charge to his diocese, two somewhat different contexts!

In the same year, he produced his 'Rules and Advices to Clergy', which went into its fourth edition in 1678. Short and simple, it speaks of the importance of prayer, self-knowledge, and decorum in worship. The demands of his new twin responsibilities and the pressures he was under to fulfil them led to a diminishing in the flow of his pen. But in 1663 he was able to produce his 'Discourse on Confirmation', which, though short by his own standards, is nonetheless probably the first and the most comprehensive treatment by an Anglican of the subject. The Restoration had brought to a head the need to defend Confirmation by the Bishop to its Reformed critics, because so many people had not been confirmed at all. Taylor entered the fray with a blend of biblical exegesis, patristic learning, and argument from tradition. Not all these grounds would pass muster today, for example his treatment of the New Testament evidence, but it was a valiant attempt, and a milestone in the long sequence of works on the subject written since then.

But Taylor still yearned for a job in England, and (perhaps unwisely) wrote to Sheldon in 1663 pleading his case, though indicating he was aware that he himself might be the main barrier to such a move. This might refer solely to the controversies of his writings, but it doubtless also echoed something along the lines of that personality trait noted years earlier by Chillingworth, a lack of courtesy with his interlocutors. Whatever was the case, no reply came, and in Ireland Taylor was to remain for the rest of his days.

He was encouraged by his episcopal colleagues to write the last main publication of his life, 'A Dissuasive against Popery' (1664), a challenge he took up with reluctance. It is not difficult to see the background to this particular work, given the deeply embedded character of Irish Catholicism. But from it emerges the kind of broad-based, tradition-centred Anglicanism that is the hallmark of much of Taylor's theology. There is, understandably for the times, a negative edge of polemic that the modern reader, in more ecumenical times, finds hard to take. But the heat of Reformation controversy was still intense, and Taylor's answer to the perennial question, 'Where was your Church before the Reformation?' is strong, confident, lucid, and unyielding, as he argues against the doctrinal innovations, moral weaknesses and political subversions, as he sees them, of the Roman Catholicism of the time.

We cannot, however, simply leave Taylor there. His last years, though tough going, were spent on visiting his parishes, rebuilding churches, and caring for those who would allow him to do so. After Bramhall's death, he was without doubt the key theological figure in Irish Anglicanism. But his health was declining. Of his two sons, one was killed in a duel, and the other died of a fever. It was shortly after his second son's funeral that he himself took ill after visiting a sick person, and he died at Lisburn on 13 August 1667. He was buried in Dromore Cathedral, which he himself had built, and the funeral sermon was preached by his old friend, George Rust (+ 1670), who was to succeed as bishop – a bold preaching of the gospel of hope and a fine account of Taylor's life, personality, and ministry.

When Sheldon heard of his death, although he had helped secure him financial assistance when he needed it, he still described him as 'a man of dangerous temper, apt to break into extravagance'.[7] Quite a lot may lie behind this verdict, both personal and theological. Fortunately, however, that is not the overall view of history. Taylor may have got across people in authority through his personal style – many great men do that to some extent or another. And he certainly rocked the theological boat over a few matters at a time when the anxiety level in the Church was understandably high. But he did, said and wrote many things that badly needed doing, saying and writing, and we in posterity are indeed the richer for it.

The main aspects of Taylor's theology

Style

There are two ways of approaching Taylor's style. One is to appreciate the sheer breadth of the reading-audiences he has in mind. Like other writers of his time and before and since, he recognizes the importance of the medium in communicating the message. Thus, 'Worthy Communicant' (1660) is written for the devout layperson, whereas 'Real Presence' (1654), for all its lively, sharp style, is intended for a more scholarly audience. While the 'Discourse on Friendship' (1657) has the inevitable format of a personal letter, 'Ductor Dubitantium' (1660), his longest work, reads like a resource to be consulted, and – unlike most of his works, which were published in octavo or, increasingly later in his life, in quarto – this one appeared in folio form. And while some of the earlier works, such as 'Episcopacy Asserted' (1642) show signs of an aspiring author still coming to terms with how to write clearly and fluently, by the time we reach 'Great Exemplar' (1649) and 'Holy Living' (1650), he seems to have mastered his trade. Reginald Askew has some of his quotations from Taylor's writings laid out in a kind of blank verse. At times it seems a little contrived, but it certainly brings out some of the linguistic devices in Taylor's use of words.

On the other hand, as many others have shown, while the verve and imagery of Taylor's prose at times seems unstoppable, there is a considerable amount of light and shade, with contrasts between the lengthy

7 Quoted in C. J. Stranks, *The Life and Writings of Jeremy Taylor*, Church Historical Society, London: SPCK, 1952, p. 216.

sentence and the pithy oneliner. 'His language comes with a rush . . . the style swoops and soars with the freedom of a bird.'[8] Some of the purple passages in 'Great Exemplar' (1649), with those repeated references to 'the holy Jesus', and the constant use of the imprecise plural, for example in 'eucharists' (which must have non-sacramental as well as sacramental references), keep carrying the reader along. And his dramatic, almost 'off-stage' passages capture the imagination, whether he is indulging in a gentle flight of fancy (the Virgin Mary's 'burden' in the young child in her womb is a light one, because it is Christ himself), or articulating a vivid understanding of the Trinity (as in the Baptism of Christ at the Jordan).

Taylor as the pastoral theologian comes across powerfully in the funeral sermon for Lady Carbery (1650). Product of the age as it is, it manages to express a depth of emotion that avoids a too overt display of it. The handsome man who was perhaps a passionate lover was someone who appreciated beauty both in other people and in the art of prose. And here, unsurprisingly but doubtless to his disappointment, while he could write prose that had poetic resonances, he was not himself a gifted creator of poetry! His efforts at hymn-writing were not successful.

Some of those long sentences that occasionally slip into anacoluthon, when he loses the thread of what he is trying to say as he presses on with the ideas he is trying to convey eventually give birth to a short and memorable 'bon mot'. A good example is in his 'Discourse on Prayer' in 'Great Exemplar' (1649): 'He [God] measures us by our needs, and we must not measure him by our impatience'; and in the accompanying exposition of the Lord's Prayer, equally full of one-liners, he follows the Syriac text at 'daily bread', which helps him produce the sequence, food for today, forgiveness for yesterday, protection in the future.[9] But although Taylor knew and thought deeply about what is often called the spiritual life, it did not give him the same kind of inside knowledge of sin as other writers such as John Donne (1571/72–1632), who perhaps had more direct personal experience of living torridly on the edge of

8 Stranks, *Life and Writings*, pp. 289–96.

9 Perhaps the most difficult area of interpretation; see general Kenneth W. Stevenson, *The Lord's Prayer: A Text in Tradition*, London: SCM and Minneapolis: Fortress Press, 2005, and esp. pp. 182–3, on Taylor, who, like other seventeenth-century Anglican writers, deals with the prayer in seven petitions (the Latin tradition), but structures it round six, merging temptation and evil, and commends the doxology (the Greek – Erasmus – Calvin tradition), not added to the Prayer Book version, and only in certain services, till 1662.

Christian practice. At times, Taylor – by any standards – 'overdoes things', but the underlying repetitions of important themes have the cumulative effect of bringing the reader along, and keeping their attention.

Theological position

Taylor's overall place in the Anglican spectrum can best be described for his own times as 'Laudian' and 'Latitudinarian', or what would nowadays be described as 'liberal Catholic'.[10] This comes across in the sacramental and ecclesiological slant in his theology and the amount of attention he gives to baptism and Eucharist and the controversies of his age that surrounded them. He will quote Augustine and John Chrysostom. But he is very much his own man, writing and preaching for his own age, and in a much plainer style, and the questions and questionings of his time are often uppermost in his mind. His Trinitariansm is deep-rooted, coming across in a number of contrasting ways, from his treatment of the baptism of Christ to his assertion that God dwells among mortals, making us 'cabinets of the mysterious Trinity' – in a strong passage near the start of 'Holy Living.' That in turn produces an equally strong pneumatology, not just in his sacramental theology, but in the Christian life.

This trait must have made him a congenial (if talkative!) companion at the Great Tew Circle, with William Chillingworth. Towards the end of his life, in the 'Dissuasive from Popery' (1664), he can lace his discussion with patristic references, but can still assert boldly that 'it is false that the testimony of the fathers . . . is infallible'. These are hardly the words of a patristic romantic. They do, however, come from someone who relied heavily upon them but who was prepared to take theological risks as well. This stemmed from a firm conviction about the use of reason, as an imaginative, God-given faculty, both in theological and moral discourse. So the parallel with later Anglicanism is probably more with the Liberal Catholic Charles Gore (1853–1932) than with the Tractarian Edward Pusey (1800–82). At a time when Anglicanism was experiencing acutely the need for self-definition, Taylor proved to be an uncomfortable (and even prophetic) figure. In the period since, those who have tried to combine the love of tradition and an openness to new questions have not always been easy to live with. But they have frequently stood the test of time.

---

10 Paul Avis, *Anglicanism and the Christian Church: Theological Resources in Historical Perspective*, Edinburgh: T & T Clark, 1989, pp. 121–7.

Platonism

Like many of his generation, such as Ralph Cudworth (1617–88), John Smith (1618–52) and others, Taylor was strongly influenced by Platonism.[11] This was part and parcel of his classical education as an undergraduate and it spilled over into his theological writings as well. This manifests itself in two particular ways. One concerns the way in which God's self-revelation is perceived. In order to illustrate this, Taylor frequently uses the image of the 'cloud', to draw out the mysteriousness of the deity and the uncertainty of human life, with repeated references to the 'cloud' that reveals the truth partially, as mystery. This is vintage Taylor, as it demonstrates both the theologian and the pastor of souls at work. It also shows how his 'holy living' theology of following Christ can embrace the whole of life, moments of revelation, in preaching and sacraments, as well as the many moments and experiences of disorientation and confusion.

The other main area where this Platonist influence is apparent is in his teaching about the Eucharist, and it comes across in both the main controvertial areas of the time – presence and sacrifice. For any seventeenth-century Anglican of Taylor's persuasion, living at the particular time he did, this whole area was a bit of a theological minefield. Following in the steps of Richard Hooker (c. 1554–1600) and Lancelot Andrewes, Taylor refuses neat definitions of either aspect of the Eucharist, especially that of presence, bringing in instead a firm but non-evasive reticence.

It is easy for theologians of a later generation, who were not immersed in the polemics of Taylor's age, to underestimate his subtlety, and to suggest (like Stranks) that he was not sure of his ground, and that his view was receptionist, and no more. For McAdoo, however, Taylor 'skims the cream off virtualism', the view that the consecrated elements, by being given and received in the sacrament, bring the virtue or efficacy of Christ's Body and Blood to the Church.[12] This also comes through in Taylor's strong view of the role of the Holy Spirit, coming from above to consecrate the elements on earth. In a particularly powerful passage in 'Worthy Communicant' (1660), he affirms that 'only the Spirit operates by the sacrament and the communicant receives it by his moral dispositions, by the hand of faith'. In comparative terms,

11 See Charles Taliaferro and Alison J. Teply (eds), *Cambridge Platonist Spirituality*, Classics of Western Spirituality, New York: Paulist Press, 2004.

12 H. R. McAdoo, *The Eucharistic Theology of Jeremy Taylor Today*, Norwich: Canterbury Press, 1988, pp. 143, 189; this is the definitive study of all aspects of Taylor's eucharistic theology.

this distances Taylor from the 'receptionist' view, where the presence of Christ is not in the consecrated elements, but the minds and souls of faithful communicants.

Taylor holds that both baptism and Eucharist are 'mysteries'. In 'Real Presence', he contends that 'as there [in baptism] natural water becomes the laver of regeneration, so here bread and wine become the body and blood of Christ; but there and here too the first substance is changed by grace, but remains the same in nature'. Later on, he discusses the patristic evidence to support this view, including Augustine's definition of sacraments as 'visible words'. He had already hit the nail on the head in 'Great Exemplar' (1649) with a brilliant one-liner: 'I suppose it to be a mistake to think whatsoever is real must be natural.'

For Taylor, above all a theologian of discipleship, sacraments and life are so closely connected that he articulates movement from one to the other. That same process can be seen in how he expresses the Eucharist as a memorial-sacrifice. Following Andrewes and others, he avoids an entirely mental approach. But his particular way is to do so by linking the Eucharist on earth with the heavenly intercession of Christ (Heb. 7.25, 8.1), a constant theme of his. Calvin himself had used this exegesis, and other writers followed him here. But it was honed considerably by Taylor, who – with others – handed it on to later Anglican (and other) writing, including in the hymns of Charles Wesley.[13] 'Worthy Communicant' (1660) puts it in characteristic language that combines the doctrinal with the devotional: 'to represent [Christ's] death, to commemorate this sacrifice, by humble prayers and thankful record; and by faithful manifestation and joyful Eucharist . . . the Church being the image of heaven; the priest, the minister of Christ; the holy table being a copy of the celestial altar; and the eternal sacrifice of the Lamb slain from the beginning of the world, being always the same; it bleeds no more after the finishing of it on the cross; but it is wonderfully represented in heaven, and graciously represented here; by Christ's action there, by his commandment here'. Such a perspective makes the Eucharist transcend both space and time. The 'heavenly altar' is without doubt a central plank in Taylor's understanding of the sacrifice.

It is no wonder, therefore, that McAdoo, Anglican Co-Chairman of the first Anglican–Roman Catholic International Commission, should see in Taylor an anticipation of the ecumenical agreements of recent

---

13 See Daniel B. Stevick, *The Altar's Fire: Charles Wesley's Hymns on the Lord's Supper, 1745: Introduction and Exposition*, Peterborough: Epworth Press, 2004, p. 22; cf. a similar view on Taylor's view of consecration, p. 17.

years, with those repeated periphrases that try to express 'anamnesis' such as 'representment', 'memorials', 'exhibiting' and 'consigning'. And from these, we gain a picture of the Eucharist as an action of the Church in history that is effected by Christ himself in heaven. It has elicited from Boone Porter and McAdoo the description of 'pleading' the sacrifice, which appears in the 1897 'Response' to the Vatican Condemnation of Anglican Orders. Although Taylor does not actually use the term, it began to appear in other writers at the time, including Henry Hammond, Simon Patrick, and the Puritan leader, Richard Baxter; and it has had a noble history in eucharistic discourse in the period since, including in the eucharistic rites both of the Church of Scotland (1940) and the Church of England (2000). All this helps to bring two necessary correctives for eucharistic faith and practice at the time: a sense of the transcendent and reverence, and a sense of the corporate nature of the Eucharist, rather than a collection of individuals hovering before the cross. But the close relationship between the earthly priest and the heavenly Saviour, in a semi-mediatorial role, can come across as too much of a hangover from mediaeval rather than patristic theology.

Covenant

It is all too easy to enter into discussions about sacramental theology in a vacuum, and throughout our treatment of Taylor, we have tried to set his writings in their context, and to do the same with how he writes about baptism and Eucharist. The same themes recur; the circumspect way he handles controversial areas, his Platonism in the dialectic between the earthly and the heavenly, and the devotional frame of reference, what McAdoo used to call the 'moral-ascetic theology' of much later seventeenth-century Anglican writing, that holds together the challenges of the gospel and the life of public worship and private prayer. It is all of a piece.

There is one important motif that Taylor uses to explain how the two dominical sacraments work and how they are different from each other – covenant. This has been explored, alongside Taylor's baptismal and eucharistic liturgies, by Bryan Spinks.[14] Although it does not figure

14 Bryan D. Spinks, 'Two Seventeenth-Century Examples of *Lex Credendi, Lex Orandi*: The Baptismal and Eucharistic Theologies and Liturgies of Jeremy Taylor and Richard Baxter', *Studia Liturgica* 21.2 (1991), pp. 165–89; see also Kenneth W. Stevenson, *The Mystery of Baptism in the Anglican Tradition*, Norwich: Canterbury Press, 1998, pp. 96–111.

in the language of the Prayer Book, it was a prominent feature of Reformed theology, and someone like Taylor would have to address it in some way, because by the middle of the seventeenth century it was common coin. Taylor's strategy is best described as softening the severity of the more Puritan approach, which could use the term to make the sacraments more restrictive (children of believing parents only) and exclusive (public debarring from communion). In this he resembles other writers of his time such as Herbert Thorndike (1598–1672) and Simon Patrick.

The covenant of grace is embarked upon by our surrender to God and a desire to glorify him, and God on his part pardons what is past and will assist us in our life of discipleship in the future. We enter that covenant sacramentally at the font and renew it at the altar; covenant figures a number of times in his baptism rite; in his eucharistic liturgy, it appears (as usual) in the words of Christ at the Last Supper, but nowhere else. Taylor likes to describe baptism as 'the laver of regeneration', where the Holy Spirit blesses the waters, as he did at the River Jordan, and where the believer is filled with heavenly blessing, to lead a 'holy life'. Taylor has a high view of baptism. It draws us into the Kingdom of God; it adopts us into a new covenant, with a strong view of obedience; it brings us into a new birth; it confers the remission of sins, including those yet to be committed; and brings us sanctification. 'By water we are sacramentally dead and buried, by the Spirit we are made alive . . . Baptism does also consign us to a holy resurrection.' Taylor's approach differs, however, from Thorndike's in that while the two dominical sacraments are foundational, Taylor fits baptism into Christian living – as a 'birth to grave' process – rather than into a more systematic 'theology of the Church', in the way of someone like Herbert Thorndike.

Taylor goes on to defend the practice of infant baptism, as the opening of the door to God, 'the first ordinary current in which the Spirit moves and descends upon us', requiring godparents (the traditional practice), not parents, as the Reformed-minded wanted. We come across the same balance that we saw in the Eucharist between sacrament and experience – 'baptism and its effect may be separated, and do not always go in conjunction . . . the Church gives the sacrament, God gives the grace of the sacrament'. Both here, in the Discourse on Baptism in 'Great Exemplar' (1649), and in his baptism liturgy are to be found references to the gift of the guardian angel, a notion which he clearly likes, but will not require as a belief.[15] His overall understanding of baptism, however, has

15 See B. A. Gerrish, *Grace and Gratitude: The Eucharistic Theology of John Calvin*, Minneapolis IL: Fortress Press, 1993, p. 167.

been described by Boone Porter as more Johannine (rebirth) than Pauline (dying and rising), with a strong emphasis on re-birth (John 3.5). It is certainly iconographic, as we have already suggested, by the way he uses the narrative of Christ's baptism as the place near which the Discourse is placed in 'Great Exemplar' (1649), and the way he (uniquely for his time) uses that narrative in his baptism rite.

For Taylor, the key to his thinking about baptism and Eucharist is the strong relationship between mystery and sacramentality. They are God-given mysteries, yet are sacraments that operate in our lives. Like many other writers down the ages (not just post-Reformation), he holds in tension divine act and human experience in what he teaches both about baptism and Eucharist. In his study of the eucharistic theology of John Calvin (1509–64), Brian Gerrish offers three models: symbolic memorialism, which locates the sacrament in the heart of the faithful recipient (which he associates with the Swiss Reformed Ulrich Zwingli, 1484–1531); symbolic parallelism, where the sacramental event is in parallel with the work of Christ (which he associates with Zwingli's successor, Heinrich Bullinger, 1504–75); and symbolic instrumentalism, where the sacraments are instruments of God's grace (which he associates with John Calvin). These terms are, of course, approximations, but they were certainly around in England (and elsewhere) from the Reformation onwards. Taylor, like other seventeenth-century writers, seems to move beyond these views to what has been described as 'effectual instrumentalism', which places a stronger emphasis on what the sacrament does, without underplaying human appropriation of the gifts of God, expressed by the strong role of the Holy Spirit as the means of consecration.[16]

Where does Confirmation fit in? He wrote learnedly on the subject, and saw it as a way of bringing Christians from other churches into the Anglican fold: he knows (and favours) communion for the young (and even their Confirmation) as an ancient practice in his early years as a priest, yet, as a bishop, requires the Prayer Book position on the matter; 'Worthy Communicant' (1660) concludes that infant communion is 'lawful' but not 'necessary'. And his reading of history enables him

---

16 I owe the term 'effectual instrumentalism' to Jeffrey Steel and his work on Lancelot Andrewes; for more on Taylor's liturgy, see W. J. Grisbrooke, *Anglican Liturgies of the Seventeenth and Eighteenth Centuries*, Alcuin Club Collections 40, London: SPCK, 1958, pp. 19–36, 183–99; also Porter, *Jeremy Taylor*, pp. 71–82.

In addition to its appearance in the Heber–Eden edition (vol. VIII), pp. 631–8, see Porter, *Jeremy Taylor*, for text of rite in facsimile between pp. 40 and 41.

to see the laying-on of hands by the bishop as a way of reconciling or drawing in Christians to the Church. But he still highlights the radically distinct functions of baptism as the start and the Eucharist as the renewal. That basic approach also enables him to be demanding but unrestrictive about who and how he baptizes, yet firm and searching in the recommendations he makes in all his writings on Holy Communion about due and proper preparation. In a line going back to Hooker, baptism is the start and Eucharist is the continuing of sacramental life. This could speak volumes to an age like ours, far more fragmented in human experience than many previous generations, that at times leans too heavily on different sorts of baptismal renewal.

Social and personal living

Taylor is a theologian of the whole human life-cycle, where it is difficult to distinguish between the public and the private. Otherwise we would not have had either 'Great Exemplar' (1649), 'Holy Living' (1650), or 'Ductor Dubitantium' (1660). 'Holy Living' opens on a note that could – mutatis mutandis – have been written for a modern personal organizer: 'he that is choice of his time will also be choice of his actions'. From that starting-point, he expounds the virtues of discipleship, prayer ('we are cabinets of the mysterious Trinity'), sobriety, temperance, chastity, humility, modesty, and contentedness. On chastity, he is more explicit than any Christian writer so far, on the basis that our bodies are temples of the Holy Spirit: 'in their permissions and licence, they must be sure to observe the order of nature, and the ends of God . . . with a desire of children, or to avoid fornication, or to lighten and ease the cares and sadnesses of household affairs, or to endear each other'.

Taylor is talking openly about sex as something good, fulfilling the design of human bodies. But saying these things was not always welcomed.[17] Sexual union can stem from a number of unexpressed motives: children, physical need, release from domestic tension and sheer delight in each other. This is a far cry from the traditional Western nervousness about reproductive fluids and when it is the right time and when it is not. It is also an advance on the three reasons for marriage in the Prayer Book – procreation, a remedy against sin, and companionship. Chastity, however, takes its place alongside the other virtues in stemming human

---

17 Criticized by Edmund Gosse, *Jeremy Taylor*, London: Longmans, 1903, p. 75.

desires and directing them aright. This is not part of our contemporary culture but we could be the better for at least some of it.

It is against this background that he deals with Christian justice, making the distinction between commutative (contracts and agreements between equals) and distributative (the command of God, or a relationship not between equals), and the importance of restitution as a social responsibility. Taylor, man of his time, is more deferential about authority than he would be today, but he nevertheless balances this with a definite emphasis on the responsibilities, moral and economic, of the one who wields power over the one who doesn't. This comes through in what he has to say about the State, and the place of the Church within it, in 'Ductor Dubitantium' (1660). When a civil contract is being negotiated, 'use not many words: for all the business of a bargain is summed up in few sentences; and he that speaks least means fairest, as having fewer opportunities to deceive' ('Holy Living', 1650). He condemns excessive profit-making, and the exploitation of the poor, and crippling others with excessive debt. In ways reminiscent of the mediaeval penitentials, manuals for priests when dealing with sinners, he makes recommendations about adultery resulting in offspring (pay for their upkeep) and murder of another man (ensure the widow is looked after properly).

Never one to play down the role of the entrepreneur, Taylor nonetheless cautions against greed and dishonesty, stressing again and again the importance of good human relationships. He does not go as far as Thomas Traherne (c. 1636–74) in condemning the trend from exchange-value to use-value, but he comes near it. Many more of these themes recur, and in more detail, in 'Ductor Dubitantium' (1660), which he begins with the story of a hungry child who had run away from home and wanted to be fed: what was the right course of action, because to refuse him by telling him to go back might mean he would die of hunger, and to feed him might indulge his desire to escape further? In the end, he decides to feed him, enough and no more, and rebukes him for leaving home, on condition that he will indeed return. Taylor's quaint habit of making a serious point from a homely image can be incisive, even if a touch sentimental. This is 'moral-ascetic' theology at its best. It is about real life, where faith in God, the virtues, and above all attention to the Word and the sacraments are seen to change not just individuals but society as a whole. That is why 'Holy Living' ends with teaching about prayer, the Eucharist, and preparation for and receiving the holy communion.

Then in 'Holy Dying' (1651), a book which carries echoes in many of his other writings, Taylor shows his reluctance to leave untouched any human predicament.[18] For a man who had suffered tragic bereavement himself, dying was an experience close to home, and in his time more social than it is today, where clinical medicine has been able to deal – however temporarily – with many of the diseases for which people in those days would have died more quickly. The dying person should meditate on the Ten Commandments, on God's grace, and the strength that can be derived from receiving the sacrament, and the spiritual counsel of a priest. Taylor also provides prayers that can be used by a layperson in the presence of a very sick and probably dying person.

This could reflect the times: clergy may not have been accessible. It may also reflect a suspicion of priestcraft born of Reformation sensibilities. But his concern with the passage from this life to the next is real, palpable, and insufficiently dealt with in pastoral writing today. Taylor must have been well aware of the 'Ars Moriendi' tradition of late mediaeval Catholicism, and writings in this area from the sixteenth century such as Thomas Becon (c. 1511–67) and William Perkins (1558–1602). But he is starting from scratch, and while some of the soul-searching may ring a shade lugubriously on modern ears, his association of sin and suffering clearly dated, and his opposition to death-bed repentance unacceptable today, it is a book that could, if abbreviated and presented in a fresh manner, provide a great deal of comfort to people who are afraid when their lives are drawing to an end.

Main areas of controversy

Controversy is the meat and drink of every creative theological writer or preacher down the ages. Taylor lived in an age of acute religious differences, and although we in our time are not without our controversies, it is sometimes hard for us to understand fully the religio-political reasons that led to the Civil War and the execution of King Charles I. Taylor wrote at a particularly nervous time in the Church's life. While many of the areas of conflict were part and parcel of living at the time, there are four in particular that stand out from the point of view of an early twenty-first century reader.

The first concerns *original sin*. We need to see this in the context of Taylor's theology, rather than isolate it as a 'problem' that he suddenly had to face with the publication of 'Unum Necessarium' in 1655. We also need to see Taylor as a moral theologian, with an edifice shaped by

18 P. G. Stanwood (ed.), *Jeremy Taylor: Holy Living and Holy Dying, vol. II: Holy Dying*, Oxford: Clarendon Press, 1989.

the materials we have observed in 'Great Exemplar' (1649) and 'Holy Living' (1650) published only half a decade before. For Taylor, to live a 'holy life' must be the starting-point, whether we are looking in the first instance at Christ's life or our own. It is then necessary to reflect either on the narrative and meaning of Christ's life and ministry or on the key virtues of godly living by faithful disciples. Once these foundations are in place, as the openings for the life of grace, then we are ready to confront ourselves and the world in the raw, aided by the sacraments, by prayer, by godly wisdom, applied to daily living.

At a time when the choice in moral theology seems to have been between neat Catholic distinctions between different sorts of sin (which Taylor rejects) and an overly Calvinist view of imputed righteousness, Taylor saw the weakness of both approaches, and courageously sought a middle line. So when 'Unum Necessarium' (1655) appeared, it was only a detailed outworking of what Taylor had already written in a different context, and what he was to go on to apply in an even wider one in 'Ductor Dubitantium' (1660) five years later. No wonder Taylor could not believe original sin was an inherent evil, but the effect of one sin, which does not destroy our liberty, and it cannot damn an infant eternally. Assessments of Taylor here vary. For Spinks, it still leaves him – and his baptism rite – open to the criticism of being too strong on obedience, and insufficiently weighted towards justification. It is the old balance between divine initiative in the gift of grace and forgiveness, and human response in repentance and good works, or as he would say, 'holy living'. For others, like Stranks and McAdoo, he has had the courage to challenge an Augustinian–Calvinist establishment that was unable to accept a different Christian anthropology. McAdoo goes so far as to contend that here, again, he was ahead of his time.[19] This is clearly an area that has been open to considerable theological debate in the period since.

The second controversy concerns *toleration*. Once again, we in our time find it hard to understand a very different world, in which people could take up arms to fight for one religious and political system only. So for Taylor to write 'Liberty of Prophesying' in 1647, well into the Civil War, was something of a risk, given his Royalist sympathies and Laudian liturgical convictions. He didn't pull his punches with the

19 See Bryan D. Spinks, *Reformation and Modern Rituals and Theologies of Baptism: From Luther to Contemporary Practices*, Liturgy Worship, Society Series, Aldershot: Ashgate, 2006, pp. 74–6; Stranks, *Life and Writings*, pp. 145–51; McAdoo, *Eucharistic Theology*, pp. 25–34.

intolerant, to say nothing of those who would use coercion to get their own way. We have already described its main intentions, and hinted at potential contradictions in the tough line he found himself having to take as a bishop nearly twenty years later in Ulster. Taylor used his considerable grasp of history to bring out the best case for variation and breadth, looking for an irreducible minimum for an orthodox faith, liturgically lived. As Boone Porter has observed, Taylor was one of the few writers of his time who saw the voluntary character of Anglicanism – it was destined to live a life alongside other Christian communities, because of the sheer impossibility of imposing one, unifying Christian Church on the entire populace. That is one of the reasons why he details the views of those whose opinions he rejects, whether it is the Anabaptists or the Roman Catholics. When, for example, televised services are broadcast nowadays to celebrate national events and tragedies that are so overtly ecumenical, we can discern how far-sighted Taylor was in this respect; this kind of view would not have been welcome to those of more stolid minds, for whom the religious controversies of their time were about winners and losers.

The third concerns *death-bed repentance*. This is a theme that recurs in Taylor's writings, and it is something that jars with an age like ours, just as it could also be said to be inconsistent with Taylor's universal view about the love of God. He devoted a whole sermon to the 'invalidity of a late of death-bed repentance', and 'Holy Dying' (1651) has some chilling words on this matter, cautioning against 'a repentance not to be repented of', because of its superficiality. Once again, this needs to be seen in the context of Taylor's age, when sickness could more easily lead to death, confronting the sufferer sometimes with a sudden fear of death. The other context is Taylor's criticism of Roman Catholic practice at the time, which he probably saw as too easy and insufficiently sincere.

And the fourth concerns *sexuality*. We have already discussed Taylor's 'Discourse on the Nature and Offices of Friendship' (1657), in effect the letter he had written to Katherine Philips, known to be a lesbian. There will be those who may well question that Taylor's intentions are as open and tolerant as we have suggested, and every age that has to grapple suddenly with something apparently new (and therefore deeply controversial) can try to find a precedent in an overlooked corner of the past. But my own view, for what it is worth, is that Taylor was well aware of the homosexual underworld that existed in seventeenth-century England, and wanted to take a 'pastoral' approach to it rather than the more usual censorious one of his time. Of course Taylor is dealing with friendship in general, but the way he writes in open code to Katherine Philips at the start is its own admission that Taylor knows exactly what he is doing and that the recipient knows as well. The fact that the 'Discourse' went into its eighth (and last) edition in 1686 – less than thirty years later – probably indicates that this item from Taylor's pen had a market. The man who wrote in such an open way about heterosexual love in 'Holy Living' (1650) only seven years before could – just possibly – be writing now in a more circumspect manner about another form of love. But even if such an interpretation is rejected, the basic tenor of what Taylor has to say about Christian friendship strikes a strong chord with an age like ours, where it scarcely figures in religious discourse, and often languishes from neglect – and suspicion – in popular culture.

Liturgical theologian – and ordination

We have mentioned on a number of occasions so far Taylor's proclivity at writing prayers. These are clearly not intended as mere intermissions. They are an essential part of Taylor's intentions. So it is not just 'Great Exemplar' (1649) that is littered with them. They appear as an integral part of 'Holy Living' (1650) and 'Holy Dying (1651), as well as in his other works. 'Holy Living' even includes a prayer for a debtor himself to use to be apprised of the importance of restitution. Admittedly, they are devotional prayers for the individual to use. But as a phenomenon, not by any means unique to Taylor, they do have the effect of showing him to be what would nowadays be called a 'liturgical theologian', as Boone Porter has suggested.

But liturgical theology is about public prayer as well, and in this connection we must mention his 'Collection of Offices' (1658). When set alongside his 'Apology for authorized and set forms of Liturgy' (1649) and 'Golden Grove (1655), it is clear that how people pray when they gather for worship was for him a self-defining aspect of the Church. How we pray expresses what we believe – or, according to the old theological adage, '*lex orandi lex credendi*', 'the rule of prayer is the rule of belief'. And that is borne out in the firm line he takes on ordination in 'Episcopacy Asserted' (1642), as well as in 'Clerus Domini' (1651) and his 'Rules and Advices to Clergy' (1661). He may not be interested in the diaconate, but he has a high view of the priestly office, ordination being required for the two dominical sacraments as well as the other five, which he clearly regards as sacramental. They function within a pastoral setting, and a set liturgical context, in which prayer, symbolic action and preaching have a central place. Bishops, moreover, Taylor sees as the successors to the apostles, even naming the 'angels of the Churches' (Rev. 2 and 3) as the local bishops, for which he has some support in certain early Christian writings. And in his own consecration sermon, he went so far as to suggest – citing the early theologian Origen, a great lover of angelology – that when bishops are consecrated, they receive an extra guardian-angel, in addition to the one they receive at their baptism. Many a bishop since would relish such a notion!

In the 'Collection of Offices' is a somewhat unusual eucharistic rite, with the Christian East forming an interesting part. These include the Beatitudes at the start of the Eucharist, as in the Byzantine Liturgy (replacing the Prayer Book's Ten Commandments), and the invocation of the Spirit in consecration. But his style was so different from Cranmer that his influence on the 1662 Prayer Book was at best minimal. The Beatitudes have continued to be used devotionally in the period since, and they re-appeared in the Church of England's *Common Worship* (2000) both as a canticle and in preparation for Holy Communion. His baptism rite, however, resembles the Prayer Book structure more closely, but carefully crafted to include covenant theology, the blessing of the water by the Holy Spirit, and a softer line on original sin. Someone with Taylor's artistry might have hoped to have been involved in the work of liturgical revision at the Restoration. It could be that his 'Collection of Offices' was under suspicion among those looking for the restoration of the Prayer Book and nothing more, even though it was only meant as a temporary substitute for it. But his liturgical projects, interesting and innovative as they are, are not where his greatness is really to be found.

How do we see Taylor now?

The best way to understand Taylor, as with any other theological writer, is to read him – and that is the main reason for this collection of extracts, long after his works have been out of print. In his funeral sermon, George Rust described him, with some understandable hyperbole, as having 'the acuteness of a school-man, the profoundness of a philosopher . . . and the piety of a saint'. Certainly, he had something of the mediaeval theologian (the 'school-men'), in being able to argue a case on the basis of mastery of detail; and like others of his time, he was an orientalist, with his knowledge – and use – of Syriac. He also had something of the philosopher, with a mind that could see the relationship between principles and issues, and draw them together. And he could see into the souls of those for whom he cared, with a prayerfulness that could only have been born of prayer and sharp observation. His memory lived on in Ireland in a special way, and it still does, and rightly so.[20] But his overall impact on the wider world was considerable, for example in the profound effect of reading 'Holy Living' and 'Holy Dying' on the young John Wesley (1703–91).[21] Not surprisingly, the works that have been most read are those that are the least controversial, perhaps because he was more comfortable authoring them.

Can we discern signs of development in his thought? 'Great Exemplar' (1649) does seem to embody the main features of his theology, which was subsequently honed by the dual experience of living through the Commonwealth and the need to respond to the reactions to some of his controversial views. Perhaps he became more conscious of the need to have a more critical use of the Fathers. He seems more confident about them in 'Episcopacy Asserted' (1642) than nearly twenty years later in 'Ductor Dubitantium' (1660).

Those characteristics, even in the atmosphere of a funeral oration, paint the picture of the man who emerges from these writings. His uniqueness stems from his ability to see through inadequacies, and to try to draw together the separate threads of theological life that were in danger of falling apart – a feature not unknown in any age, especially at a time of deep controversy. McAdoo, one of his great admirers, persistently regarded him as a great 'moral-ascetic' theologian, and with that we entirely agree. Taylor took the risk of drawing together these two aspects of the Christian enterprise. His stress on the importance of free will always stood in tension with his view of God as a moral Being. In some areas, he paid the price for such a risk, writing perhaps too frequently and too candidly, and in ways that could be disturbing.

With whom should we compare him? Of his near-contemporaries, Robert Sanderson (1587–1663), Restoration Bishop of Lincoln, stands out as a moral theologian with similar instincts and aspirations, who

---

20 F. R. Bolton, *The Caroline Tradition of the Church of Ireland with particular reference to Jeremy Taylor*, London: Longmans, 1958.

21 L. Tyerman, *The Life and Times of John Wesley*, vol. 1, London: Hodder and Stoughton, 1870, p. 36.

undoubtedly left his mark on him.[22] But the two figures he most resembles are contrasting figures, whom we have encountered already, and whom Taylor must have influenced. One is Simon Patrick, Bishop of Ely from 1691, another Cambridge Platonist, a pastorally minded theologian with a flowing pen, who wrote on the sacraments and published many sermons, but who was a less creative and comprehensive thinker than Taylor, yet a more adept ecclesiastical statesman.[23] The other is a different figure altogether, Thomas Traherne, a priest-poet many of whose writings have been recovered, identified and published only in the past hundred years, but who shared many of the features of Taylor's theology, mystical as well as social, his talkative nature and angular frame of mind, yet who shared none of Taylor's concerns over church order or sacramental theology.[24]

We do not write like this today, and nor should we. But Taylor would be baffled by the fragmentation of knowledge that is such a feature of our own age, not helped by the lamentable gap that exists between church and academy. First, his contribution to the evolution of seventeenth-century moral theology was unique, because he was able to ground the exercise in reason and revelation, thus making natural law more accessible to new situations, and rescuing it from the control of a church hierarchy, or the personal whim of the individual's fervent faith. 'Ductor Dubitantium' (1660), after all, ends with a strong warning against legalistic religion.

Then his contribution identified by McAdoo to what we would nowadays call ecumenical theology is shown in the method he brings to such areas as baptism and Eucharist, where ecclesial act and human experience are seen not as irreconcilable contrasts but as a complementary whole, powerful without being wooden, yet personal without being wholly subjective. Taylor's reading of the Fathers attuned him to the importance of baptismal catechesis, and the significance of ancient sym-

22 A point made by H. R. McAdoo, *The Structure of Caroline Moral Theology*, London: Longmans, 1949, pp. 67ff.

23 Stevenson, *Covenant of Grace Renewed*, pp. 149–63 and *The Mystery of Baptism in the Anglican Tradition*, pp. 125–38; on encouragement for increased frequency of the Eucharist at the Restoration, to which Taylor and Patrick (among many others) contributed, see John Spurr, *The Restoration Church of England, 1646–1690*, New Haven and London: Yale University Press, 1991.

24 Denise Inge (ed.), *Happiness and Holiness: Thomas Traherne and His Writings*, Canterbury Studies in Spiritual Theology, Norwich: Canterbury Press, 2008 and *Wanting Like a God: Desire and Freedom in Thomas Traherne*, London: SCM Press, 2009.

bolism lost at the Reformation, such as chrism; and he saw in the patristic notion of 'anamnesis' the true heart of the eucharistic action.[25]

Finally, however, it is his contribution to devotional theology that is without question immense. If he has a theological starting-point it is in life lived – hence the significance of 'Great Exemplar' (1649) and 'Holy Living' (1650) – the life of Christ into which we are called, and the life of the believer redeemed by the grace of discipleship. Taylor may be verbose at times in his determination to cover as much as he possibly he can. But he always has the praying, thinking, self-disciplined believer in his sights, precisely because he believes that prayer, reflection, and practical living have the potential to be transformative, not just for the individual but for society as a whole. Like so many of the seventeenth-century writers, Taylor's aim was to give theology to the *laity* and to ensure the proper interplay of scripture, tradition and reason in the process. For Taylor, faith and reason have an intrinsic relationship – which is a lesson that badly needs learning again in our time, in a world where the two are frequently driven apart, and the believer and the non-believer – and half-believer – suffer in consequence. For Taylor, such a relationship needed to be worked out in the day-to-day task of Christian discipleship. 'A following holy life' sums up all his teaching in the 'Discourse on Repentance', by far the lengthiest in 'Great Exemplar' (1649). That's not a bad place to locate it.

25 See Thomas K. Carroll, 'Jeremy Taylor: Liturgist and Ecumenist: a study of Taylor's sacramental theology and its ecumenical implications', doctoral dissertation, Angelicum University, Rome, 1970.

Taylor's Works Listed Chronologically

Roman and Arabic numerals refer to the relevant volume and page numbering in the Heber–Eden edition. Some of the datings have to be checked against the Gathorne-Hardy and Proctor Williams Bibliography, while others are occasionally published together in different assortments, as was common practice at the time.

1 Gunpowder Sermon, 1638, VIII, pp. 451–96.
2 Episcopacy Asserted, 1642, V, pp. 1–226.
3 The Psalter of David, and Devotions, 1644 – attributed to Taylor.
4 Discourse on Prayer Extempore, 1646, rewritten and expanded as Apology for Liturgy, 1649 (see 7 below).
5 New Institution of Grammar, 1647, I, pp. 62–3.
6 Liberty of Prophesying, 1647, V, pp. 341–608.
7 Apology for Liturgy, 1649, V, pp. 229–314.
8 The Great Exemplar, 1649, II, (whole volume).
9 Holy Living, 1650, III, pp. 1–256.
10 Funeral Sermon for Lady Frances Carbery, 1650, VIII, pp. 425–50.
11 Clerus Domini, 1651, I, pp. 1–61.
12 Twenty-Eight Sermons, 1651, IV, pp. 323–672.
13 Holy Dying, 1651, III, pp. 257–455.
14 A Short Catechism, 1652; reprinted with Golden Grove, 1655, VII, pp. 593–9, and other parts.
15 Discourse on Baptism, 1652, II, pp. 229–76; Syriac prayer, with translation, added 1657, pp. 277–9.
16 Twenty-Five Sermons, 1653, IV, pp. 1–322 – also published with Twenty-Eight Sermons as 'Eniautos', 1653.
17 Real Presence, 1654, VI, pp. 3–170.
18 Golden Grove, 1655, VII, pp. 589–648.
19 Unum Necessarium, 1655, VII, pp. 3–494.
20 Further Explanation of Original Sin, 1656, VII, pp. 301–90 (inserted into subsequent editions of Unum Necessarium).

21 Answer to a Letter Concerning the Chapter on Original Sin, 1656, VII, pp. 541–70.
22 Deus Justificatus, 1656, VII, pp. 495–540.
23 Discourse on Friendship, 1657, I, pp. 69–98.
24 Five Letters to Persons tempted to change in their religion, 1657, VI, pp. 645–70.
25 Collection of Offices, 1658, VIII, pp. 573–701.
26 Funeral Sermon for Sir George Dalston, 1658, VIII, pp. 541–70.
27 Ductor Dubitantium, 1660, IX and X (both volumes).
28 Worthy Communicant, 1660, VIII, pp. 3–244.
29 Consecration Sermon, 1661, VIII, pp. 303–32.
30 Parliament Sermon, 1661, VIII, pp. 333–58.
31 Rules and Advice to the Clergy, 1661, I, pp. 99–114.
32 Via Intelligentiae (University Sermon), 1662, VIII, pp. 359–92.
33 The Righteousness Evangelical (Three Sermons), 1663, VIII, pp. 247–65.
34 Funeral Sermon of Archbishop John Bramhall, 1663, VIII, pp. 393–424.
35 Discourse on Confirmation, 1663, V, pp. 609–70.
36 Seven Sermons (A Supplement to the 'Eniautos'), 1663 = 33, 29, 30, 32, 34, and (usually) 31.
37 Dissuasive from Popery, 1664, VI, pp. 171–288.
38 Second Part of Dissuasive from Popery, 1667, VI, pp. 289–644.
39 Christ's Yoke (Two Sermons), 1675, I, pp. 115–27.
40 On Reverence due to the Altar, 1848, V, pp. 315–40.

Heber's 'Life of Taylor', I, pp. i–cccvii.
George Rust's Funeral Sermon for Taylor, I, pp. cccix–cccxxvii.

About the Extracts

Sources

All the extracts come from the ten-volume Heber–Eden edition.

Presentation

Each extract is followed by a citation to the Heber–Eden edition, giving volume number and page references.

In the case of 'Holy Living' (1650) and 'Holy Dying' (1651), the only two works that have appeared in accurate, modern editions, with seventeenth-century spelling by Stanwood, an extra reference, preceded by 'S', will be given: this applies to Chapter 2. These, the popular works of Taylor, have also been the most frequently, and often inaccurately, printed, edited and abbreviated over the years.

Selection

With an author like Taylor, who wrote about so many matters, arrangement of material has to be somewhat pragmatic. The four chapters are arranged in themes and sub-themes as follows:

1 The Life of Christ – 'Great Exemplar' (1649)
2 Discipleship – 'Holy Living' (1650), 'Holy Dying' (1651), 'Doctor Dubitantium' (1660)
3 Eucharist, Confirmation, Ordination, Liturgy, Preaching – 'Real Presence' (1654), 'Worthy Communicant' (1660); 'Episcopacy Asserted' (1642), 'Cleris Domini (1651), 'Rules and Advices' (1661), 'Discourse on Confirmation' (1663), 'Apology for Liturgy' (1647), 'Collection of Offices' (1658), 'Enactors' (1651–55), 'Supplement' (1663)

4 Sermons, Friendship, Toleration, Against becoming Roman Catholic, Original Sin: 'Eniautos' (1651–55), 'Supplement to Eniautos' (1663), 'Discourse on Friendship' (1657), 'Liberty of Prophesying' 1647), 'Golden Grove' (1655), Dissuasive from Popery' (1664), 'Two Letters' (1657), 'Unum Necessarium' (1655), 'Deus Justificatus' (1656)

I

The Life of Christ

The opening words of the 'Dedication' – in the year of the execution of Charles I, a time for theology that is practical, not polemical

When interest divides the church, and the calentures of men breathe out in problems and inactive discourses, each part, in pursuance of its own portion, follows that proposition which complies with and bends in all the flexures of its temporal ends; and while all strive for truth, they hug their own opinions dressed up in her imagery, and they dispute for ever; and either the question is indeterminable, or, which is worse, men will never be convinced. For such is the nature of disputings, that they begin commonly in mistakes, they proceed with zeal and fancy, and end not at all but in schisms and uncharitable names, and too often dip their feet in blood. In the mean time, he that gets the better of his adversary oftentimes gets no good to himself, because, although he hath fast hold upon the right side of the problem, he may be an ill man in the midst of his triumphant disputations. And therefore it was not here that God would have man's felicity to grow; for our condition had been extremely miserable if our final state had been placed upon an uncertain hill, and the way to it had been upon the waters upon which no spirit but that of contradiction and discord did ever move: for the man should have tended to an end of an uncertain dwelling, and walked to it by ways not discernible, and arrived thither by chance; which, because it is irregular, would have discomposed the pleasures of a Christian hope, as the very disputing hath already destroyed charity, and disunited the continuity of faith; and in the consequent there would be no virtue, and no felicity. But God, who never loved that man should be too ambitiously busy in imitating His wisdom (and man lost paradise for it,) is most desirous we should imitate His goodness, and transcribe copies of those excellent emanations from His holiness whereby, as He communicates Himself to us in mercies, so He propound Himself, imitable by us in graces: and in order to this, God has described our way plain, certain, and determined;

and although He was pleased to leave us undetermined in the questions of exterior communion, yet He put it past all question that we are bound to be charitable. He hath placed the question of the state of separation in the dark, in hidden and undiscerned regions; but He hath opened the windows of heaven, and given great light to us, teaching how we are to demean ourselves in the state of conjunction. Concerning the salvation of the heathens He was not pleased to give us account; but He hath clearly described the duty of Christians, and tells upon what terms alone we shall be saved. And although the not inquiring into the ways of God and the strict rules of practice have been instrumental to the preserving them free from the serpentine enfoldings and labyrinths of dispute, yet God also, with a great design of mercy, hath writ His commandments in so large characters, and engraven them in such tables, that no man can want the records, nor yet skill to read the hand-writing upon this wall, if he understands what he understands, that is, what is placed in his own spirit. For God was therefore desirous that human nature should be perfected with moral not intellectual excellencies, because these only are of use and compliance with our present state and conjunction, If God had given to eagles an appetite to swim, or to the elephant strong desires to fly, He would have ordered that an abode in the sea and the air respectively should have been proportionable to their manner of living; for so God hath done to man, fitting him with such excellencies which are useful to him in his ways and progress to perfection. And man hath great use and need of justice, and all the instances of morality serve his natural and political ends; he cannot live without them, and be happy: but the filling the rooms of the understanding with airy and ineffective notions is just such an excellency as it is in a man to imitate the voice of birds; at his very best, the nightingale shall excel him, and it is of no use to that end which God designed him in the first intentions of creation.

In pursuance of this consideration, I have chosen to serve the purposes of religion by doing assistance to that part of theology which is wholly practical; that which makes us wiser therefore because it makes us better.

II.1–2

'Preface' – Christianity and Natural Law

For certain it is, Christianity is nothing else but the most perfect design that ever was to make a man be happy in his whole capacity: and as the law was to the Jews, so was philosophy to the gentiles, a schoolmaster to bring them to Christ, to teach them the rudiments of happiness, and the first and lowest things of reason; that when Christ was come, all mankind might become perfect; that is, be made regular in their appetites, wise in their understandings, assisted in their duties, directed to, and instructed in, their great ends. And this is that which the apostle calls "being perfect men in Christ Jesus;" perfect in all the intendments of nature, and in all the designs of God: and this was brought to pass by discovering, and restoring, and improving the law of nature and by turning it all into religion.

For the natural law being a sufficient and a proportionate instrument and means to bring a man to the end designed in his creation, and this law being eternal and unalterable, (for it ought to be as lasting and as unchangeable as the nature itself, so long as it was capable of a law,) it was not imaginable that the body of any law should make a new morality, new rules and general proportions, either of justice, or religion, or temperance, or felicity; the essential parts of all these consisting in natural proportions, and means toward the consummation of man's last end, which was first intended and is always the same. It is, as if here were a new truth in an essential and a necessary proposition. For although the instances may vary, there can be no new justice, no new temperance, no new relations, proper and natural relations, and intercourses, between God and us, but what always were; in praises and prayers, in adoration and honour, and in the symbolical expressions of God's glory and our needs.

II.20

On how Christ perfects Natural Law

Thus the holy Jesus perfected and restored the natural law, and drew it into a system of propositions, and made them to become of the family of religion. For God is so zealous to have man attain to the end to which He first designed him, that those things which He hath put to the natural order to attain that end, He hath bound fast upon us, not only by the order of things by which it was that he that prevaricated did naturally fall short of felicity, but also by bands of religion; He hath now made Himself a party, and an enemy to those that will not be happy. Of old, religion was but one of the natural laws, and the instances of religion were distinct from the discourses of philosophy. Now, all the law of nature is adopted into religion, and by our love and duty to God we are tied to do all that is reason, and the parts of our religion are but pursuances of the natural relation between God and us. And beyond all this, our natural condition is, in all senses, improved by the consequents and adherences of this religion: for although nature and grace are opposite, that is, nature depraved by evil habits, by ignorance, and ungodly customs, is contrary to grace, that is, to nature restored by the gospel, engaged to regular living by new revelations, and assisted by the Spirit; yet it is observable that the law of nature and the law of grace are never opposed. "There is a law of our members," saith St. Paul; that is an evil necessity introduced into our appetites by perpetual evil customs, examples, and traditions of vanity; and there is a law of sin, that answers to this; and they differ only as inclination and habit, vicious desires and vicious practices. Bt then contrary to these are, first "a law of my mind," which is the law of nature and right reason, and then the law of grace, that is, of Jesus Christ, who perfected and restored the first law, and by assistances reduced it into a law of holy living: and these two differ as the other; the one is in order to the other, as imperfection and growing degrees and capacity are to perfection and consummation. The law of the mind had been so rased and obliterate, and we, by some means or other, so disabled from observing it exactly, that until it was turned into the law of grace, (which is a law of pardoning infirmities, and assisting us in our choices and elections,) we were in a state of deficiency from the perfective state of man to which God intended us.

II. 28–9

Exhortation to the imitation of Christ

I consider, that the imitation of the life of Jesus is a duty of that excellency and perfection, that we are helped in it, not only by the assistance of a good and great example, which possibly might be too great, and scare our endeavours and attempts; but also by its easiness, compliance, and proportion to us. For Jesus, in His whole life, conversed with men with a modest virtue, which, like a well kindled fire fitted with just materials, casts a constant heat; not like an inflamed heap of stubble, glaring with great emissions, and suddenly stooping into the thickness of smoke. His piety was even, constant, unblamable, complying with civil society, without affrightment of precedent, or prodigious instances of actions greater than the imitation of men. For if we observe our blessed Saviour in the whole story of His life, although He was without sin, yet the instances of His piety were the actions of a very holy, but of an ordinary life; and we may observe this difference in the story of Jesus from ecclesiastical writings of certain beatified persons, whose life is told rather to amaze us and to create scruples, than to lead us in the evenness and serenity of a holy conscience.

II.41

Considerations upon the Annunciation and the Conception: The Incarnation

And if we consider the reasonableness of the thing, what can be given more excellent for the redemption of man than the blood of the Son of God? And what can more ennoble our nature, than that by the means of His holy humanity it was taken up into the cabinet of the mysterious Trinity? What better advocate could we have for us, than He that is appointed to be our judge? And what greater hopes of reconciliation can be imagined, than that God, in whose power it is to give an absolute pardon, hath taken a new nature, entertained an office, and undergone a life of poverty, with a purpose to procure our pardon?

II.52

On the Annunciation

The holy Virgin, when she saw an angel and heard a testimony from heaven of her grace and piety, was troubled within herself at the salutation and the manner of it: for she had learned, that the affluence of divine comforts and prosperous successes should not exempt us from fear, but make it the more prudent and wary, lest it entangle us in a vanity of spirit; God having ordered that our spirits should be affected with dispositions in some degrees contrary to exterior events, that we be fearful in the affluence of prosperous things, and joyful in adversity; as knowing that this may produce benefit and advantage; and the changes that are consequent to the other are sometimes full of mischiefs, but always of danger. But her silence and fear were her guardians; that, to prevent excrescences of joy; this, of vainer complacency.

And it is not altogether inconsiderable to observe, that the holy Virgin came to a great perfection and state of piety by a few, and those modest and even, exercises and external actions. St. Paul travelled over the world, preached to the gentiles, disputed against the Jews, confounded heretics, writ excellently learned letters, suffered dangers, injuries, affronts, and persecutions to the height of wonder, and by these violences of life, action, and patience, obtained the crown of an excellent religion and devotion. But the holy Virgin, although she was engaged sometimes in an active life, and in the exercise of an ordinary and small economy and government or ministries of a family, yet she arrived to her perfections by the means of a quiet and silent piety, the internal actions of love, devotion, and contemplation; and instructs us, that not only those who have opportunity and powers of a magnificent religion, or a pompous charity, or miraculous conversion of souls, or assiduous and effectual preachings, or exterior demonstrations of corporal mercy, shall have the greatest crowns, and the addition of degrees and accidental rewards; but the silent affections, the splendours of an internal devotion, the unions of love, humility, and obedience, the daily offices of prayer and praises sung to God, the acts of faith and fear, of patience and meekness, of hope and reverence, repentance and charity, and those graces which walk in a veil and silence, make great ascents to God, and as sure progress to favour and a crown, as the more ostentatious and laborious exercises of a more solemn religion. No man needs to complain of want of power or opportunities for religious perfections: a devout woman in her closet, praying with much zeal and affections for the conversion of souls, is in the same order to a "shining like the stars in glory," as he who by excellent discourses puts it into a more forward disposition to be actually performed. And possibly her prayers obtained energy and force to my sermon, and made the ground fruitful, and the seed spring up to life eternal. Many times God is present in the still voice and private retirements of a quiet religion, and the constant spiritualities of an ordinary life, when the loud and impetuous winds, and the shining fires of a more laborious and expensive actions, are profitable to others only, like a tree of balsam, distilling precious liquor for others, not for its own use.

II.54–5

Considerations concerning the circumstances of the interval between the conception and the nativity

When the holy Virgin had begun her journey she made haste over the mountains, that she might not only satisfy the desires of her joy by a speedy gratulation, but lest she should be too long abroad under the dispersion and discomposing of her retirements; and therefore she hastens to an enclosure, to her cousin's house, as knowing that all virtuous women, like tortoises, carry their house on their heads, and their chapel in their heart, and their danger in their eye, and their souls in their hands, and God in all their actions. And indeed her very little burden, which she bare, hindered her not but she might make haste enough; and as her spirit was full of cheerfulness and alacrity, so even her body was made airy and vegete, for there was no sin in her burden to fill it with natural inconveniences. And there is this excellency in all spiritual things, that they do no disadvantage to our persons, nor retard our just temporal interests: and the religion by which we carry Christ within us, is neither so peevish as to disturb our health, nor so sad as to discompose our just and modest cheerfulness, nor so prodigal as to force us to needs and ignoble trades; but recreates our body by the medicine of holy fastings and temperance, fills us full of serenities and complacencies by the sweetnesses of a holy conscience and joys spiritual, promotes our temporal interests, by the gains and increases of the rewards of charity, and by securing God's providence over us while we are in the pursuit of the heavenly kingdom. And as in these dispositions she climbed the mountains with much facility, so there is nothing in our whole life of difficulty so great, but it may be managed by those assistances we receive from the holiest Jesus, when we carry Him about us; as the valleys are exalted, so the mountains are made plain before us.

II.58–9

Considerations upon the birth of our Blessed Saviour Jesus Christ

Here then are concentred the prodigies of greatness and goodness, of wisdom and charity, of meekness and humility, and march all the way in mystery and incomprehensible mixtures; if we consider Him in the bosom of His Father, where He is seated by the postures of love and essential felicity; and in the manger, where love also placed Him, and an infinite desire to communicate His felicities to us. As he is God, His throne is in the heaven, and He fills all things by His immensity: as He is man, He is circumscribed by an uneasy cradle, and cries in a stable. As He is God, He is seated upon a super-exalted throne; as man, exposed to the lowest estate of uneasiness and need. As God clothed in a robe of glory, at the same instant when you may behold and wonder at His humanity, wrapped in cheap and unworthy cradle-bands. As God, He is encircled by millions of angels; as man, in the company of beasts. As God, He is the eternal Word of the Father, eternal, sustained by Himself, all-sufficient, and without need: and yet He submitted Himself to a condition imperfect, inglorious, indigent, and necessitous. And this consideration is apt and natural to produce great affections of love, duty, and obedience, desires of union and conformity to His sacred person, life, actions, and laws; that we resolve all our thoughts, and finally determine all our reason and our passions and capacities, upon that saying of St. Paul, "He that loves not the Lord Jesus Christ, let him be accursed." [1 Cor. 16.22]

II.68

The great and glorious accidents happening about the birth of Jesus

The wise men . . . "fell down and worshipped Him," after the manner of the easterlings when they do veneration to their kings, not with an empty *Ave* and gay blessing of fine words, but "they bring presents and come into His courts;" for "when they had opened their treasures, they presented unto Him gifts, gold, frankincense, and myrrh." And if these gifts were mysterious, beyond the acknowledgment of Him to be the king of the Jews, and Christ, that should come into the world; frankincense might signify Him to be acknowledged a God, myrrh to be a man, and gold to be a king: unless we choose by gold to signify the acts of mercy; by myrrh, the chastity of minds and purity of our bodies, to the incorruption of which myrrh is especially instrumental; and by incense we intend our prayers, as the most apt presents and oblations to the honour and service of this young king. But however the fancies of religion may represent variety of ideas, the act of adoration was direct and religious, and the myrrh was medicinal to His tender body: the incense possibly no more than was necessary in a stable, the first throne of His humilty: and the gold was a good antidote against the present indigencies of His poverty: presents such as were used in all the Levant (especially in Arabia and Saba, to which the growth of myrrh and frankincense were proper) in their addresses to their God and to their king; and were instruments with which, under the veil of flesh, they worshipped the eternal Word; the wisdom of God, under infant innocency; the almighty power, in so great weakness; and under the lowness of human nature, the altitude of majesty and the infinity of divine glory.

II.86–7

Considerations upon the apparition of the angels to the shepherds

But the angels also had other motions: for besides the pleasures of that joy, which they had in beholding human nature so highly exalted, and that God was man, and man was God; they were transported with admiration at the ineffable counsel of God's predestination, prostrating themselves with adoration and modesty, seeing God so humbled, and man so changed, and so full of charity, that God stooped to the condition of man, and man was inflamed beyond the love of seraphim, and was made more knowing than cherubim, more established than thrones, more happy than all the orders of angels. The issue of this consideration teaches us to learn their charity, and to exterminate all the intimations and beginnings of envy, that we may as much rejoice at the good of others as of ourselves: for then we love good for God's sake, when we love good wherever God has placed it: and that joy is charitable which overflows our neighbours' fields when ourselves unconcerned in the personal accruements; for so we are "made partakers of all that fear God," when charity unites their joy to ours, as it makes us partakers of their common sufferings.

And now the angels, who had adored the holy Jesus in heaven, come also to pay their homage to Him upon earth; and laying aside their flaming swords, they take into their hands instruments of music, and sing, "Glory be to God on high:" first signifying to us that the incarnation of the holy Jesus was a very great instrument of the glorification of God, and those divine perfections in which He is chiefly pleased to communicate Himself to us were in nothing manifested so much as in the mysteriousness of this work: secondly; and in vain doth man satisfy himself with complacencies and ambitious designs upon earth, when he sees before him God in the form of a servant, humble, and poor, and crying, and an infant full of need and weakness.

II.88

Considerations upon the Circumcision: our fault not all Adam's

For though the fall of Adam lost to him all those supernatural assistances which God put into our nature by way of grace, yet it is by accident that we are more prone to many sins than we are to virtue. Adam's sin did discompose his understanding and affections: and every sin we do does still make us more unreasonable, more violent, more sensual, more apt still to the multiplication of the same or the like actions: the first rebellion of the inferior faculties against the will and understanding, and every victory flesh gets over the spirit, makes the inferior insolent, strong, tumultuous, domineering, and triumphant upon the proportionable ruins of the spirit; blinding our reason and binding our will; and all these violations of our powers are increased by the perpetual ill customs and false principles and ridiculous guises of the world, which make the later ages to be worse than the former, unless some other accident do intervene to stop the ruin and declension of virtue; such as are God's judgments, the sending of prophets, new imposition of laws, messages from heaven, diviner institutions, such as in particular was the great discipline of Christianity. And even in this sense here is origination enough for sin and impairing of the reasonable faculties of human souls, without charging our faults upon Adam.

II.191

Discourse of obedience: free will

If you will be secure, remove your tent, dwell farther off. God hath given us more liberty than we may safely use; and although God is so gracious as to comply much with our infirmities, yet if we do so too, as God's goodness in indulging liberty to us was to prevent our sinning, our complying with ourselves will engage us in it: but if we imprison and confine our affections into a narrower compass, then our extravagancies may be imperfect, but will not easily be criminal. The dissolution of a scrupulous and strict person is not a vice, but into a less degree of virtue. He that makes a conscience of loud laughter, will not easily be drawn into the wantonness of balls and revellings, and the longer and more impure carnivals. This is the way to secure our obedience; and no men are so curious of their health as they that are scrupulous of the air they breathe in.

II.115

Considerations upon the Presentation in the Temple: Purification and sexual relations

The turtle-doves were offered also with the signification of another mystery. In the sacred rites of marriage, although the permissions of natural desires are such as are most ordinate to their ends, the avoiding fornication, the alleviation of economical cares and vexations, and the production of children, and mutual comfort and support; yet the apertures and permissions of marriage have such restraints of modesty and prudence, that all transgression of the just order to such ends is a crime: and besides these, there may be degrees of inordination or obliquity of intention, or too sensual complacency, or unhandsome preparations of mind, or unsacramental thoughts; in which particulars, because we have no determined rule but prudence, and the analogy of the rite, and the severity of our religion, which allow in some cases more, in some less, and always uncertain latitudes, for aught we know there may be lighter transgressions, something that we know not of: and for these at the purification of the woman, it is supposed, the offering was made, and the turtles, by being an oblation, did deprecate a supposed irregularity; but by being a chaste and marital emblem, they professed the obliquity (if any were) was within the protection of the sacred bands of marriage, and therefore so excusable as to be expiated by a cheap offering. And what they did in hieroglyphic, Christians must do in the exposition; be strict observers of the main rites and principal obligations, and not neglectful to deprecate the lesser unhandsomenesses of the too sensual applications.

II.127

Discourse of meditation

Note here the threefold process of memory, understanding, and will.

For meditation is an attention and application of spirit to divine things; a searching out all instruments to a holy life, a devout consideration of them, and a production of those affections which are in a direct order to the love of God and a pious conversation. Indeed meditation is all that great instrument of piety whereby it is made prudent, and reasonable, and orderly, and perpetual: for supposing our memory instructed with the knowledge of such mysteries and revelations as are apt to entertain the spirit, the understanding is first and best employed in the consideration of them, and then the will in their reception, when they are duly prepared and so transmitted; and both these in such manner, and to such purposes, that they become the magazine and great repositories of grace, and instrumental to all designs of virtue.

II.130

Considerations upon the disputation of Jesus with the doctors in the Temple: Jesus 'removed' from his own

But we often give God cause to remove and for a while to absent Himself, and His doing of it sometimes upon the just provocations of our demerits makes us at other times with good reason to suspect ourselves even in our best actions. But sometimes we are vain, or remiss, or pride invades us in the darkness and incuriousness of our spirits, and we have a secret sin which God would have us to enquire after; and when we suspect every thing, and condemn ourselves with strictest and most angry sentence, then, it may be, God will with a ray of light break through the cloud; if not, it is nothing the worse for us: for although the visible remonstrance and face of things in all the absences and withdrawings of Jesus be the same, yet if a sin be the cause of it, the withdrawing is a taking away His favour and His love: but if God does it to secure thy piety and to enflame thy desires, or to prevent a crime, then He withdraws a gift only, nothing of His love, and yet the darkness of the spirit and sadness seem equal. It is hard in these cases to discover the cause, as it is nice to judge the condition of the effect; and therefore it is prudent to ascertain our condition by improving our care and our religion, and in all accidents to make no judgment concerning God's favour by what we feel, but by what we do.

II.162

The history of the baptism and temptation of Jesus: John's baptism transformed all three Persons of the Trinity

But the holy Jesus, who came (as Himself, in answer to the Baptist's question, professed) "to fulfil all righteousness," would receive that rite which His Father had instituted in order to the manifestation of His Son. For although the Baptist had a glimpse of Him by the first irradiations of the Spirit, yet John professed that he therefore came baptizing with water, that "Jesus might be manifested to Israel;" and it was also a sign given to the Baptist himself, that "on whomsoever he saw the Spirit descending and remaining," He is the person "that baptizeth with the holy Ghost." And God chose to actuate the sign at the waters of Jordan, in great and religious assemblies convened there at John's baptism; and therefore Jesus came to be baptized, and by his baptism became know to John, who, as before he gave to Him an indiscriminate testimony, so now he pointed out the person in his sermons and discourses, and by calling Him the Lamb of God, prophesied of His passion, and preached Him to be the world's Redeemer and the sacrifice for mankind. He was now manifest to Israel: He confirmed the baptism of John; He sanctified the water to become sacramental and ministerial in the remission of sins: He by a real event declared, that to them who should rightly be baptized the kingdom of heaven should certainly be opened: He inserted Himself by that ceremony into the society and participation of holy people, of which communion Himself was head and prince; and He did in a symbol purify human nature, whose stains and guilt He had undertaken.

As soon as John had performed his ministry, and Jesus was baptized, He prayed, and the heavens were opened, and the air clarified by a new and glorious light; "and the holy Ghost, in the manner of a dove, alighted upon" His sacred head, and God the Father gave "a voice from heaven, saying, Thou art My beloved Son, in whom I am well pleased." This was the inauguration and proclamation of the Messias, when He began to be the great prophet of the new covenant. And this was the greatest meeting that ever was upon earth, where the whole cabinet of the mysterious Trinity was opened and shewn, as much as the capacities of our present imperfections will permit: the second Person in the veil of humanity, the third in the shape or with the motion of a dove: but the first kept His primitive state; and as to the Israelites He gave notice by way of caution, "Ye saw no shape, but ye heard a voice," so now also God the Father gave testimony to His holy Son and appeared, only in a voice without any visible representment.

II.190–1

The significance of the transformation: the Spirit consecrates the waters

After the holy Jesus was baptized, and had prayed, the heavens opened, the holy Ghost descended, and a voice from heaven proclaimed Him to be the Son of God, and one in whom the Father was well pleased; and the same ointment that was cast upon the head of our High priest, went unto His beard, and thence fell to the borders of His garment: for as Christ our Head felt these effects in manifestation, so the church believes God does to her and to her meanest children, in the susception of the holy rite of baptism in right, apt, and holy dispositions. For the heavens open too upon us; and the holy Ghost descends, to sanctify the waters, and to hallow the catechumen, and to pardon the past and repented sins, and to consign him to the inheritance of sons, and to put on his military girdle, and give him the sacrament and oath of fidelity; for all this is understood to be meant by those frequent expressions of scripture, calling baptism, "the laver of regeneration, illumination, a washing away the filth of the flesh, and the answer of a good conscience, a being buried with Christ," and many others of the like purpose and signification. But we may also learn hence, sacredly to esteem the rites of religion, which He first sanctified by His own personal susception, and then made necessary by His own institution and command; and God hath made to be conveyances of blessing and ministries of the holy Spirit.

II.196

Discourse of baptism: the origins of baptism

The holy Jesus having found His way ready prepared by the preaching of John, and by his baptism and the Jewish manner of adopting proselytes and disciples into the religion a way chalked out for Him to initiate disciples into His religion, took what was so prepared, and changed it into a perpetual sacrament. He kept the ceremony, that they who were led only by outward things might be the better called in, and easier enticed into the religion, when they entered by a ceremony which their nation always used in the like cases: and therefore without change of the outward act, He put into it a new spirit, and gave it a new grace, and a proper efficacy; He sublimed it to higher ends, and adorned it with stars of heaven; He made it to signify greater mysteries, to convey greater blessings, to consign the bigger promises, to cleanse deeper than the skin, and to carry proselytes farther than the gates of the institution. For so He was pleased to do in the other sacrament: He took the ceremony which He found ready in the custom of the Jews, where the *major domo*, after the paschal supper, gave bread and wine to every person of his family; He changed nothing of it without, but transferred the rite to greater mysteries, and out His own spirit to their sign, and it became a sacrament evangelical. It was so also in the matter of excommunication, where the Jewish practice was made to pass into Christian discipline: without violence and noise "old things became new," while He fulfilled the law, making it up in full measures of the Spirit.

II.232

Baptism and covenant, gift of the Spirit, and forgiveness

It is a grace which, by virtue of the covenant consigned in baptism, does like a centre transmit effluxes to all the periods and portions of our life; our whole life, all the periods of our succeeding hopes, are kept alive by this. This consideration is of great use, besides many other things, to reprove the folly of those who in the primitive church deferred their baptism till their death-bed; because baptism is a laver of sanctification, and drowns all our sins, and buries them in the grave of our Lord, they thought they might sin securely upon the stock of an after baptism; for unless they were strangely prevented by a sudden accident, a death-bed baptism they thought would secure their condition: but early some of them durst not take it, much less in the beginning of their years, that they might at least gain impunity for their follies and heats of their youth. Baptism hath influence into the pardon of all our sins committed in all the days of our folly and infirmity; and so long as we have not been baptized, so long we are out of the state of pardon: and therefore an early baptism is not to be avoided upon this mistaken fancy and plot upon heaven: it is the greater security towards the pardon of our sins, if we have taken it at the beginning of our days. . . .

The holy Ghost descends upon the waters of baptism, and makes them prolifical, apt to produce children unto God: and therefore St. Leo compares the font of baptism to the womb of the blessed Virgin, when it was replenished with the holy Spirit. And this is the baptism of our dearest Lord: His ministers baptize with water; our Lord at the same time verifies their ministry with giving the holy Spirit: they are joined together by St. Paul; "we are by one Spirit baptized into one body," that is, admitted into the church by baptism of water and the Spirit. This is that which our blessed Lord calls "a being born of water and of the Spirit;" by water we are sacramentally dead and buried, by the Spirit we are made alive. But because these are mysterious expressions, and, according to the style of scripture, high and secret in spiritual significations, therefore that we may understand what these things signify, we must consider it by its real effects, and what it produces upon the soul of a man.

It is the suppletory of original righteousness by which Adam was at first gracious with God, and which he lost by his prevarication. It was in him a principle of wisdom and obedience, a relation between God and himself, a title to the extraordinary mercies of God, and a state of friendship. When he fell, he was discomposed in all; the links of the golden chain and blessed relation were broken; and it so continued in the whole life of man, which was stained with the evils of this folly and the consequent mischiefs. And therefore when we began the world again, entering into the articles of a new life, God gave us His Spirit, to be an instrument of our becoming gracious persons, and of being in a condition of obtaining that supernatural end which God at first designed to us. And therefore as our baptism is a separation of us from unbelieving people, so the descent of the holy Spirit upon us in our baptism is a consigning or marking us for God, as the sheep of His pasture, as the soldiers of His army, as the servants of His household. We are so separated from the world that we are appropriated to God; so that God expects of us duty and obedience, and all sins are acts of rebellion and undutifulness. Of this nature was the sanctification of Jeremy, and John the baptist, from their mother's womb; that is, God took them to His own service by an early designation, and His Spirit marked them to a holy ministry. To this also relates that of St. Paul, whom God by a decree separated from his mother's womb to the ministry of the gospel; the decree did antedate the act of the Spirit, which did not descend upon him until the day of his baptism. What these persons were in order to exterior ministries, that all the faithful are in order to faith and obedience; consigned in baptism by the Spirit of God to a perpetual relation to God, in a continual service and title to His promises.

II.240–1

The guardian-angel given at baptism

It is more considerable, which is generally and piously believed by very many eminent persons in the church, that at our baptism God assigns an angel-guardian; for then the catechumen, being made a servant and a brother to the Lord of angels, is sure not to want the aids of them who "pitch their tents round about them that fear the Lord;" and that this guard and ministry is then appointed when themselves are admitted into the inheritance of the promises and their title to salvation, is hugely agreeable to the words of St. Paul, "are they not all ministering spirits, sent forth to minister to them who shall be heirs of salvation?" where it appears that the title to the inheritance is the title to this ministry, and therefore must begin and end together. But I insist not on this, though it seems to me hugely probable.

II.244–5

Baptism briefly described

So God is made a father to the man, and the holy church a mother. Faith and repentance strip the old man naked, and make him fit for baptism; and then the holy Spirit, moving upon the waters, cleanses the soul, and makes it put on the new man, who grows up to perfection, and a spiritual life, to a life of glory, by our verification of our undertaking in baptism in our part, and the graces of the Spirit on the other.

II.247

Discourse on baptism: on baptizing infants: the sacrament obligatory, regardless of experience of faith

When the ordinary effect of a sacrament is done already by some other efficiency or instrument, yet the sacrament is still as obligatory as before, not for so many reasons or necessities, but for the same commandment. Baptism is the first ordinary current in which the Spirit moves and descends upon us: and where God's Spirit is, there are the sons of God, for Christ's Spirit descends upon none but them that are His: and yet Cornelius, who had received the holy Spirit, and was heard by God, and visited by an angel, and accepted in his alms, and fastings, and prayers, was tied to the susception of baptism. To which may be added, that the receiving the effects of baptism beforehand was used as an argument the rather to administer baptism. The effect of which consideration is this, that baptism and its effect may be separated, and do not always go in conjunction; the effect may be before, and therefore much rather may it be after its susception; the sacrament operating in the virtue of Christ, even, "as the Spirit shall move:" according to that saying of St. Austin,

. . . 'the work of regeneration, that is begun in the ministry of baptism, is perfected in some sooner, in some later,' — 'we may soon be washed, but to be healed is a work of a long cure.'

II. 248

Infants and the covenant

Baptism is not to be estimated as one act, transient and effective to single purposes, but it is an entrance to a conjugation and a state of blessings. All our life is to be transacted by the measures of the gospel covenant, and that covenant is consigned by baptism; there we have our title and adoption to it: and the grace that is then given to us is like a piece of leaven put into a lump of dough, and faith and repentance do in all the periods of our life put it into fermentation and activity. Then the seed of God is put into the ground of our hearts, and repentance waters it, and faith makes it *subactum solum*, the ground and furrows apt to produce fruits; and therefore faith and repentance are necessary to the effect of baptism, not to its susception; that is, necessary to all those parts of life, in which baptism does operate, not to the first sanction or entering into the covenant. The seed may lie long in the ground, and produce fruits in its due season, if it be refreshed with "the former and the latter rain," that is, the repentance that first changes the state, and converts the man, and afterwards returns him to his title, and recalls him from his wanderings, and keeps him in the state of grace and within the limits of the covenant: and all the way faith gives efficacy and acceptation to this repentance, that is, continues our title to the promise of not having righteousness exacted by the measures of the law, but by the covenant and promise of grace into which we entered in baptism, and walk in the same all the days of our life.

II.252–3

Defence of infant baptism

These sayings concerning baptism in the like manner are to be so understood, that they cannot exclude all persons from the sacrament that have not all those real effects of the sacrament at all times, which some men have at some times, and all men must have at some time or other, viz. when the sacrament obtains its last intention: but he that shall argue from hence that children are not rightly baptized, because they cannot in a spiritual sense put on Christ, concludes nothing, unless these propositions did signify universally, and at all times, and in every person, and in every manner; which can no more pretend to truth than that all Christians are God's elect, and all that are baptized are saints, and all that are called are justified, and all that are once justified shall be saved finally. These things declare only the event of things, and their order, and the usual effect, and the proper design, in their proper season, in their limited proportions.

II.255

Considerations touching the vocation of five disciples, and of the first miracle of Jesus done at Cana: calling of Christians embraces marriage

When Jesus had chosen these few disciples to be witnesses of succeeding accidents, every one of which was to be a probation of His mission and divinity, He entered into the theatre of the world at a marriage feast, which He now first hallowed to a sacramental signification, and made to become mysterious: He now began to choose His spouse out from the communities of the world, and did mean to endear her by unions ineffable and glorious, and consign the sacrament by His blood, which He first gave in a secret representment, and afterwards in a letter and apparent effusion. And although the holy Jesus did in His own person consecrate celibate and abstinence, and chastity in His mother's; yet by His presence He also hallowed marriage, and made it honourable, not only in civil account and the rites of heraldry, but in a spiritual sense, He having new sublimed it by making it a sacramental representment of the union of Christ and His spouse the church. And all married persons should do well to remember what the conjugal society does represent, and not break the matrimonial bond, which is a mysterious ligament of Christ and His church; for whoever dissolves the sacredness of the mystery, and unhallows the vow by violence and impurity, he dissolves his relation to Christ: to break faith with a wife or husband is a divorce from Jesus, and that is a separation from all possibilities of felicity. In the time of the Mosaical statutes, to violate marriage was to do injustice and dishonour, and a breach to the sanctions of nature, or the first constitutions: but two bands more are added in the gospel, to make marriage more sacred; for now our bodies are made "temples of the holy Ghost," and the rite of marriage is made significant and sacramental: and every act of adultery is profanation and irreligion; it desecrates a temple, and deflowers a mystery.

II.292

Discourse of faith: will more than understanding

For the faith of a Christian hath more in it of the will than of the understanding. Faith is that great mark of distinction which separates and gives formality to the covenant of the gospel, which is a "law of faith." The faith of a Christian is his religion, that is, it is that whole conformity to the institution or discipline of Jesus Christ which distinguishes him from the believers of false religions. And to be one of the faithful signifies the same with being a disciple; and that contains obedience as well as believing. For to the same sense are all those appellatives in scripture, "the faithful, brethren, believers, the saints, disciples," all representing the duty of a Christian. A believer, and a saint, or a holy person, is the same thing; 'brethren' signifies charity, and 'believers,' faith in the intellectual sense: the 'faithful' and 'disciples' signify both: for besides the consent to the proposition, the first of them is also used for perseverance and sanctity, and the greatest of charity mixed with a confident faith up to the height of martyrdom, "Be faithful unto the death," said the holy Spirit, "and I will give you the crown of life." And when the apostles, by way of abbreviation, express all the body of Christian religion, they call it "faith working by love;" which also St. Paul in a parallel place calls a "new creature;" it is "a keeping of the commandments of God. That is the faith of a Christian, into whose definition charity is ingredient, whose sense is the same with keeping of God's commandments; so that if we define faith, we must first distinguish it. The faith of a natural person, or the faith of devils, is a mere believing a certain number of propositions upon conviction of the understanding: but the faith of a Christian, the faith that justifies and saves him, is "faith working by charity," or "faith keeping the commandments of God." They are distinct faiths, in order to different ends, and therefore of different constitution; and the instrument of distinction, is charity or obedience.

II.296–7

Discourse of repentance: the covenant of grace and the Church as human

So that now the hopes of lapsed sinners rely upon another bottom: and as in Moses' law there was no revelation of repentance, but yet the Jews had hopes in God, and were taught the succours of repentance by the homilies of the prophets and other accessory notices: so in the gospel the covenant was established upon faith and repentance, but was consigned in baptism, and was verifiable only in the integrity of a following holy life according to the measures of a man; not perfect, but sincere; not faultless, but heartily endeavoured. But yet the mercies of God, in pardoning sinners lapsed after baptism, was declared to us by collateral and indirect occasions: by the sermons if the apostles, and the commentaries of apostolical persons who understood the meaning of the Spirit and the purposes of the divine mercy, and those other significations of His will which the blessed Jesus left upon record in other parts of His testament, as in codicils annexed, besides the precise testament itself. And it is certain, if in the covenant of grace there be the same involution of an after-repentance, as there is of present pardon upon past repentance and future sanctity, it is impossible to justify that a holy life and a persevering sanctity is enjoined by the covenant of the gospel: if, I say, in its first intention it be declared that we may as well, and upon the same terms, hope for pardon upon a recovery hereafter, as upon the perseverance in the present condition.

II.359

Baptism and forgiveness

And yet this discourse is no otherwise to be understood than according to the design of the thing itself and the purpose of God; that is, that it be a deep engagement and an effectual consideration for the necessity of a holy life; but at no hand let it be made an instrument of despair, nor an argument to lessen the influences of the divine mercy. For although the nicety and limits of the covenant, being consigned in baptism, are fixed upon the condition of a holy and persevering uninterrupted sanctity; and our redemption is wrought but once, completed but once, we are but once absolutely, entirely, and presentially forgiven, and reconciled to God, this reconciliation being in virtue of the sacrifice, and this sacrifice applied in baptism is one, as "baptism is one," and as the sacrifice is one: yet the mercy of God, besides this great feast, hath fragments, which the apostles and ministers spiritual are to gather up in baskets, and minister to the after-needs of indigent and necessitous disciples.

II.361

Baptism and confirmation

This consideration I intend should relate to all Christians of the world; and although by the present custom of the church we are baptized in our infancy, and do not actually reap that fruit of present pardon which persons of a mature age in the primitive church did, (for we yet need it not, as we shall when we have past the calentures of youth, which was the time in which the wisest of our fathers in Christ chose for their baptism, as appears in the instance of St. Ambrose, St. Austin, and divers others;) yet we must remember that there is a baptism of the Spirit as well as of water: and whenever this happens, whether it be together with that baptism of water, as usually it was when only men and women of years of discretion were baptized; or whether it be ministered in the rite of confirmation, which is an admirable suppletory of an early baptism, and intended by the holy Ghost for a corroborative of baptismal grace, and a defensative against danger; or that, lastly, it be performed by an internal and merely spiritual ministry, when we by acts of our own election verify the promise made in baptism, and so bring back the rite by receiving the effect of baptism; that is, whenever the "filth of our flesh is washed away," and that we have "the answer of a pure conscience towards God," which St. Peter affirms to be the true baptism, and which by the purpose and design of God it is expected we should not defer longer than a great reason or a great necessity enforces; when our sins are first expiated, and the sacrifice and death of Christ is made ours, and we made God's by a more immediate title, which at some time or other happens to all Christians that pretend to any hopes in heaven: then let us look to our standing, and "take heed lest we fall." When we once have "tasted of the heavenly gift, and are made partakers of the holy Ghost, and have tasted the good word of God, and the powers of the world to come," that is, when we are redeemed by an actual mercy and presential application, which every Christian that belongs to God is at some time or other of his life; then a fall into a deadly crime is highly dangerous, but a relapse into a contrary estate is next to desperate.

II.365

Death-bed repentance condemned

For God hath made no covenant with us on our death-bed distinct from that He made with us in our life and health. And since in our life and present abilities, good purposes and resolutions and vows (for they are but the same thing in differing degrees) did signify nothing till they came to act, and no man was reconciled to God by good intentions, but by doing the will of God; can we imagine that such purposes can more prevail at the end of a wicked life than at the beginning? that less piety will serve our turns after fifty or sixty years' impiety, than after but five or ten? that a wicked and sinful life should by less pains be expiated than an unhappy year? For it is not in the state of grace as in other exterior actions of religion or charity, where God will accept the will for the deed, when the external act is inculpably out of our powers, and may also be supplied by the internal; as bendings of the body by the prostration of the soul, alms by charity, preaching by praying for conversion. These things are necessary because they are precepts, and obligatory only in certain circumstances, which may fail, and we be innocent and disobliged. But it is otherwise in the essential parts of our duty, which God hath made the immediate and next condition of our salvation, such which are never out of our power but by our own fault.

II.379

Considerations upon the Sermon on the Mount: The Eight Beatitudes: spiritual hunger and thirst

Fourthly: "Blessed are they that hunger and thirst after righteousness; for they shall be filled." This grace is the greatest indication of spiritual health, when our appetite is right, strong, and regular; when we are desirous of spiritual nourishment, when we long for *manna*, and "follow Christ for loaves," not of a low and terrestrial gust, but of that "bread which came down from heaven." Now there are two sorts of holy repast which are the proper objects of our desires. The bread of heaven, which is proportioned to our hunger: that is, all those immediate emanations from Christ's pardon of our sins, and redemption from our former conversation, holy laws, and commandments. To this food there is also a spiritual beverage to quench our thirst: and this is the effects of the holy Spirit, who first "moved upon the waters" of baptism, and afterwards became to us "the breath of life," giving us holy inspirations and assistances, refreshing our wearinesses, cooling our fevers, an allaying all our intemperate passions, making us holy, humble, resigned and pure, "according to the pattern in the mount," even "as our Father is pure." So that the first redemption and pardon of us by Christ's merits is the bread of life, for which we must hunger; and the refreshments and daily emanations of the Spirit, who is the spring of comforts and purity, is that drink which we must thirst after: a being first reconciled to God by Jesus, and a being sanctified and preserved in purity by the holy Spirit, is the adequate object of our desires. Some to hunger and thirst best fancy the analogy and proportion of the two sacraments, the waters of baptism, and the food of the eucharist: some, the bread of the paten, and the wine of the chalice. But it is certain they signify one desire, expressed by the most impatient and necessary of our appetites, hungering and thirsting: and the object is, whatsoever is the principle or the effect, the beginning, or the way, or the end of righteousness; that is, the mercies of God, the pardon of Jesus, the graces of the Spirit, a holy life, and a holy death, and a blessed eternity.

II.400–1

Discourse of Prayer – the Lord's Prayer, its shape and meaning

Our Father, which art in heaven

[I]t is observable that Christ, here speaking concerning private prayer, does describe it in the form of plural signification; to tell us that we are to draw into the communication of our prayers all those who are confederated in the common relation of sons the same Father.

II. 466

Hallowed be Thy Name

[T]he name of God is representative of God himself, and it signifies: Be Thou worshipped and adored, be Thou thanked and celebrated; with honour and eucharist.

II. 467

Thy Kingdom come

[T]he address of this prayer being to God the Father, it is proper to observe, that the kingdom of grace, or of the gospel, is called the kingdom of the Son; and that of glory, in the style of Scripture, is the kingdom of the Father.

II. 467

Thy will be done in earth, as it is in heaven.

That is, the whole economy and dispensation of thy providence, be the guide of the world, and the measure of our desires.

II. 468

These three petitions are addressed to God, by way of adoration. In the first, the soul puts on the affections of a child, and divests itself of its own interest, offering itself up wholly to the designs and glorifications of God. In the second, it puts on the relations and duties of a subject to her legitimate prince, seeking the promotion of his regal interest. In the third, she puts on the affections of a spouse, loving the same love, and choosing the same objects; and delighting in unions and conformities.

II. 468

Give us this day our daily bread

Give unto us all that is necessary for the support of our lives, the bread of our necessity, so the Syriac interpreter reads this.

II. 468–9

But there is also a bread that came down from heaven, a diviner nutriment of our souls, the food and wine of angels, Christ himself, as he communicates himself in the expresses of his word and sacraments.

II. 469

Forgive us our trespasses, as we forgive them that trespass against us.

Not only those sins of infirmity, invasion, and sudden surprise, which, like excrescences of luxuriant trees, adhere to many actions by inadvertency, and either natural weakness or accidental prejudice; but also those great sins, which were washed off from our souls, and the stain taken away in baptism; or when by choice, and after the use of reason, we gave up our names to Christ, when we first received the adoption of sons.

II. 470

And lead us not into temptation

We are to pray, that we enter not into the possession of the temptation, that we be not overcome by it.

II.471

But deliver us from evil

Deliver us from the evil one, who is interested, as an enemy, in every hostility, and in every danger.

II. 471

In these last petitions, which concern ourselves, the soul hath the affections proper to her own needs; as in the former, proportion to God's glory. In the first of these, the affections of a poor, indigent and necessitous beggar; in the second, of a delinquent and penitent servant; and in the last, of a person in affliction or danger. And after all this, the reason of our confidence is derived from God.

II. 471

For thine is the kingdom, the power, and the glory, for ever

These which we beg are for the honour of thy Kingdom, for the manifestations of thy power, and the glory of thy name and mercies; and it is an express doxology or adoration, which is apt and fit to conclude all our prayers and addresses to God.

II. 471

And on prayer in general

Prayer is an abstract and summary of the Christian religion.

II. 464

The matter of our prayers is best taught us, in the form Our Lord taught his disciples; which, because it is short, mysterious, and, like the treasures of the Spirit, full of wisdom and latent senses, it is not improper to draw forth those excellencies, which are intended and signalled by every petition; that, by so excellent an authority, we may know what is lawful to beg of God.

II.466

The special sin of uncharitableness makes the biggest cloud, for he who is softened with apprehension of his own needs of mercy, will be tender hearted towards his brother.

II. 473

That prayer perishes to which the man gives no degree of actual attention.

II. 476

God's blessings, though they come infallibly, yet not always speedily.

II. 478

Only we must not make our accounts for God according to the course of the sun, but the measures of eternity. He measures us by our needs; and we must not measure Him by our impatience.

II.478–9

Those repetitions are vain which repeat the words, not the devotion which renew the expression, and not the desire.

II. 479

Prayer is public, or private: in the communion or society of saints, or in our closets: these prayers have less temptation to variety; the others have more advantage of charity, example, fervour, and energy. In public offices we avoid singularity, in private we avoid hypocrisy.

II. 481

Mental prayer is the best remedy against lightness, and indifferency of affections; but vocal prayer is the aptest instrument of communion.

II.483

Discourse of the certainty of salvation: moments of revelation and then withdrawal

Every man that is in this condition of a confirmed grace does not always know it; but sometimes God draws aside the curtains of peace and shews him His throne and visits him with irradiations of glory, and sends him a little star to stand over his dwelling, and then again covers it with a cloud.

II. 554

Considerations upon some accidents preparatory to the passion

The blessed Jesus had never but two days of triumph in His life: the one was His transfiguration upon mount Tabor; the other, this His riding into the holy city. But that it may appear how little were His joys and present exterior complancencies, in the day of His transfiguration, Moses and Elias appeared to Him, telling Him what great things He was to suffer; and in this day of His riding to Jerusalem, He wet the palms with a dew sweeter than the moistures upon mount Hermon, or the drops of *manna*: for to allay the little warmth of a springing joy He let down a shower of tears, weeping over undone Jerusalem in the day of His triumph, leaving it disputable whether He felt more joy or sorrow in the acts of love; for He triumphed to consider that the redemption of the world was so near, and wept bitterly that men would not be redeemed; His joy was great, to consider that Himself was to suffer so great sadness for our good; and His sorrow was very great, to consider that we would not entertain that good that He brought and laid us by His passion.

II.621–2

Considerations upon the washing of the disciples' feet

And indeed our blessed Lord, knowing that examples are like maps and perfect schemes, in which the whole continent may at once be represented to the eye to all the purposes of art and benefit, did in the latter end of his life draw up the dispersions and larger harvest of His precepts, binding them in the bundle of great examples, and casting them into actions as into sums total: for so this act of washing the feet of His own ministers, and then dying for them, and for all His enemies, did preach the three great sums of evangelical perfection with an admirable energy and abbreviature; humility, and charity, and sufferings, being to Christianity, as the body, and the soul, and the spirit, are to the whole man. For no man brings a sad funeral into the theatre to make his spectators merry, nor can well preach chastity in the impurity of the Bordelli, or persuade temperance when himself is full of wine and luxury, and enters into the baths to boil his undigested meat that he may return to his second supper, and breathes forth impure belchings together with his homily; a poor eremite, or a severely living philosopher, into whose life his own precepts have descended, and his doctrine is mingled with his soul, mingles also effect and virtue with homilies, and incorporates his doctrine in the hearts of his disciples. And this the holy Jesus did in His own person, bearing the burden first upon His own shoulders, that we may with better alacrity undergo what our blessed Lord bears with us, and for us. But that we may the better understand what our blessed Lord designed to us in this lecture, let us consider the proper acts of humility which integrate the virtue.

II.630

Discourse of the Lord's Supper: presence

Some so observe the literal sense of the words that they understand them also in a natural; some so alter them by metaphors and prenatural significations that they will not understand them at all in a proper.

We see it, we feel it, we taste it, and we smell it to be bread; and by philosophy we are led into a belief of that substance whose accidents these are, as we are to believe that to be fire which burns, and flames, and shines: but Christ also affirmed concerning it, "This is My body:" and if faith can create an assent as strong as its object is infallible, or can be as certain in its conclusion as sense is certain in its apprehensions, we must at no hand doubt but that it is Christ's body. Let the sense of that be what it will, so that we believe those words, and (whatsoever that sense is which Christ intended) that we no more doubt in our faith than we do in our sense; then our faith is not reprovable. It is hard to do so much violence to our sense as not to think it bread; but it is more unsafe to do so much violence to our faith as not to believe it to be Christ's body. But it would be considered, that no interest of religion, no saying of Christ, no reverence of opinion, no sacredness of the mystery, is disavowed, if we believe both what we hear and what we see. He that believes it to be bread, and yet verily to be Christ's body, is only tied also by implication to believe God's omnipotence, that He who affirmed it can also verify it. And they that are forward to believe the change of substance, can intend no more but that it be believed verily to be the body of our Lord. And if they think it impossible to reconcile its being bread with the verity of being Christ's body, let them remember that themselves are put to more difficulties, and to admit of more miracles, and to contradict more sciences, and to refuse the testimony of sense, in affirming the special manner of transubstantiation. And therefore it were safer to admit the words in their first sense, in which we shall no more be at war with reason, nor so much with sense, and not at all with faith. And for persons of the contradictory persuasion, who to avoid the natural sense affirm it only to be figurative, since their design is only to make this sacrament to be Christ's body in the sense of faith and not of philosophy, they may remember that its being really present does not hinder but that all that reality may be spiritual; and if it be Christ's body, so it be not affirmed such in a natural sense and manner, it is still only the object of faith and spirit; and if it be affirmed only to be spiritual, there is then no danger to faith in admitting the words of Christ's institution, "This is My body." I suppose it to be a mistake to think whatsoever is real must be natural; and it is no less to think spiritual to be only figurative: that's too much, and this is too little. Philosophy and faith may well be reconciled; and whatsoever objection can invade this union may be cured by modesty. And if we profess we understand not the manner of this mystery, we say no more but that it is a mystery; and if it had been necessary we should have construed it into the most latent sense, Christ himself would have give a *clavis*, and taught the church to unlock so great a secret. Christ said, "this is My body, — this is My blood:" St. Paul said, "the bread of blessing that we break is the communication of the body of Christ, and the chalice which we bless is the communication of the blood of Christ;" and, "we are all one body, because we eat of one bread." One proposition, as well as the other, is the matter of faith, and the latter of them is also of sense; one is as literal as the other: and he that distinguishes in his belief, as he may place the impropriety upon which part he please, and either say it is improperly called 'bread,' or improperly called 'Christ's body;' so he can have nothing to secure his proposition from error, or himself from boldness, in decreeing concerning mysteries against the testimonies of sense, or beyond the modesty and simplicity of christian faith. Let us love and adore the abyss of divine wisdom and goodness, and entertain the sacrament with just and holy receptions; and then we shall receive all those fruits of it which an earnest disputer or a peremptory dogmatizer, whether he happen right or wrong, hath no warrant to expect upon the interest of his opinion.

II.638–40

Sacrifice

There He sits, a high priest continually, and offers still the same one perfect sacrifice; that is, still represents it as having been once finished and consummate, in order to perpetual and never-failing events. And this also His ministers do on earth; they offer up the same sacrifice to God, the sacrifice of the cross, by prayers, and a commemorating rite and representment, according to His holy institution. And as all the effects of grace and the titles of glory were purchased for us on the cross, and the actual mysteries of redemption perfected on earth, but are applied to us, and made effectual to single persons and communities of men, by Christ's intercession in heaven; so also they are promoted by acts of duty and religion here on earth, that we may be "workers together with God," as St. Paul expresses it, and in virtue of the eternal and all-sufficient sacrifice may offer up our prayers and our duty; and by representing that sacrifice may send up, together with our prayers, an instrument of their graciousness and acceptation. The funerals of a deceased friend are not only performed at his first interring, but in the monthly minds and anniversary commemorations; and our grief returns upon the sight of a picture, or upon any instance which our dead friend desired us to preserve as his memorial: we celebrate and "exhibit the Lord's death" in sacrament and symbol; and this is that great express, which when the church offers to God the Father, it obtains all those blessings which that sacrifice purchased. Themistocles snatched up the son of king Admetus, and held him between himself and death, to mitigate the rage of the king; and prevailed accordingly. Our very holding up the Son of God; and representing Him to His Father, is the doing an act of mediation and advantage to ourselves, in the virtue and efficacy of the Mediator.

II.643

Pledge of glory

The holy sacrament is the pledge of glory and the earnest of immortality; for when we have received Him who hath "overcome death, and henceforth dies no more," He becomes to us like the tree of life in paradise; and the consecrated symbols are like the seeds of an eternal duration, springing up in us to eternal life, nourishing our spirits with grace, which is but the prologue and the infancy of glory, and differs from it only as a child from a man. But God first raised up His Son to life, and by giving Him to us hath also consigned us to the same state; for "our life is hid with Christ, in God." When we lay down and cast aside the impurer robes of flesh, they are then but preparing for glory; and "if by the only touch of Christ bodies were redintegrate and restored to natural perfections; how shall not we live for ever who eat His flesh and drink His blood?" it is the discourse of St. Cyril. Whatsoever the Spirit can convey to the body of the church, we may expect from this sacrament; for as the Spirit is the instrument of life and action, so the blood of Christ is the conveyance of His Spirit. And let all the mysterious places of holy scripture concerning the effects of Christ communicated in the blessed sacrament be drawn together in one scheme, we cannot but observe that, although they are so expressed as that their meaning may seem intricate and involved, yet they cannot be drawn to any meaning at all but it is as glorious in its sense as it is mysterious in the expression: and the more intricate they are, the greater is their purpose; no words being apt and proportionate to signify this spiritual secret, and excellent effects of the Spirit.

II.645

Reception of the sacrament

Love and religion are boundless, and all acts of grace relating to the present mystery are fit and proportioned entertainments of our Lord. This only remember, that we are by the mystery of 'one bread' confederated into one body, and the communion of saints, and that the sacrifice which we then commemorate was designed by our Lord for the benefit of all His church: let us be sure to draw all faithful people into the society of the present blessing, joining with the holy man that ministers in prayers, and offerings of that mystery, for the benefit of all sorts of men, of Christ's catholic church.

II.653

Considerations upon the scourging and other accidents from the apprehension till the crucifixion

But nothing prevailing, nor the innocence of Jesus, not His immunity from the sentence of Herod, nor the industry and diligence of Pilate, nor the misery, nor the sight of the afflicted Lamb of God, at last (for so God decreed to permit it and Christ to suffer it) Pilate gave sentence of death upon Him, having first washed his hands; of which God served His end, to declare the innocence of His Son, of which in this whole process He was most curious, and suffered not the least probability to adhere to Him; yet Pilate served no end of his, nor preserved any thing of his innocence. He that rails upon a prince, and cries, Saving your honour you are a tyrant; and he that strikes a man upon the face and cries him mercy, and undoes him and says it was in jest, does just like that person that sins against God, and thinks to be excused by saying it was against his conscience; that is washing our hands when they are stained in blood, as if a ceremony of purification were enough to cleanse a soul from the stains of a spiritual impurity. So some refuse not to take any oath in times of persecution, and say it obliges not because it was forced and done against their wills; as if the doing of it were washed off by protesting against it, whereas the protesting against it declares me criminal, if I rather choose not death than that which I profess to be a sin.– But all the persons which co-operated in this death were in this life consigned to a fearful judgment after it. The Jews took the blood (which Pilate seemed to wash off) "upon themselves and their children," and the blood of this paschal Lamb stuck upon their forehead, and marked them, not to escape, but to fall under the sword of the destroying angel, and they perished either by a more hasty death, or shortly after in the extirpation and miserable ruin of their nation. And Pilate, who had a less share in the crime, yet had a black character of a secular judgment; for not long after he was by Vitellius, the president of Syria, sent to Rome, to answer to the crimes objected against him by the Jews, whom to please he had done so much violence to his conscience; and by Cæsar's sentence he was banished to Vienna deprived of all his honours, where he lived ingloriously, till by impatience of his calamity he killed himself with his own hand. And thus the blood of Jesus, shed for the salvation of the world, became to them a curse; and that which purifies the saints stuck to them that shed it and mingled it not with the tears of repentance, to be a leprosy loathsome and incurable, So manna turns to worms, and the wine of angels to vinegar and lees, when it is received into impure vessels, or tasted by wanton palates; and the sun himself produces rats and serpents, when it reflects upon the dirt of Nilus.

II.678–9

Considerations upon the crucifixion: the death of Jesus

In the midst of two thieves, three long hours the holy Jesus hung, clothed with pain, agony, and dishonour, all of them so eminent and vast, that He who could, not but hope, whose soul was enchased with divinity, and dwelt in the bosom of God, and in the cabinet of the mysterious Trinity, yet had a cloud of misery so thick and black drawn before Him, that He complained as if God had forsaken Him: but this was "the pillar of cloud" which conducted Israel into Canaan. And as God behind the cloud supported the holy Jesus, and stood ready to receive Him into the union of His glories; so His soul in that great desertion had internal comforts proceeding from consideration of all those excellent persons which should be adopted into the fellowship of His sufferings, which should imitate His graces, which should communicate His glories. And we follow this cloud to our country, having Christ for our guide: and though He trod the way, leaning upon the cross, which, like the staff of Egypt, pierced His hands; yet it is to us a comfort and support, pleasant to our spirits as the sweetest canes, strong as the pillars of the earth, and made apt for our use by having been borne and made smooth by the hands of our elder brother.

In the midst of all His torments, Jesus made only one prayer of sorrow, to represent His sad condition to His Father; but no accent of murmur, no syllable of anger against His enemies; instead of that, He sent up a holy charitable, and effective prayer for their forgiveness, and by that prayer obtained of God that within fifty-five days eight thousand of His enemies were converted. So potent is the prayer of charity, that it prevails above the malice of men, turning the arts of Satan into the designs of God; and when malice occasions the prayer, the prayer becomes an antidote to malice. And by this instance our blessed Lord consigned that duty to us, which in his sermons He had preached, That we should forgive our enemies, and pray for them: and by so doing ourselves are freed from the stings of anger, and the storms of a revengeful spirit; and we oftentimes procure servants to God, friends to ourselves, and heirs to the kingdom of heaven.

II.708–9

The Virgin Mary

By the cross of Christ stood the holy Virgin-mother, upon whom old Simeon's prophecy was now verified: for now she felt a sword passing through her very soul: she stood without clamour and womanish noises; sad, silent, and with a modest grief, deep as the waters of the abyss but smooth as the face of a pool; full of love, and patience, and sorrow, and hope. Now she was put to it to make use of all those excellent discourse her holy Son had used to build up her spirit, and fortify it against this day. Now she felt the blessings and strengths of faith; and she passed from the griefs of the passion to the expectation of the resurrection; and she rested in this death, as in a sad remedy; for she knew it reconciled God with all the world. But her hope drew a veil before her sorrow; and though her grief was great enough to swallow her up, yet her love was greater, and did swallow up her grief. But the sun also had a veil upon his face, and taught us to draw a curtain before the passion, which would be the most artificial expression of its greatness; whilst by silence and wonder we confess it great beyond our expression, or, which is all one, great as the burden and baseness of our sins. And with this veil drawn before the face of Jesus, let us suppose Him at the gates of paradise, calling with His last words in a loud voice to have them opened, that "the King of glory might come in."

II.710

A devotional prayer

O dearest Saviour, I adore Thy mercies and Thy incomparable love expressed in Thy so voluntary susception and affectionate suffering such horrid and sad tortures, which cannot be remembered without a sad compassion; the waters of bitterness entered into Thy soul, and the storms of death, and Thy Father's anger, broke Thee all in pieces: and what shall I do, who by my sins have so tormented my dearest Lord? what contrition can be great enough, what tears sufficiently expressive, what hatred and detestation of my crimes can be equal and commensurate to those sad accidents which they have produced? Pity me, O Lord; pity me, dearest God; turn those Thy merciful eyes towards me, O most merciful Redeemer; for my sins are great, like unto Thy passion; full of sorrow and shame, and a burden too great for me to bear. Lord, who hast done do much for me, now only speak the word, and Thy servant shall be whole. Let Thy wounds heal me, Thy virtues amend me, Thy death quicken me; that I in this life suffering the cross of a sad and salutary repentance, in the union and merits of Thy cross and passion may die with Thee, and rest with Thee, and rise again with Thee, and live with Thee for ever, in the possession of Thy glories, O dearest Saviour Jesus. Amen.

II.711

Considerations upon the accidents happening in the interval after the death of the holy Jesus, until His resurrection

But the apparitions which Jesus made were all upon the design upon laying the foundation of all Christian graces; for the begetting and establishing faith and an active confidence in their persons, and building them up on the great fundamentals of the religion. And therefore He appointed a general meeting upon the mountain in Galilee, that the number of witnesses might not only disseminate the fame, but establish the article, of the resurrection; for upon that are built all the hopes of a Christian; and "if the dead rise not, then we are of all men most miserable," in quitting the present possessions, and entertaining injuries and affronts without hope of reparation. But we lay two gages in several repositiories; the body in the bosom of the earth, the soul in the bosom of God: and as we here live by faith and lay them down with hope; so the resurrection is a restitution of them both, and a state of re-union. And therefore, although the glory of our spirits, without the body, were joy great enough to make compensation for more than the troubles of the world; yet because one shall not be glorified without the other, they being of themselves incomplete substances, and God having revealed nothing clearly concerning actual and complete felicities till the day of judgement, when it is promised our bodies shall rise; therefore it is that the resurrection is the great article on which we rely, and which Christ took so much care to prove and ascertain to so many persons, because if that should be disbelieved with which all our felicities ate to be received, we have nothing to establish our faith, or entertain our hope, or satisfy our desires, or make retribution for that state of secular inconveniences in which by the necessities of our nature, and humility and patience of our religion, we are engaged.

II. 725

2

Discipleship

From *Holy Living*

From the Preface – 'Men are apt to prefer a prosperous error before an afflicted truth'

My Lord,
I have lived to see religion painted upon banners, and thrust out of churches, and the temple turned into a tabernacle, and that tabernacle made ambulatory, and covered with skins of beasts and torn curtains, and God to be worshipped, not as He is, the Father of our Lord Jesus, an afflicted Prince, the King of sufferings; nor as the God of peace; which two appellatives God newly took upon Him in the New testament, and glories in for ever but He is owned now rather as the Lord of hosts, which title He was pleased to lay aside when the kingdom of the gospel was preached by the Prince of peace. But when religion puts on armour, and God is not acknowledged by His New testament titles, religion may have in it the power of the sword, but not the power of godliness; and we may complain of this to God, and amongst them that are afflicted, but we have no remedy but what we must expect from the fellowship of Christ's sufferings, and the returns of the God of peace. In the mean time, and now that religion pretends to stranger actions upon new principles, and men are apt to prefer a prosperous error before an afflicted truth, and some will think they are religious enough if their worshippings have in them the prevailing ingredient; and the ministers of religion are so scattered, that they cannot unite to stop the inundation, and from chairs or pulpits, from their synods or tribunals, chastise the iniquity of the error, and the ambition of evil guides, and the infidelity of the willingly seduced multitude, and that those few good people who have no other plot in their religion but to serve God and save their souls, do want such assistances of ghostly counsel as may serve their emergent needs, and assist their endeavours in the acquist of virtues, and relieve their dangers when they are tempted to sin and death; I thought I had reasons enough inviting me to draw into one body those advises, which the several necessities of many men must use at some time or other, and many of them daily: that by a collection of

holy precepts they might less feel the want of personal and attending guides, and that the rules for conduct of souls might be committed to a book, which they might always have; since they could not always have a prophet at their needs, nor be suffered to go up to the house of the Lord to enquire of the appointed oracles.

III. 1–2/S.55–6

Use of time

He that is choice of his time will also be choice of his company, and choice of his actions: lest the first engage him in vanity and loss; and the latter, by being criminal, be a throwing his time and himself away, and a going back in the accounts of eternity.

God lath given to man a short time here upon earth, and yet upon this short time eternity depends; but so that for every hour of our life, after we are persons capable of laws and know good from evil, we must give account to the great Judge of men and angels. And this is it which our blessed Saviour told us, that we must account for every idle word: not meaning that every word which is not designed to edification, or is less prudent, shall be reckoned for a sin; but that the time which we spend in our idle talking and unprofitable discoursings, that time which might and ought to have been employed to spiritual and useful purposes, that is to be accounted for.

For we must remember that we have a great work to do, many enemies to conquer, many evils to prevent, much danger to run through, many difficulties to be mastered, many necessities to serve, and much good to do, many children to provide for, or many friends to support, or many poor to relieve, or many diseases to cure, besides the needs of nature and of relation, our private and our public cares, and duties of the world which necessity and the providence of God hath adopted into the family of Religion.

And that we need not fear this instrument to be a snare to us, or that the duty must end in scruple, vexation, and eternal fears, we must remember that the life of every man may be so ordered, and indeed must, that it may be a perpetual serving of God: the greatest trouble and most busy trade and worldly incumbrances, when they are necessary, or charitable, or profitable in order to any of those ends which we are bound to serve, whether public or private, being a doing God's work. For God provides the good things of the world to serve the needs of nature by the labours of the ploughman, the skill and pains of the artisan, and the dangers and traffic of the merchant: these men are in their calling the ministers of the divine providence, and the stewards of the creation, and servants of a great family of God, the world, in the employment of procuring necessaries for food and clothing, ornament and physic. In their proportions also a king and a priest and a prophet, a judge and an advocate, doing the works of their employment according to their proper rules, are doing the work of God, because they serve those necessities, which God hath made, and yet made no provisions for them but by their ministry. So that no man can complain that his calling takes him off from religion: his calling itself and his very worldly employment in honest trades and offices is a serving of God; and if it be moderately pursued, and according to the rules of Christian prudence, will leave void spaces enough for prayers and retirements of a more spiritual religion.

III. 9–10/S.19–20

Prayer and Action

Let every action of concernment be begun with prayer, that God would not only bless the action, but sanctify your purpose; and make an oblation of the action to God: holy and well intended actions being the best oblations and presents we can make to God; and when God is entitled to them, He will the rather keep the fire upon the altar bright and shining.

III. 18/S.29

'We are also cabinets of the mysterious Trinity'

God is especially present in the hearts of His people, by His Holy Spirit and indeed the hearts of holy men are temples in the truth of things, and in type and shadow they are heaven itself. God reigns in the hearts of His servants: there is His kingdom. The power of grace hath subdued all His enemies: there is His power. They serve Him night and day, and give Him thanks and praise: that is His glory. This is the religion and worship of God in the temple. The temple itself is the heart of man; Christ is the high priest, who from thence sends up the incense of prayers, and joins them to His own intercession, and presents all together to His Father; and the Holy Ghost, by His dwelling there, hath also consecrated it into a temple; and God dwells in our hearts by faith, and Christ by His spirit, and the Spirit by His purities: so that we are also cabinets of the mysterious Trinity; and what is this short of heaven itself, but as infancy is short of manhood, and letters of words? The same state of life it is, but not the same age. It is heaven in a looking-glass, dark but yet true, representing the beauties of the soul, and the graces of God, and the images of His eternal glory, by the reality of a special presence.

III. 24/S.37

Sensual pleasures

A longing after sensual pleasures is a dissolution of the spirit of a man, and makes it loose, soft, and wandering; unapt for noble, wise, or spiritual employments; because the principles upon which pleasure is chosen and pursued, are sottish, weak, and unlearned, such as prefer the body before the soul, the appetite before reason, sense before the spirit, the pleasures of a short abode before the pleasures of eternity.

III. 44/S.37

Marriage and sexual relations

Concerning married persons, besides the keeping of their mutual faith and contract with each other, these particulars are useful to be observed.

Although their mutual endearments are safe within the protection of marriage, yet they that have wives or husbands must be as though they had them not; that is, they must have an affection greater to each other, than they have to any person in the world, but not greater than they have to God, but that they be ready to part with all interest in each other's person rather than sin against God.

In their permissions and licence, they must be sure to observe the order of nature, and the ends of God. He is an ill husband that uses his wife as a man treats a harlot, having no other end but pleasure. Concerning which our best rule is, that although in this, as in eating and drinking, there is an appetite to be satisfied, which cannot be done without pleasing that desire; yet since that desire and satisfaction was intended by nature for other ends, they should never be separate from those ends, but always be joined with all or one of these ends, with a desire of children, or to avoid fornication, or to lighten and ease the cares and sadnesses of household affairs, or to endear each other; but never with a purpose, either in act or desire, to separate the sensuality from these ends which hallow it. Onan did separate his act from its proper end, and so ordered his embraces that his wife should not conceive, and God punished him.

Married persons must keep such modesty and decency of treating each other, that they never force themselves into high and violent lusts with arts and misbecoming devices; always remembering that those mixtures are most innocent, which are most simple and most natural, most orderly and most safe.

It is a duty of matrimonial chastity to be restrained and temperate in the use of their lawful pleasures: concerning which although no universal rule can antecedently be given to all persons any more than to all bodies one proportion of meat and drink; yet married persons are to estimate the degree of their licence according to the following proportions; that it be moderate, so as to consist with health; that it be so ordered as not to be too expensive time, that precious opportunity of working out our salvation; that when duty is demanded, it be always paid (so far as is in our power and election) according to the foregoing measures; and that it be with a temperate affection, without violent transporting desires, or too sensual applications. Concerning which a man is to make judgment by proportion to other actions, and the severities of his religion and the sentences of sober and wise persons: always remembering that marriage is a provision for supply of the natural necessities of he body, not for the artificial and procured appetites of the mind; and it is a sad truth that many married persons, thinking that the flood-gates of liberty are set wide open without measures or restraints, so they sail in that channel, have felt the final rewards of intemperance and lust, by their unlawful using of lawful permissions. Only let each of them be temperate, and both of them be modest. Socrates was wont to say that those women to whom nature had not been indulgent in good features and colours, should make it up themselves with excellent manners; and those who were beautiful and comely, should be careful that so fair a body be not polluted with unhandsome usages. To which Plutarch adds, that a wife, if she be unhandsome, should consider how extremely ugly she would be, if she wanted modesty; but if she be handsome, let her think how gracious that beauty would be if she superadds chastity.

Married persons by consent are to abstain from their mutual entertainments at solemn times of devotion; not as a duty of itself necessary, but as being the most proper act of purity which in their condition they can present to God, and being a good advantage for attending their preparation to the solemn duty and their demeanour in it. It is St. Paul's counsel, that "by consent for a time they should abstain, that they may give themselves to fasting and prayer." And though when Christians did receive the holy communion every day, it is certain they did not abstain, but had children; yet when the communion was more seldom, they did with religion abstain from the marriage-bed during the time of their solemn preparatory devotions, as anciently they did from eating and drinking, till the solemnity of the day was past.

III.62–4/S.81–3

Arguments against pride

Our body is weak and impure, sending out more uncleannesses from its several sinks than could be endured if they were not necessary and natural: and we are forced to pass that through our mouths, which as soon as we see upon the ground, we loathe like rottenness and vomiting.

Our strength is inferior to that of many beasts, and our infirmities so many that we are forced to dress and tend horses and asses, that they may help our needs and relieve our wants.

Our beauty is in colour inferior to many flowers, and in proportion of parts it is no better than nothing; for even a dog hath parts as well proportioned and fitted to his purposes and the designs of his nature, as we have: and when it is most florid and gay, three fits of an ague can change it into yellowness and leanness, and the hollowness and wrinkles of deformity.

Our learning is then best when it teaches most humility: but to be proud of learning is the greatest ignorance in the world. For our learning is so long in getting, and so very imperfect, that the greatest clerk knows not the thousandth part of what he is ignorant; and knows so uncertainly what he seems to know, and knows no otherwise than a fool or a child even what is told him or what he guesses at, that except those things which concern his duty, and which God hath revealed to him, which also every woman knows so far as is necessary, the most learned man hath nothing to be proud of, unless this be a sufficient argument to exalt him, that he uncertainly guesses at some more unnecessary things than many others, who yet know all that concerns them, and mind other things more necessary for the needs of life and commonwealths.

III.68–9/S.87–8

Humility

Give God thanks for every weakness, deformity and imperfection, and accept it as a favour and grace of God, and an instrument to resist pride, and nurse humility; ever remembering that when God, by giving thee a crooked back, hath also made thy spirit stoop or less vain, thou art more ready to enter the narrow gate of heaven, than by being straight, and standing upright, and thinking highly. Thus the apostles rejoiced in their infirmities, not moral, but natural and accidental, in their being beaten and whipt like slaves, in their nakedness and poverty.

III.73/S.93

Contentedness

Virtues and discourses are, like friends, necessary in all fortunes; but those are the best, which are friends in our sadnesses, and support us in our sorrows and sad accidents; and in this sense, no man that is virtuous can be friendless; nor hath any man reason to complain of the divine providence, or accuse the public disorder of things, or his own infelicity, since God hath appointed one remedy for all the evils in the world, and that is a contented spirit: for this alone makes a man pass through tire, and not be scorched; through seas, and not be drowned; through hunger and nakedness, and want nothing. For since all the evil in the world consists in the disagreeing between the object and the appetite, as when a man hath what he desires not, or desires what be hath not, or desires amiss; he that composes his spirit to the present accident, hath variety of instances for his virtue, but none to trouble him; because his desires enlarge not beyond his present fortune; and a wise man is placed in the variety of chances, like the nave or centre of a wheel in the midst of all the circumvolutions and changes of posture, without violence or change, save that it turns gently in compliance with its changed parts, and is indifferent which part is up, and which is down.

III.84/S.106

A prayer for a contented spirit, and the grace of moderation and patience

O almighty God, Father and Lord of all the creatures, who hast disposed all things and all chances so as may best glorify Thy wisdom, and serve the ends of Thy justice, and magnify Thy mercy, by secret and undiscernible ways bringing good out of evil; I most humbly beseech Thee to give me wisdom from above, that I may adore Thee, and admire Thy ways and footsteps, which are in the great deep and not to be searched out: teach me to submit to Thy providence in all things, to be content in all changes of person and condition; to be temperate in prosperity, and to read my duty in the lines of Thy mercy; and in adversity to be meek, patient, and resigned; and to look through the cloud, that I may wait for the consolation of the Lord, and the day of redemption: in the mean time doing my duty with an unwearied diligence and an undisturbed resolution, having no fondness for the vanities or possessions of this world, but laying up my hopes in heaven and the rewards of holy living, and being strengthened with the spirit of the inner man, through Jesus Christ our Lord. Amen.

III.114/S.140

Obedience

There is no sin in the world which God hath punished with so great severity and high detestation, as this of disobedience. For the crime of idolatry God sent the sword amongst his people; but it was never heard that the earth opened and swallowed up any but rebels against their prince.

Obedience is better than the particular actions of religion; and he serves God better that follows his prince in lawful services, than he that refuses his command upon pretence he must go say his prayers. But rebellion is compared to that sin, which of all sin seems the most unnatural and damned impiety; "rebellion is as the sin of witchcraft."

Obedience is a complicated act of virtue, and many graces are exercised in one act of obedience. It is an act of humility, of mortification and self-denial, of charity to God, of care of the public, of order and charity to ourselves and all our society, and a great victory over the most refractory and unruly passions.

III.120/S.147

Law and Civil Authority – implicit criticism of authoritarian monarchy?

Princes of the people, and all that have legislative power, must provide useful and good laws, for the defence of propriety, for the encouragement of labour, for the safeguard of their persons, for determining controversies, for reward of noble actions and excellent arts and rare inventions, for promoting trade and enriching their people.

In the making laws, princes must have regard to the public dispositions, to the affections and disaffections of the people, and must not introduce a law with public scandal and displeasure; but consider the public benefit, and the present capacity of affairs, and general inclinations of men's minds. For he that enforces a law upon a people against their first and public apprehensions, tempts them to disobedience, and makes laws to become snares and hooks to catch the people, and to enrich the treasury with the spoil and tears and curses of the commonalty, and to multiply their mutiny and their sin.

Princes must provide that the laws be duly executed, for a good law without execution is like an unperformed promise; and therefore they must be severe exactors of accounts from their delegates and ministers of justice.

III.123/S.150

Rules and measures of justice in bargaining

In making contracts, use not many words; for all the business of a bargain is summed up in few sentences: and he that speaks least, means fairest, as having fewer opportunities to deceive.

Lie not at all, neither in a little thing nor in a great, neither in the substance nor in the circumstance, neither in word nor deed; that is, pretend not what is false, cover not what is true and let the measure of your affirmation or denial be the understanding of your contractor; for he that deceives the buyer or the seller by speaking what is true in a sense not intended or understood by the, other, is a liar and a thief; for in bargains you are to avoid not only what is false, but that also which deceives.

In prices of bargaining concerning uncertain merchandises, you may buy as cheap ordinarily as you can, and sell as dear as you can, so it be, first, without violence and secondly, when you contract on equal terms with persons in all senses, as to the matter and skill of bargaining, equal to yourself, that is, merchants with merchants, wise men with wise men, rich with rich; and thirdly, when there is no deceit, and no necessity, and no monopoly: for in these cases, viz., when the contractors are equal, and no advantage on either side, both parties are voluntary, and therefore there can be no injustice or wrong to either. But then add also this consideration, that the public be not oppressed by unreasonable and unjust rates: for which the following rules are the best measure.

Let your prices be according to that measure of good and evil which is established in the fame and common accounts of the wisest and most merciful men, skilled in that manufacture or commodity; and the gain such which without scandal is allowed to persons in all the same circumstances.

Let no prices be heightened by the necessity or unskilfulness of the contractor: for the first is direct uncharitableness to the person, and injustice in the thing, because the man's necessity could not naturally enter into the consideration of the value of the commodity; and the other is deceit and oppression: much less must any man make necessities, as by engrossing a commodity, by monopoly, by detaining corn, or the like indirect arts; for such persons are unjust to all single persons with whom in such cases they contract, and oppressors of the public.

In intercourse with others, do not do all which you may lawfully do, but keep something within thy power: and because there is a latitude of gain in buying and selling, take not thou the utmost penny that is lawful, or which thou thinkest so; for although it be lawful, yet it is not safe; and he that gains all that he can gain lawfully this year, possibly next year will be tempted to gain something unlawfully.

III.130–1/S.157–9

Faith

The consideration of the divine omnipotence and infinite wisdom, and our own ignorance, are great instruments of curing all doubting, and silencing the murmurs of infidelity.

Avoid all curiosity of enquiry into particulars and circumstances and mysteries: for true faith is full of ingenuity and hearty simplicity, free from suspicion, wise and confident, trusting upon generals, without watching and prying into unnecessary or indiscernible particulars. No man carries his bed into his field to watch how his corn grows, but believes upon the general order of providence and nature; and at harvest finds himself not deceived.

In time of temptation, be not busy to dispute, but rely upon the conclusion, and throw yourself upon God: and contend not with Him but in prayer, and in the presence and with the help of a prudent untempted guide; and be sure to esteem all changes of belief which offer themselves in the time of your greatest weakness, contrary to the persuasions of your best understanding, to be temptations, and reject them accordingly.

III.149/S.178–9

Hope

Let your hope be moderate; proportioned to your state, person, and condition, whether it be for gifts or graces, or temporal favours. It is an ambitious hope for persons whose diligence is like them that are least in the kingdom of heaven, to believe themselves endeared to God as the greatest saints; or that they shall have a throne equal to St. Paul, or the blessed Virgin Mary. A stammerer cannot with moderation hope for the gift of tongues, or a peasant to become learned as Origen; or if a beggar desires, or hopes, to become's king, or asks for a thousand pound a year, we call him impudent, not passionate, much less reasonable. Hope that God will crown your endeavours with equal measures of that reward, which He indeed freely gives, but yet gives according to our proportions. Hope for good success according to, or not much beyond, the efficacy of the causes and the instrument; and let the husbandman hope for a good harvest, not for a rich kingdom, or a victorious army.

III.151/S.179–80

Love of God

Love is the greatest thing that God can give us, for Himself is love; and it is the greatest thing we can give to God, for it will also give ourselves, and carry with it all that is ours. The apostle calls it the band of perfection; it is the old, and it is the new, and it is the great commandment, and it is all the commandments; for it is the fulfilling of the law. It does the work of all other graces, without any instrument but its own immediate virtue. For as the love to sin makes a man sin against all his own reason, and all the discourses of wisdom, and all the advices of his friends, and without temptation, and without opportunity; so does the love of God; it makes a man chaste without the laborious arts of fasting and exterior disciplines, temperate in the midst of feasts, and is active enough to choose it without any intermedial appetites, and reaches at glory through the very heart of grace, without any other arms but those of love. It is a grace that loves God for Himself, and our neighbours for God. The consideration of God's goodness and bounty, the experience of those profitable and excellent emanations from Him, may be, and most commonly are, the first motive of our love; but when we are once entered, and have tasted the goodness of God, we love the spring for its own excellency, passing from passion to reason, from thanking to adoring, from sense to spirit, from considering ourselves to an union with God: and this is the image and little representation of heaven; it is beatitude in picture, or rather the infancy and beginnings of glory.

III.156/S.181

Fasting

Fasting if it be considered in itself, without relation to spiritual `ends, is a duty no where enjoined or counselled; but christianity hath to do with it as it may be made an instrument of the spirit, by subduing the lusts of the flesh, or removing any hindrances of religion. And it hath been practised by all ages of the church, and advised in order to three ministries; to prayer; to mortification of bodily lusts; and to repentance.

III.147/S.196

Sunday Worship

The memories of the saints are precious to God, and therefore they ought also to be so to us; and such persons who serve God by holy living, industrious preaching, and religious dying, ought to have their names preserved in honour, and God be glorified in them, and their holy doctrines and lives published and imitated; and we by so doing give testimony to the article of the communion of saints. But in these cases as every church is to be sparing in the number of days, so also should she be temperate in her injunctions, not imposing them but upon voluntary and unbusied persons, without snare or burden. But the holy day is best kept by giving God thanks for the excellent persons, apostles or martyrs, we then remember, and by imitating their lives; this all may do: and they that can also keep the solemnity, must do that too when it is publicly enjoined.

III.175/S.208

Motives to prayer

I cannot say any thing beyond this very consideration and its appendages to invite christian people to pray often. But we may consider that, first, it is a duty commanded by God and His holy Son; secondly, it is an act of grace and highest honour, that we, dust and ashes, are admitted to speak to the eternal God, to run to Him as to a father, to lay open our wants, to complain of our burdens, to explicate our scruples, to beg remedy and ease, support and counsel, health and safety, deliverance and salvation: and thirdly, God hath invited us to it by many gracious promises of hearing us; fourthly, He hath appointed His most glorious Son to the the precedent of prayer, and to make continual intercession for us to the throne of grace; fifthly, He hath appointed an angel to present the prayers of His servants; and sixthly, Christ unites them to His own, and sanctifies them, and makes them effective and prevalent; and seventhly, hath put it into the hands of men to rescind, or alter, all the decrees of God which are of one kind, that is, conditional, and concerning ourselves and our final estate, and many instances of our intermedial or temporal, by the power of prayers; and eighthly, the prayers of men have saved cities and kingdoms from ruin: prayer hath raised dead men to life, hath stopped the violence of fire, shut the mouths of wild beasts, hath altered the course of nature, caused rain in Egypt, and drought in the sea: it made the sun to go from west to east, and the moon to stand still, and rocks and mountains to walk; and it cures diseases without physic, and makes physic to do the work of nature, and nature to do the work of grace, and grace to do the work of God, and it does miracles of accident and event. And yet prayer that does all this is of itself nothing but an ascent of the mind to God, a desiring things fit to be desired, and an expression of this desire to God, as we can, and as becomes us: and our unwillingness to pray, is nothing else but a not desiring what we ought passionately to long for; or if we do desire it, it is a choosing rather to miss our satisfaction and felicity, than to ask for it.

III.176/S.209–10

Concentration in prayer

Learn to abstract your thoughts and desires from pleasures and things of the world; for nothing is a direct cure to this evil but cutting off all other loves and adherences. Order your affairs so that religion may be propounded to you as a reward, and prayer as your defence, and holy actions as your security, and charity and good works as your treasure. Consider that all things else are satisfactions but to the brutish part of a man, and that these are the refreshments and relishes of that noble part of us by which we are better than beasts; and whatsoever other instrument, exercise, or consideration, is of use to take our loves from the world, the same is apt to place them upon God.

III.185/S.222

Anger

Consider that anger is a professed enemy to counsel; it is a direct storm, in which no man can be heard to speak or call from without: for if you counsel gently, you are despised: if you urge it and be vehement, you provoke it more. Be careful therefore to lay up beforehand a great stock of reason and prudent considerations, that like a besieged town you may be provided for and be defensible from within, since you are not likely to be relieved from without. Anger is not to be suppressed but by something that is as inward as itself and more habitual.

III.199/S.238

Repentance

True repentance is a punishing duty, and acts its sorrow; and judges and condemns the sin by voluntary submitting to such sadnesses as God sends on us, or, to prevent the judgment of God, by judging ourselves, and punishing our bodies and our spirits by such instruments of piety as are troublesome to the body; such as are fasting, watching, long prayers, troublesome postures in our prayers, expensive alms, and all outward acts of humiliation. For he that must judge himself, must condemn himself if he be guilty; and if he be condemned, he must be punished; and if he be so judged, it will help to prevent the judgment of the Lord, St. Paul instructing us in this particular. But I before intimated that the punishing actions of repentance are only actions of sorrow, and therefore are to make up the proportions of it. For our grief may be so full of trouble as to outweigh all the burdens of fasts and bodily afflictions, and then the other are the less necessary; and when they are used, the benefit of them is to obtain of God a remission or a lessening of such temporal judgments which God hath decreed against the sins, as it was in the case of Ahab; but the sinner is not by any thing of this reconciled to the eternal favour of God, for as yet this is but the introduction to repentance.

III.208/S.248

The Eucharist

The celebration of the holy sacrament is the great mysteriousness of the christian religion, and succeeds to the most solemn rite of natural and Judaical religion, the law of sacrificing. For God spared mankind, and took the sacrifice of beasts, together with our solemn prayers, for an instrument of expiation. But these could not purify the soul from sin, but were typical of the sacrifice of something that could. But nothing could do this, but either the offering of all that sinned, that every man should be the *anathema* or devoted thing;' or else by some one of the same capacity, who by some superadded excellency might in his own personal sufferings have a value great enough to satisfy for all the whole kind of sinning persons. This the Son of God, Jesus Christ, God and man, undertook, and finished by a sacrifice of Himself upon the altar of the cross.

This sacrifice, because it was perfect, could be but one, and that once: but because the needs of the world should last as long as the world itself, it was necessary that there should be a perpetual ministry established, whereby this one sufficient sacrifice should be made eternally effectual to the several new arising needs of all the world, who should desire it or in any sense be capable of it.

To this end Christ was made a priest for ever; He was initiated or consecrated on the cross, and there began His priesthood, which was to last till His coming to judgment. It began on earth, but was to last and be officiated in heaven, where He sits perpetually representing and exhibiting to the Father that great effective sacrifice which He offered on the cross, to eternal and never-failing purposes.

As Christ is pleased to represent to His Father that great sacrifice as a means of atonement and expiation for all mankind, and with special purposes and intendment for all the elect, all that serve Him in holiness: so He hath appointed that the same ministry shall be done upon earth too, in our manner, and according to our proportion: and therefore hath constituted and separated an order of men who, by "showing forth the Lord's death" by sacramental representation, may pray unto God after the same manner that our Lord and High Priest does, that is, offer to God and represent in this solemn prayer and sacrament Christ as already offered; so sending up a gracious instrument whereby our prayers may, for His sake and in the same manner of intercession, be offered up to God in our behalf, and for all them for whom we pray, to all those purposes for which Christ died.

As the ministers of the sacrament do in a sacramental manner present to God the sacrifice of the cross by being imitators of Christ's intercession; so the people are sacrificers too in their manner: for besides that by saying 'Amen' they join in the act of him that ministers, and make it also to be their own; so when they eat and drink the consecrated and blessed elements worthily, they receive Christ within them, and therefore may, also offer Him to God, while in their sacrifice of obedience and thanksgiving they present themselves to God with Christ, whom they have spiritually received, that is, themselves with that which will make them gracious and acceptable. The offering their bodies and souls and services to God, in Him, and by Him, and with Him, who is His Father's well-beloved, and in whom He is well pleased, cannot but be accepted to all the purposes of blessing, grace, and glory.

This is the sum of tie greatest mystery of our religion; it is the copy of the passion, and the ministration of the great mystery of our redemption: and therefore whatsoever entitles us to the general privileges of Christ's passion, all that is necessary by way of disposition to the celebration of the sacrament of His passion, because this celebration is our manner of applying or using it.

III.214–15/S.254–6

A prayer to be said upon our birthday or day of baptism

O blessed and eternal God, I give Thee praise and glory for Thy great mercy to me, in causing me to be born of christian parents, and didst not allot to me a portion with misbelievers and heathen that have not known Thee. Thou didst not suffer me to be strangled at the gate of the womb, but Thy hand sustained and brought me to the light of the world, and the illumination of baptism, with Thy grace preventing my election, and by an artificial necessity and holy prevention engaging me to the profession and practices of christianity. Lord, since that, I have broken the promises made in my behalf, and which I confirmed by my after-act; I went back from them by an evil life: and yet Thou hast still continued to me life and time of repentance, and didst not cut me off in the beginning of my days and the progress of my sins. O dearest God, pardon the errors and ignorances, the vices and vanities, of my youth, and the faults of my more forward years, and let me never more stain the whiteness of my baptismal robe: and now that by Thy grace I still persist in the purposes of obedience, and do give up my name to Christ, and glory to be a disciple of Thy institution and a servant of Jesus, let me never fail of Thy grace; let no root of bitterness spring up, and disorder my purposes, and defile my spirit. O let my years be so many degrees of nearer approach to Thee: and forsake me not, O God, in my old age, when I am greyheaded; and when my strength faileth me, be Thou my strength and my guide unto death; that I may reckon my years, and apply my heart unto wisdom; and at last, after the spending a holy and a blessed life, I may be brought unto a glorious eternity, through Jesus Christ our Lord. Amen.

III.239–40/S.283–4

From *Holy Dying*

Shortness of life

A man is a bubble, said the Greek proverbs; which Lucian represents with advantages and its proper circumstances, to this purpose; saying, that all the world is a storm, and men rise up in their several generations, like bubbles descending *a Jove pluvio*, from God and the dew of heaven, from a tear and drop of man, from nature and Providence: and some of these instantly sink into the deluge of their first parent, and are hidden in a sheet of water, having had no other business in the world but to be born that they might be able to die: others float up and down two or three turns, and suddenly disappear, and give their place to others: and they that live longest upon the face of the waters, are in perpetual motion, restless and uneasy; and being crushed with the great drop of a cloud sink into flatness and a froth; the change not being great, it being hardly possible it should be more a nothing than it was before. So is every man: he is born in vanity and sin; he comes into the world like morning mushrooms, soon thrusting up their heads into the air, and conversing with their kindred of the same production, and as soon they turn into dust and forgetfulness some of them without any other interest in the affairs of the world but that they made their parents a little glad, and very sorrowful: others ride longer in the storm; it may be until seven years of vanity be expired, and then peradventure the sun shines hot upon their heads, and they fall into the shades below, into the cover of death and darkness of the grave to hide them. But if the bubble stands the shock of a bigger drop, and outlives the chances of a child of a careless nurse, of drowning in a pail of water, of being overlaid by a sleepy servant, or such little accidents, then the young man dances like a bubble, empty and gay, and shines like a dove's neck, or the image of a rainbow, which hath no substance, and whose very imagery and colours are fantastical; and so he dances out the gaiety of his youth, and is all the while in a storm, and endures only because he is not knocked on the head by a drop of bigger rain, or crushed by the pressure of a load of indigested meat, or quenched by the disorder of an ill-placed humour: and to preserve a man alive in the midst of so many chances and hostilities, is as great a miracle as to create him; to preserve him from rushing into nothing, and at first to draw him up from nothing, were equally the issues of an almighty power. And therefore the wise men of the world have contended who shall best fit man's condition with words signifying his vanity and short abode.

III.265–6/S.19–20

Preparation for death

Let no man extend his thoughts or let his hopes wander towards future and far-distant events and accidental contingencies. This day is mine and yours, but ye know not what shall be on the morrow; and every morning creeps out of a dark cloud, leaving behind it an ignorance and silence deep as midnight, and undiscerned as are the phantasms that make a chrisom-child to smile: so that we cannot discern what comes hereafter, unless we had a light from heaven brighter than the vision of an angel, even the spirit of prophecy. Without revelation we cannot tell whether we shall eat tomorrow, or whether a squinzy shall choke us: and it is written in the unrevealed folds of divine predestination that many who are this day alive shall tomorrow be laid upon the cold earth, and the women shall weep over their shroud, and dress them for their funeral.

III.273/S.19–20

Reflecting on one's life

In taking the accounts of your life, do not reckon by great distances, and by the periods of pleasure, or the satisfaction of your hopes, or the stating your desires; but let every intermedial day and hour pass with observation. He that reckons he hath lived but so many harvests, thinks they come not often enough, and that they go away too soon: some lose the day with longing for the night, and the night in waiting for the day. Hope and fantastic expectations spend much of our lives: and while with passion we look for a coronation, or the death of an enemy, or a day of joy, passing from fancy to possession without any intermedial notices, we throw away a precious year, and use it but as the burden of our time, fit to be pared off and thrown away, that we may come at those little pleasures which first steal our hearts, and then steal our life.

A strict course of piety is the way to prolong our lives in the natural sense, and to add good portions to the number of our years: and sin is sometimes by natural causality, very often by the anger of God and the divine judgment, a cause of sudden and untimely death. Concerning which I shall add nothing to what I have somewhere else said of this article, but only the observation of Epiphanius; that for three thousand three hundred and thirty-two years, even to the twentieth age, there was not one example of a son that died before his father; but the course of nature was kept, that he who was first born in the descending line did first die (I speak of natural death, and therefore Abel cannot be opposed to this observation), till that Terah the father of Abraham taught the people a new religion, to make images of clay and worship them; and concerning him it was first remarked, that "Haran died before his father Terah in the land of his nativity;" God by an unheard-of judgment and a rare accident punishing his newly invented crime by the untimely death of his son.

III.283/S.39

Self-examination

A frequent examination of our actions will intenerate and soften our consciences, so that they shall be impatient of any rudeness or heavier load: and he that is used to shrink when he is pressed with a branch of twining osier, will not willingly stand in the ruins of a house when the beam dashes upon the pavement. And provided that our nice and tender spirit be not vexed into scruple, nor the scruple turn into unreasonable fears, nor the fears into superstition; he that by any arts can make his spirit tender and apt for religious impressions, hath made the fairest seat for religion, and the unaptest and uneasiest entertainment for sin and eternal death, in the whole world.

A frequent examination of the smallest parts of our lives is the best instrument to make our repentance particular, and a fit remedy to all the members of the whole body of sin. For our examination put off to our death-bed of necessity brings us into this condition, that very many thousands of our sins must be (or not be at all) washed off with a general repentance, which the more general and indefinite it is, it is ever so much the worse. And if he that repents the longest and the oftenest, and upon the most instances, is still during his whole life but an imperfect penitent, and there are very many reserves left to be wiped off by God's mercies, and to be eased by collateral assistances, or to be groaned for at the terrible day of judgment; it will be but a sad story to consider that the sins of a whole life, or of very great portions of it, shall be put upon the remedy of one examination, and the advises of one discourse, and the activities of a decayed body and a weak and an amazed spirit. Let us do the best we can, we shall find that the mere sins of ignorance and unavoidable forgetfulness will be enough to be intrusted to such a bank; and that if a general repentance will serve towards their expiation, it will be an infinite mercy: but we have nothing to warrant our confidence if we shall think it to be enough on our death-bed to confess the notorious actions of our lives, and to say, "the Lord be merciful unto me for the infinite transgresssions of my life which I have wilfully or carelessly forgot."

III.299/S.57

Exercising love

He that would die well and happily must in his life-time according to all his capacities exercise charity; and because religion is the life of the soul, and charity is the life of religion, the same which gives life to the better part of man, which never dies, may obtain of God a mercy to the inferior part of man in the day of its dissolution.

Charity is the great channel through which God passes all His mercy upon mankind. For we receive absolution of our sins in proportion to our forgiving our brother: this is the rule of our hopes, and the measure of our desire in this world; and in the day of death and judgment the great sentence upon mankind shall be transacted according to our alms, which is the other part of charity. Certain it is that God cannot, will not, never did, reject a charitable man in his greatest needs and in his most passionate prayers; for God himself is love, and every degree of charity that dwells in us is the participation of the divine nature: and therefore when upon our death-bed a cloud covers our head, and we are enwrapped with sorrow; when we feel the weight of a sickness, and do not feel the refreshing visitations of God's loving-kindness; when we have many things to trouble us, and looking round about us we see no comforter; then call to mind what injuries you have forgiven, how apt you were to pardon all affronts and real persecutions, how you embraced peace when it was offered you, how you followed after peace when it ran from you: and when you are weary of one side, turn upon the other, and remember the alms that by the grace of God and His assistances you have done, and look up to God, and with the eye of faith behold Him coming in the cloud, and pronouncing the sentence of doomsday according to His mercies and thy charity.

III.302–3/S.61–2

Impatience

Silence and still composures, and not complaining, are no parts of a sick man's duty; they are not necessary parts of patience. We find that David roared for the very disquietness of his sickness, and he lay chattering like a swallow, and his throat was dry with calling for help upon his God. That's the proper voice of sickness: and certain it is that the proper voices of sickness are expressly vocal and petitory in the ears of God, and call for pity in the same accent as the cries and expressions of widows and orphans do for vengeance upon their persecutors, though they say no collect against them. For there is the voice of man, and there is the voice of the disease, and God hears both; and the louder the disease speaks, there is the greater need of mercy and pity, and therefore God will the sooner bear it. Abel's blood had a voice, and cried to God; and humility hath a voice, and cries so loud to God that it pierces the clouds; and so hath every sorrow and every sickness: and when a man cries out, and complains but according to the sorrows of his pain, it cannot be any part of a culpable impatience, but an argument for pity.

Some men's senses are so subtile, and their perceptions so quick and full of relish, and their spirits so active, that the same load is double upon them to what it is to another person: and therefore comparing the expressions of the one to the silence of the other, a different judgment cannot be made concerning their patience. Some natures are querulous, and melancholic, and soft, and nice, and tender, and weeping, and expressive; others are sullen, dull, without apprehension, apt to tolerate and carry burdens: and the crucifixion of our blessed Saviour, falling upon a delicate and virgin body of curious temper, and strict, equal composition, was naturally more full of torment than that of the ruder thieves, whose proportions were coarser and uneven.

III.311/S.71

Complaining

Our complaints in sickness must be without peevishness. This sins against civility, and that necessary decency which must be used toward the ministers and assistants. By peevishness we increase our own sorrows, and are troublesome to them that stand there to ease ours. It hath in it harshness of nature and ungentleness, wilfulness and fantastic opinions, morosity and incivility.

Against it are opposed obedience, tractability, easiness of persuasion, aptness to take counsel. The acts of this part of patience are, first, to obey our physicians; secondly, to treat our persons with respect to our present necessities; thirdly, not to be ungentle and uneasy to the ministers and nurses that attend us, but to take their diligent and kind offices as sweetly as we can, and to bear their indiscretions or unhandsome accidents contentedly and without disquietness within, or evil language or angry words without; fourthly, not to use unlawful means for our recovery.

If we secure these particulars, we are not lightly to be judged of by noises and postures, by colours and images of things, by paleness, or tossings from side to side. For it were a hard thing that those persons who are loaden with the greatest of human calamities should be strictly tied to ceremonies and forms of things. He is patient, that calls upon God; that hopes for health or heaven; that believes God is wise and just in sending him afflictions; that confesses his sins, and accuses himself, and justifies God; that expects God will turn this into good; that is civil to his physicians and his servants; that converses with the guides of souls, the ministers of religion; and in all things submits to God's will, and would use no indirect means for his recovery, but had rather be sick and die than enter at all into God's displeasure.

III.313/S.73–4

Remedies against impatience

Prevent the violence and trouble of thy spirit by an act of thanksgiving, for which in the worst of sicknesses thou canst not want cause, especially if thou rememberest that this pain is not an eternal pain; bless God for that; but take heed also lest you so order your affairs, that you pass from hence to an eternal sorrow: if that be hard, this will be intolerable; but as for the present evil, a few days will end it.

III.321/S.83

Fear of death

There is nothing which can make sickness unsanctified, but the same also will give us cause to fear death. If therefore we so order our affairs and spirits that we do not fear death, our sickness may easily become our advantage; and we can then receive counsel, and consider, and do those acts of virtue which are in that state the proper services of God; and such which men in bondage and fear are not capable of doing, or of advices how they should, when they come to the appointed days of mourning. And indeed if men would but place their design of being happy in the nobleness, courage, and perfect resolutions of doing handsome things, and passing through our unavoidable necessities, in the contempt and despite of the things of this world, and in holy living, and the perfective desires of our natures, the longings and pursuances after heaven; it is certain they could not be made miserable by chance and change, by sickness and death. But we are so softened and made effeminate with deliberate thoughts, and meditations of ease, and brutish satisfactions; that if our death comes before we have seized upon a great fortune, or enjoy the promises of the fortune-tellers, we esteem ourselves to be robbed of our goods, to be mocked, and miserable. Hence it comes that men are impatient of the thoughts of death: hence come those arts of protraction and delaying the significations of old age: thinking to deceive the world, men cozen themselves, and by representing themselves youthful, they certainly continue their vanity till Proserpina pull the peruke from their heads. We cannot deceive God and nature for a coffin is a coffin, though it be covered with a pompous veil; and the minutes of our time strike on, and are counted by angels, till the period comes which must cause the passing bell to give warning to all the neighbours, that thou art dead, and they must be so: and nothing can excuse or retard this. And if our death could be put off a little longer, what advantage can it be in thy accounts of nature or felicity? They that three thousand years agone died unwillingly, and stopped death two days, or stayed it a week, what is their gain? where is that week ? And poor-spirited men use arts of protraction, and make their persons pitiable, but their condition contemptible; being like the poor sinners at Noah's flood: the waters drove them out of their lower rooms; then they crept up to the roof, having lasted half a day longer, and then they knew not how to get down: some crept upon the top branch of a tree, and some climbed up to a mountain, and stayed, it may be, three days longer; but all that while they endured a worse torment than death: they lived with amazement, and were distracted with the ruins of mankind, and the horror of a universal deluge.

III.335–6/S.99–100

As in health, so in sickness

In pursuance of this rule, let a man consider that whatsoever must be done in sickness ought to be done in health; only let him observe that his sickness as a good monitor chastises his neglect of duty, and forces him to live as he always should; and then all these solemnities and dressings for death are nothing else but the part of a religious life; which he ought to have exercised all his days; and if those circumstances can affright him, let him please his fancy by this truth, that then he does but begin to live.

III.351/S.117

You cannot choose your illness

Do not choose the kind of thy sickness, or the manner of thy death; but let it be what God pleases, so it be no greater than thy spirit or thy patience: and for that you are to rely upon the promise of God, and to secure thyself by prayer and industry: but in all things else let God be thy chooser, and let it be thy work to submit indifferently, and attend thy duty. It is lawful to beg of God that thy sickness may not be sharp or noisome, infectious or unusual, because these are circumstances of evil which are also proper instruments of temptation: and though it may well concern the prudence of thy religion to fear thyself, and keep thee from violent temptations, who hast so often fallen in little ones; yet even in these things be sure to keep some degrees of indifferency that is, if God will not be entreated to ease thee or to change thy trial, then be importunate that thy spirit and its interest be secured, and let Him do what seemeth good in His eyes. But as in the degrees of sickness, thou art to submit to God, so in the kind of it (supposing equal degrees) thou art to be altogether incurious whether God call thee by a consumption or an asthma, by a dropsy or a palsy, by a fever in thy humours or a fever in thy spirits; because all such nicety of choice is nothing but a colour to legitimate impatience, and to make an excuse to murmur privately, and for circumstances, when in the sum of affairs we durst not own impatience. I have known some persons vehemently wish that they might die of a consnmption; and some of these had a plot upon heaven, and hoped by that means to secure it after a careless life, as thinking a lingering sickness would certainly infer a lingering and a protracted repentance, and by that means they thought they should be safest: others of them dreamed it would be an easier death; and have found themselves deceived, and their patience hath been tired with a weary spirit and a useless body, by often conversing with healthful persons and vigorous neighbours, by uneasiness of the flesh and the sharpness of their bones, by want of spirits and a dying life; and in conclusion have been directly debauched by peevishness and a fretful sickness: and these men had better have left it to the wisdom and goodness of God; for they both are infinite.

III.356/S.123–4

Repentance

Men generally do very much dread sudden death, and pray against it passionately; and certainly it hath in it great inconveniences accidentally to men's estates, to the settlement of families, to the culture and trimming of souls, and it robs a man of the blessings which may be consequent to sickness, and to the passive graces and holy contentions of a Christian, while he descends to his grave without an adversary or a trial: and a good man may be taken at such a disadvantage that a sudden death would be a great evil, even to the most excellent person, if it strikes him in an unlucky circumstance. But these considerations are not the only ingredients into those men's discourse, who pray violently against sudden deaths. For possibly if this were all, there may be in the condition of sudden death something to make recompense for the evils of the over hasty accident: for certainly it is a less temporal evil to fall by the rudeness of a sword, than the violences of a fever, and the axe is much a less affliction than a strangury; and though a sickness tries our virtues, yet a sudden death is free from temptation: a sickness may be more glorious, and a sudden death more safe. The deadest deaths are best, the shortest and least premeditate.

III.371/S.140

Articulating love and justice

Let the sick man set his house in order before he die; state his cases of conscience, reconcile the fractures of his family, reunite brethren, cause right understandings, and remove jealousies; give good counsels for the future conduct of their persons and estates, charm them into religion by the authority and advantages of a dying person; because the last words of a dying man are like the tooth of a wounded lion, making a deeper impression in the agony, than in the most vigorous strength.

Let the sick man discover every secret of art, or profit, physic, or advantage to mankind, if he may do it without the prejudice of a third person. Some persons are so uncharitably envious that they are willing that a secret receipt should die with them, and be buried in their grave, like treasure in the sepulchre of David: but this, which is a design of charity, must therefore not be done to any man's prejudice; and the mason of Herodotus the king of Egypt, who kept secret his notice of the king's treasure, and when he was a-dying, told his son, betrayed his trust then when he should have kept it most sacredly, for his own interest. In all other cases let thy charity outlive thee, that thou mayest rejoice in the mansion of rest, because by thy means many living persons are eased or advantaged.

III.395/S.167–8

Visitation of the sick

God, who hath made no new covenant with dying persons distinct from the covenant of the living, hath also appointed no distinct sacraments for them, no other manner of usages but such as are common to all the spiritual necessities of living and healthful persons. In all the days of our religion, from our baptism to the resignation and delivery of our soul, God hath appointed His servants to minister to the necessities, and eternally to bless, and prudently to guide, and wisely to judge concerning souls; and the Holy Ghost, that anointing from above, descends upon us in several effluxes, but ever by the ministries of the church. Our heads are anointed with that sacred unction, baptism, not in ceremony, but in real and proper effect; our foreheads in confirmation, our hands in ordinations, all our senses in the visitation of the sick; and all by the ministry of especially deputed and instructed persons: and we, who all our lifetime derive blessings from the fountains of grace by the channels of ecclesiastical ministries, must do it then especially when our needs are most pungent and actual.

We cannot give up our names to Christ, but the holy man that ministers in religion must enrol them, and present the persons, and consign the grace; when we beg for God's spirit, the minister can best present our prayers, and by his advocation hallow our private desires, and turn them into public and potent offices.

If we desire to be established and confirmed in the grace and religion of our baptism, the holy man whose bands were anointed by a special ordination to that and its symbolical purposes, lays his hands upon the catechumen, and the anointing from above descends by that ministry.

If we would eat the body and drink the blood of our Lord, we must address ourselves to the Lord's table, and he that stands there to bless and to minister can reach it forth, and feed thy soul; and without his ministry thou canst not be nourished with that heavenly feast, nor thy body consigned to immortality, nor thy soul refreshed with the sacramental bread from heaven; except by spiritual suppletories, in cases of necessity and an impossible communion.

If we have committed sins, the spiritual man is appointed, to restore us, and to pray for us, and to receive our confessions, and to enquire into our wounds, and to infuse oil and remedy, and to pronounce pardon.

III.401–2/S.175–6

The role of 'The Spiritual Man'

The spiritual man will find in the conduct of this duty many cases and varieties of accidents, which will alter his course and forms of proceedings. Most men are of a rude indifferency, apt to excuse themselves, ignorant of their condition, abused by evil principles, content with a general and indefinite confession; and, if you provoke them to it by the foregoing considerations, lest their spirits should be a little uneasy, or not secured in their own opinions, will be apt to say, they are sinners, as every man hath his infirmity, and he as well as any man: but, God be thanked, they bear no ill will to any man, or are no adulterers, or no rebels, or they have fought on the right side; and God be merciful to them, for they are sinners. But you shall hardly open their breasts further: and to enquire beyond this, would be to do the office of an accuser.

III.408/S.182–3

Confession

The ministers of religion must take care that the sick man's confession be as minute and particular as it can, and that as few sins as may be be entrusted to the general prayer of pardon for all sins; for by being particular and enumerative of the variety of evils which have disordered his life, his repentance is disposed to be more pungent and afflictive, and therefore more salutary and medicinal: it hath in it more sincerity, and makes a better judgment of the final condition of the man; and from thence it is certain the hopes of the sick man can be more confident and reasonable.

The spiritual man that assists at the repentance of the sick, must not be inquisitive into all the circumstances of the particular sins, but be content with those that are direct parts of the crime, and aggravations of the sorrow; such as frequency, long abode, and earnest choice in acting them; violent desires, great expense, scandal of others; dishonour to the religion, days of devotion, religious solemnities, and holy places; and the degrees of boldness and impudence, perfect resolution and the habit. If the sick person be reminded or enquired into concerning these, it may prove a good instrument to increase his contrition, and perfect his penitential sorrows, and facilitate his absolution, and the means of his amendment. But the other circumstances, as of the relative person in the participation of the crime, the measures or circumstances of the impure action, the name of the injured man or woman, the quality or accidental condition: these and all the like are but questions springing from curiosity, and producing scruple, and apt to turn into many inconveniences.

III.414/S.189

Communion

It is the minister's office to invite sick and dying persons to the holy sacrament; such whose lives were fair and laudable, and yet their sickness sad and violent, making them listless and of slow desires, and slower apprehensions; that such persons who are in the state of grace, may lose no accidental advantages of spiritual improvement, but may receive into their dying bodies the symbols and great consignations of the resurrection, and into their souls the pledges of immortality; and may appear before God their Father in the union and with the impresses and likeness of their elder brother. But if the persons be of ill report, and have lived wickedly, they are not to be invited; because their case is hugely suspicious, though they then repent and call for mercy: but if they demand it, they are not to be denied: only let the minister in general represent the evil consequence of an unworthy participation; and if the penitent will judge himself unworthy, let him stand candidate for pardon at the hands of God, and stand or fall by that unerring and merciful sentence: to which his severity of condemning himself before men will make the easier and more hopeful address. And the strictest among the Christians, who denied to reconcile lapsed persons after baptism, yet acknowledged that there were hopes reserved in the court of heaven for them, though not here: since we, who are easily deceived by the pretences of a real return, are tied to dispense God's graces as He hath given us commission, with fear and trembling, and without too forward confidences; and God hath mercies which we know not of, and therefore because we know them not, such persons were referred to God's tribunal, where he would find them, if they were to be had at all.

III.422/S.198–9

Last stages

Then let the sick man be called upon to rehearse the articles of his faith; or if he be so weak he cannot, let him (if he have not before done it) be called to say, Amen, when they are recited, or to give some testimony of his faith and confident assent to them.

After which it is proper, if the person be in capacity, that the minister examine him, and invite him to confession, and all the parts of repentance, according to the foregoing rules: after which he may pray this prayer of absolution;

> Our Lord Jesus Christ, who hath given commission to His church in His name to pronounce pardon to all that are truly penitent; He of His mercy pardon and forgive thee all thy sins, deliver thee from all evils past, present, and future, preserve thee in the faith and fear of His holy name to thy life's end, and bring thee to His everlasting kingdom to live with Him for ever and ever. Amen.

Then let the sick man renounce all heresies, and whatsoever is against the truth of God or the peace of the church, and pray for pardon for all his ignorances and errors, known and unknown.

After which let him, if all other circumstances be fitted, be disposed to receive the blessed sacrament, in which the curate is to minister according to the form prescribed by the church.

When the rites are finished, let the sick man in the days of his sickness be employed with the former offices and exercises before described; and when the time draws near of his dissolution, the minister may assist by the following order of recommendation of the soul.

O holy and most gracious Saviour Jesus, we humbly recommend the soul of Thy servant into Thy hands, Thy most merciful hands; let Thy blessed angels stand in ministry about Thy servant, and defend him from the violence and malice of all his ghostly enemies, and drive far from hence all the spirits of darkness. Amen.

III.440/S.219–20

Last prayers

O spare us a little, that we may recover our strength before we go hence and be no more seen. Amen.

Cast us not away in the time of age, O forsake us not when strength faileth. Amen.

Grant that we may never sleep in sin or death eternal, but that we may have our part of the first resurrection, and that the second death may not prevail over us. Amen.

Grant that our souls may be bound up in the bundle of life, and in the day when Thou bindest up Thy jewels, remember Thy servants for good and not for evil, that our souls may be numbered amongst the righteous. Amen.

Grant unto all sick and dying Christians mercy and aids from heaven, and receive the souls returning unto Thee whom Thou hast redeemed with Thy most precious blood. Amen.

Grant into Thy servants to have faith in the Lord Jesus, a daily meditation of death, a contempt of the world; a longing desire after heaven; patience in our sorrows; comfort in our sicknesses; joy in God; a holy life and a blessed death; that our souls may rest in hope, and my body may rise in glory, and both may be beatified in the communion of saints, in the kingdom of God, and the glories of the Lord Jesus. Amen.

The blessing

Now the God of peace, that brought again from the dead our Lord Jesus, that great Shepherd of the sheep, through the blood of the everlasting covenant, make you perfect in every good work to do His will, working in you that which is pleasing in His sight; to whom be glory, for ever and ever. Amen.

The doxology

To the blessed and only potentate, the King of kings and the Lord of lords, who only hath immortality, dwelling in the light which no man can approach unto, whom no man hath seen nor can see, be honour and power everlasting. Amen.

III.442–3/S.222–3

From *Ductor Dubitantium*

The need for casuistic theology

The reformation of religion in the western churches hath been so violently, so laboriously, so universally opposed by evil spirits and evil men, by wilfulness and ignorance, by prejudice and interest, by error and partiality; and itself also hath been done so imperfectly in some places, and so unskilfully in some others, because the thick and long incumbent darkness had made it impossible to behold the whole light in all its splendour; that it was found to be work enough for the ministers of religion to convince the gainsayers, to oppose their witty arts by the advantageous representment of wise truths, so to keep the people from their temptations. But since there were found not many able to do this but such which had other cures to attend, the conduct of souls in their public and private charges, and the consequent necessity of preaching and catechising, visiting the sick, and their public daily offices; it was the less wonder that in the reformed churches there hath been so great a scarcity of books of cases of conscience: though it is not to be denied but the careless and needless neglect of receiving private confessions hath been too great a cause of our not providing materials apt for so pious and useful a ministration. But besides this, it is certain that there was a necessity of labouring to other purposes than formerly: and this necessity was present and urgent, and the hearts and heads of men ran to quench that fire, and left the government of the house more loosely, till they could discern whether the house would be burnt or no by the flames of contention which then brake out: only this duty was supplied by excellent preachings, by private conferences, by admonitions and answers given when some more pious and religious persons came to confessions, and as they were upon particular occasions required and invited. But for any public provisions of books of casuistical theology, we were almost wholly unprovided, and like the children of Israel in the days of Saul and Jonathan, we were forced to go down to the forges of the Philistines to sharpen every man his share and his coulter, his axe and his mattock. We had swords and spears of our own, enough for defence, and more than enough for disputation: but in this more necessary part of the conduct of consciences we did receive our answers from abroad, till we found that our old needs were sometimes very ill supplied, and new necessities did every day arise.

IX.ix

Purpose of writing

But now shall I desire that he who reads my book will not expect this book to be a collective body of particular cases of conscience; for I find that they are infinite, and my life is not so, and I shall never live to write them all, or to understand them all: and if I should write some and not all, I should profit I know not whom, and do good but to a very few, and that by chance too; and it may be that their cases being changed by circumstances would not be fitted by my indefinite answers. I therefore resolved upon another way, which although no man before me hath trod in writing cases of conscience, yet I cannot say it is new; for I took my pattern from Tribonianus the lawyer, who out of the laws of the old Romans collected some choice rules which give answer to very many cases that happen. And after I had considered and tried many others, I found this most reasonable, most useful, and most comprehensive, of all matters relating to my present undertaking. For I intend here to offer the world a general instrument of moral theology.

IX.xix

Book I Conscience and its definitions

God and conscience

The sum is this: God is supreme, and conscience is His viceregent and subordinate. Now it is certain, that the law of an inferior cannot bind against the command of a superior when it is known: but when the superior communicates the notices of his will by that inferior, and no otherwise, the subject is to obey that inferior; and in so doing he obeys both. But the vicegerent is to answer for the misinformation, and the conscience for its error, according to the degree of its being culpable.

IX.139

The adversary

In the other way an adversary supposes himself to prevail when he can answer the arguments singly, and the discourses in that method are like the servants sent singly to gather fruits of the husbandmen, they killed them as fast as they came, and a man may kill a whole kingdom over, if the opponents come by single persons; but a moral demonstration is like an army which can lose single persons and yet prevail, but yet cannot be beaten unless it be beaten all.

IX.156

The hungry little child – a case study

A little child came to my door for alms, of whom I was told he was run from his mother's house and his own honest employment; but in his wandering he was almost starved: I found that if I relieved him, he would not return to his mother, if I did not relieve him, he would not be able. I considered that indeed his soul's interests were more to be regarded and secured than his body, and his sin rather to be prevented than his sickness, and therefore not to relieve him seemed at first the greater charity. But when I weighed against these considerations, that his sin is uncertain, and future, and arbitrary, but his need is certain, and present, and natural; that he may choose whether he will sin or no; but cannot in the present case choose whether he will perish or no; that if he be not relieved he dies in his sin, but many things may intervene to reform his vicious inclination; that the natural necessity is extreme, but that he will sin is no way necessary, and hath in it no degrees of unavoidable necessity; and above all, that if he abuses my relief to evil purposes which I intended not, it is his fault, not mine; but the question being concerning my duty not his, and that to relieve him is my duty and not his, and that that therefore if I do not relieve him, the sin is also mine and not his; and that by bidding of him to do his duty I acquit myself on one side, but by bidding him to be warm and fed, I cannot be acquitted on the other, I took that side which was at least equally sure and certainly more charitable.

IX.229

A doubtful conscience

A doubtful conscience is no guide of human actions, but a disease, and it is to be cured by prayer and prudent advices, and the proper instruments of resolution and reasonable determination; but for those things which are called doubts, and the resolution of which is the best way to cure the infirmity of conscience, they must be derived from their several heads and categories. For these discourses or advises of conscience in general, are intended but as directions how to take our physic, and what order to observe *in diebus custodiæ*; but the determining of the several doubts is like preparing and administering the medicines which consist of very many ingredients.

IX.262

Book II – Divine Laws

Unreasonable not always unlawful

The breach of commandment is a surer rule to judge of sins than the doing against a natural reason. For there are many things which are unreasonable which are not unlawful, and some things which are in some circumstances reasonable, but yet in the law forbidden and irregular; such are all those things which are permitted for the hardness of our hearts. So was polygamy to the patriarchs and to the Jews. So is the breach of laws by an universal deficiency of the people; which though it be infinitely unlawful, yet for the unreasonableness in punishing all, it becomes permitted to as. Therefore to estimate the goodness or badness of an action by its being reasonable or unreasonable is infinitely fallacious, unless we take in other measures. It is unreasonable that a man should marry when he is fourscore years old, but it is not unlawful.

It is unreasonable for an old man to marry a young maiden, but I find no sin in it. Nothing is more against nature than to marry June and December, and it is unnatural to make productions by the mixture of an horse and an ass, and yet it is done without scruple. But in these and the like cases, the commandment and nothing else is the measure of right and wrong.

IX.328

God and divine power

I am willing publicly to acknowledge that I was always, since I understood it, a very great enemy to all those questions of the school which enquire into the power of God: as whether by God's absolute power a body can be in two places; whether God can give leave to a man to sin; and very many there are of them to as little purpose. But yet here I am willing to speak in the like manner of expression, because the consequent and effect of it goes not to a direct enquiry concerning the divine power; for it intends to remonstrate that because God does actually dispense in His own law, this prime law of God, or the law of nature, is nothing else but the express and declared will of God in matters proportionable to right reason and the nature of man.

IX.333

Divine law and the importance of reason

[I]n the sanction of the divine laws the reason obliges more than the letter: for since the change of the reason is the ground of all mutation and dispensation in laws, it is certain that the reason and the authority, that in the thing, this in God, are the soul and the spirit of the law; and though this must not be used so as to neglect the law when we fancy a reason, yet when the letter and the reason are in opposition, this is to be preferred before that. If the reason ceases it is not enough of warrant to neglect the law, unless a contrary reason arises, and that God cannot be served by obedience in that instance; but when the case is not only otherwise but contrary to what it was before, let the design of God be so observed as that the letter be obeyed in that analogy and proportion. It is a natural law that we should not deceive our neighbour, because his interest and right is equal to any man's else; but if God have commanded me to kill him, and I cannot by force get him into my hand, I may deceive him whom God hath commanded me to kill, if without such a snare I cannot obey the command of God. But this is but seldom practicable, because the reasons in all natural laws are so fixed and twisted with the accidents of every man's life, that they cannot alter but by miracle, or by an express command of God; and therefore we must in the use of this rule wholly attend upon the express voice of God.

It hence also will follow, that if an angel from heaven, or any prophet, or dreamer of dreams, any teacher and pretendedly illuminate person shall teach or persuade to any act against any natural law, that is, against any thing which is so reasonable and necessary that it is bound upon our natures by the Spirit of God, and the light of our reason, he is not to be heard: for until God changes His own establishments, and turns the order of things into new methods and dispositions, the natural obligations are sacred and inviolable.

IX.339–40

The Law of Nature cannot be dispensed with by any human power

The reason is because nature and her laws have both the same author, and are relative to each other; and these as necessary to the support and improvement of human nature, as nourishment to the support of human bodies: and as no man can create new appetites, or make hay or stones to be our nourishment, so neither can he make that our nature should be maintained in its well-being without these laws. The laws of nature being bound upon us by the law of God, cannot be dispensed withal, unless by a power equal or the same, or superior to that which made the sanction: but that cannot be at all; therefore neither can they be dispensed with at all, unless it be by God himself. Natural laws are all the dictates of natural reason, and he that dispenses with the law must have power to alter the reason; which because it can never be done but by superinducing something upon nature greater than her own natural need, and none can do this but God, therefore none but He can dispense.

IX.341

No dispensing with the positive laws of Christ

[T]here is no necessity that a power of dispensing in the positive laws of Christ should be intrusted to any man, or to any society. Because the law needs it not, and the subjects need it not: and he that dispenses must either do it when there is cause, or when there is none. If he dispenses when there is no cause, he makes himself superior to the power of God by exercising dominion over His laws; if he dispenses when there is cause, he dispenses when there is no need. For if the subject can obey, he must obey, and man cannot untie what God hath bound; but if he cannot obey, he is not bound, and therefore needs to be untied; he may as well go about to unbend a strait line, or to number that which is not, as to dispense in a law to which in such cases God exacts no obedience.

IX.560

Book III – Human Laws

Law and obedience in extreme situations

The lawgiver expressly requires our fortitude and resistance; for unless it be in such cases, though the law can bind, yet it does not. The sum is this, when death is likely to be consequent of obedience by accident and the chance of things, or the providence of God abstractly, then it is not to be expounded to be contempt. Because in such cases God tempts not: but when an enemy or a tyrant power tempts with the fear of death, he does it in defiance of the law or the authority, and therefore here we must obey and die. And this distinction is very much to be regarded: for if a prince or an ecclesiastic superior make a law, it is to be presumed that they do it not (for they have no interest to do it) in despite of chance to bind to obedience in the danger of death; and therefore it is a rack of their power to extend it to such a case. But they may have interest and public necessity to exact this obedience when an opposite power threatens death that they may destroy the law.

X.36

Civil power over ecclesiastical power

These instances are more than enough to prove that if religion be governed by any hand with which the civil power hath nothing to do, it may come to pass that the civil power shall have no hands at all, or they shall be in bands. The consequence of these is this, that if the supreme civil power be sufficient to preserve itself, it can provide against the evil use of the spiritual sword, and consequently can conduct all religion that can by evil men be abused, so as to keep it harmless. If by excommunications the bishop can disturb the evil interest, the civil power can hold his hands that he shall not strike with it, or if he does, can take out the temporal sting, that it shall not venom and fester. If by strange doctrines the ecclesiastics can aliene the hearts of subjects from their duty, the civil power can forbid those doctrines to be preached. If the canons of the church be seditious or peevish or apt for trouble, the civil power can command them to be rescinded, or may refuse to verify them, and make them into laws.

X.251–2

'Ecclesiastical state to remain firm'

We therefore being placed in the kingdom by God, having received from Him the care both of the religion and the prosperity of the subject, we have hitherto endeavoured by our care and by our forces to keep in perpetual union: and for the safety of the republic we are intent to the profit of our subjects, and diligently watch for the conservation of true religion; but especially we strive that they may live holily, as becomes holy persons, taking care, as it befits us, even of both (for it is impossible we should take good care of one if we neglect the other). But above the rest, we are careful that the ecclesiastical state may remain firm, so as is fit to relate to God, and to be in our time, and may have tranquillity by the consent of all men, and may be quiet by the peace of the ecclesiastic affairs; and that true religion may be kept unreprovable, and the lives of the inferior clergy and the bishops may be free from blame.

X.255

The power of the keys

But the use of the keys does differ from proper jurisdiction in this great thing, that if the keys be rightly used they do bind or loose respectively;

but if they err, they do nothing upon the subject, they neither bind nor loose. Now in proper jurisdiction it is otherwise: for, right or wrong, if a man be condemned he shall die for it; and if he be hanged he is hanged. But the church gives nothing but the sentence of God, and tells upon what terms God will or will not pardon. If the prince minister rightly, and judge according to the will and laws of God, the subject, shall find that sentence made good in heaven by the real events of the other world, which the priest pronounces here upon earth. But if the priest be deceived, he is deceived for himself and for nobody else; he alters nothing of the state of the soul by his quick absolution, or his unreasonable binding.

X.272

Ecclesiastical and legislative institutions

So that now upon this account the ecclesiastical laws are as obligatory to the conscience as those which are made in a civil matter; and there is no difference but in the matter only: but for that there will be some advantage; for as the civil power hath authority in ecclesiastical mattes, so the spiritual power hath a share in the legislative: the matter is handled by the ecclesiastics, and the law is established by the secular. And therefore if it be thought that the cognizance of these things is not proper for seculars, those that think so may be satisfied that the bishops have judged the thing already; and they that think the bishops have no power of making the law, may learn to obey, because the prince hath by his legislative established it. So one hand helps another, and both are lift up to God, but will fall heavy upon the disobedient.

X.295

Exclusion from Communion

For it is to be observed that in this affair one part concerns the criminal, and another concerns the people. The criminal is bound to abstain from the communion: that duty is incumbent upon him, because he is judged to be unworthy of it by that authority which he is bound to trust, in case there be no apparent error. But to be thrust from civil society is not directly any duty of his, but is incumbent on the people. Now though the bishop can in some cases advise this, yet in a christian commonwealth he cannot without leave command it: and therefore the censure or judgment of the church is to have effort upon the conscience of the guilty, and this invades no man's right; it is for his good that is concerned, and is wholly a spiritual power, and intrenches not upon the civil right of any man, much less upon the public and supreme power. In the lesser excommunication, if the subjects be not voluntary, or be not subjected by him that hath the power over them, that is, the king, they cannot be compelled by the bishop to any external act or abstention. But if they do themselves submit, or are submitted by their supreme, they are bound not only to obey the censure of the church, but themselves to go away from company that know not of this calamity: as I have already instanced.

X.315

Variations in tradition and reason

And the same is the case in baptism, in which that which was necessary is that the person be baptized in water, and in the name of the Father, Son, and Holy Ghost: but whether the priest shall say, *Ego te baptizo,* as the Latins do, or *Baptizetur servus Christi,* as the Greeks do, is indifferent: and if the apostles had used any other little variety of words, yet if there was not in the first churches an unity and universality of practice, it is certain the apostles did not by their not or canon intend to oblige all christendom; but themselves did it with liberty, and therefore so might the churches after them.

For excepting those things which the apostles received from Christ, in which they were ministers to all ages, once for all conveying the mind of Christ to the generations to come, in all other things they were but ordinary ministers, to govern the churches in their own times, and left all that ordinary power to their successors, with a power to rule their churches, such as they had; and therefore whatever they conveyed as from Christ, a part of His doctrine or any thing of His appointment, this was to bind for ever; for Christ only is our lawgiver, and what He said was to last for ever: in all things which He said not, the apostles could not be lawgivers, they had no such authority; and therefore whatsoever they ordered by their own wisdom, was to abide as long as the reason did abide; but still with the same liberty with which they appointed it; for of all men in the world they would least put a snare upon the disciples, or tie fetters upon christian liberty. But in divine commandments, and in what were the appointed ministries of grace, they were but the mouth of Christ and ministers of His holy Spirit; and in those things, what they told to the churches is our law for ever.

X.338

Custom and reasonability

But if a contrary custom could justly abrogate a law, then it were no matter who had the legislative power, for whatever the prince please, the people shall choose whether it be a law or no; which because it is a perfect destruction to all government, must needs proceed from an intolerable principle. To which I add this consideration, that whatever effect in law and external regiment a custom may be admitted to have, of which I am not concerned to give accounts, yet if the custom be against law, it is certain the conscience can have no safety and no peace but in the obedience to the law. For besides that there are so many difficult and indeterminable questions in the conduct of the matter of customs, as whether the custom be reasonable, and who is to judge of that, and by what measures; what are the sufficient causes of custom, whether there must be some inequality or pressure or iniquity in the matter, or is it sufficient that the multitude is willing to introduce a custom against law? what time and continuance is required to prescribe a custom, and when it begins to be innocent, and how long it is disobedience; how many must concur to the making of it, and whether the dissent of a few does interrupt its coalition and growing into a custom, and how shall we know whether all or no do consent? or how are we sure that a greater part. is sufficient, and that we have the greater part with us? whether for the abrogation of the law a mere desuetude or omission is sufficient, or must the custom be contrary to the Jaw and matter of fact? and if that be sufficient to annul an affirmative precept, how many things and circumstances of things will be further required for the removing the obligation of a negative commandment? and very many more to the same purposes, that is, to no purposes:—besides this, I say, the conscience can never be warranted in any thing but obedience, because it is impossible to tell the precise time in which the law is actually abrogated by the custom; and therefore a man can never know by all that is before him in this affair whether he be worthy of love or hatred.

X.540–1

Book IV – The Nature of Good and Evil

Freewill and the grace of God

Let the will of man be enabled by what means it please God to choose for it, without God's grace we are sure it cannot do its work; but we are sure also that we can do our work that God requires of us, and we can let it alone: and therefore as sure as God's grace and help is necessary, so sure it is that we have that help that is necessary; for if we had not we could not be commanded to work, and there were no need of arguments or of reason, of deliberation or enquiry.

X.549

Freewill and consequent actions

And yet beyond this heap of things there is another reason by a man can be good or bad only by the act of his will, and not of any other faculty, because the act of the will produces material and permanent events; it is acquisitive and effective, or recusative and destructive, otherwise than it is in any other faculties. For the other faculties are like the eye and ear, they can see or hear foul things and be never the worse, and good things and be never the better: but the will of a man is like the hand and the mouth and the belly, if they touch foul things they are defiled, and if they eat poison they die; so is the will of man, it becomes all one with its object. For it works only by love or hatred, and therefore changes by the variety of the object it entertains. He that loves a lie is a liar; but he that only understands it is never the worse.

X.554

God's judgement

It follows also from hence that no unavoidable calamity, no being born of evil parents, no being born from illegitimate embraces, no unjust sentences of men, can irreconcile us to God, or prejudice our eternal interest. God will judge us according to our works, not according to his or any man's else, or by any measures but by His own law and our obedience.

X.555

Intention

[I]f a prince pardons a thief, or a friend begs his pardon that killed a man, although he could not have stolen any more without that pardon, yet that after theft or murder is not imputable to him that gave or to him that begged the pardon, unless they did it with that very intention; for the pardon is not in any natural order to any such consequent action, and therefore without his own actual or designed conjunction and intuition cannot convey the crime and guiltiness.

X.580

Games of chance lawful, but not without serious pitfalls

Now that cards and dice are of themselves lawful I do not know any reason to doubt. For if they be unlawful, it is because they are forbidden, or because there is in them something that is forbidden. They are nowhere of themselves forbidden: and what is in them that is criminal or suspicious? Is it because there is chance and contingency in them? There is so in all human affairs; in merchandise, in laying wagers, in all consultations and wars, in journeys and agriculture, in teaching and learning, in putting children to school or keeping them at home, in the price of the market and the vendibility of commodities. And if it be said that there is in all these things an overruling providence; though no man can tell in what manner or by what means the divine providence brings such things to a determinate event, yet it is certain that every little thing as well as every great thing is under God's government, and our recreations as well as our wages. But what if it be, and what if it be not? He can never be suspected in any criminal sense to tempt the divine providence, who by contingent things recreates his labour, and having acquired his refreshment, hath no other end to serve, and no desires to engage the divine providence to any other purpose: and this end is sufficiently secured by whatsoever happens. I know nothing else that can be pretended to render the nature of these things suspicious; and this is perfectly nothing: and as for the evil appendages which are so frequently attending upon these kinds of games, besides that they also are as near to other exercises as to these, as to bowling, horse-racing, cock-fighting, the fight of quails and of partridges, bull-baiting, pall-mall, billiards, and all other games for money and victory, to some more and to some less; besides this, I say, the evil appendages are all separable from these games, and till they be separated they are not lawful.

X.592–3

3

Eucharist, Confirmation, Ordination, Liturgy

Eucharist

Spiritual Presence

The doctrine of the church of England and generally of the protestants in this article, is, that after the minister of the holy mysteries hath ritely [sic] prayed, and blessed or consecrated the bread and the wine, the symbols become changed into the body and blood of Christ, after a SACRAMENTAL, that is, in a SPIRITUAL, REAL manner; so that all that worthily communicate do by faith receive Christ really, effectually, to all the purposes of His passion: the wicked receive not Christ, but the bare symbols only; but yet to their hurt, because the offer of Christ is rejected, and they pollute the blood of the covenant by using it as an unholy thing. The result of which doctrine is this: it is bread, and it is Christ's body: it is bread in substance, Christ in the sacrament; and Christ is as really given to all that are truly disposed, as the symbols are; each as they can Christ as Christ can be given; the bread and wine as they can, and to the same real purposes to which they are designed; and Christ does as really nourish and sanctify the soul as the elements do the body. It is here as in the other sacrament; for as there natural water becomes the laver of regeneration, so here bread and wine become the body and blood of Christ; but there and here too the first substance is changed by grace, but remains the same in nature.

VI.13–14

Presence and reception

So that now the question is not whether the symbols be changed into Christ's body and blood or no, for it is granted on all sides; but whether this conversion be sacramental and figurative, or whether it be natural and bodily: nor is it whether Christ be really taken, but whether He be taken in a spiritual or in a natural manner. We say the conversion is figurative, mysterious, and sacramental; they say it is proper, natural, and corporal: we affirm that Christ is really taken by faith, by the spirit, to all real effects of His passion; they say He is taken by the mouth, and that the spiritual and the virtual taking Him in virtue or effect is not sufficient, though done also in the sacrament.

VI.20

The Bread remains bread

The sum of all is this; if of bread Christ said, 'This is My body,' because it cannot be true in a proper natural sense, it implying a contradiction that it should be properly bread and properly Christ's body, it must follow that it is Christ's body in a figurative improper sense. But if the bread does not remain bread, but be changed by blessing into our Lord's body; this also is impossible to be in any sense true but by affirming the change to be only in use, virtue and condition, with which change the natural being of bread may remain. For he that supposes that by the blessing the bread ceases so to be, that nothing of it remains, must also necessarily suppose that the bread being no more, it neither can be the body of Christ nor any thing else. For it is impossible that what is taken absolutely from all being, should yet abide under a certain difference of being, and that that thing which is not at all should yet be after a certain manner. Since therefore (as I have proved) the bread remains, and of bread it was affirmed, 'This is My body,' it follows inevitably that it is figuratively, not properly and naturally spoken of bread, that it is the flesh or body of our Lord.

VI.59

The Last Supper not the whole story

[I]f- Christ gave His body properly in the last supper, and not only figuratively and in sacrament, then it could not be a representment or sacrament of His passion, but a real exhibition of it; but that it was a sacrament only, appears by considering that it was then alive, that the passion was future, that the thing was really to be performed upon the cross, that then He was to be delivered for the life of the world. In the last supper all this was in type and sacrament, because it was before, and the substance was to follow after.

VI.68

Transubstantiation an unnecessary miracle

[I]n the words of institution there is nothing that can be pretended to prove the conversion of the substance of bread into the body of Christ, but the same will infer the conversion of the whole into the whole, and therefore of the accidents of the bread into the accidents of the body. And in those little pretences of philosophy which these men sometimes make to cozen fools into a belief of the possibility, they pretend to no instance but to such conversions in which if the substance is changed, so also are the accidents: sometimes the accident is changed in the same remaining substance; but if the substance be changed, the accidents never remain the same individually; or in kind, unless they be symbolical, that is, are common to both, as in the change of elements, of air into fire, of water into earth. Thus when Christ changed water into wine, the substances being changed, the accidents also were altered, and the wine did not retain the colour and taste of water; for then though it had been the stranger miracle that wine should be wine, and yet look and taste like water, yet it would have obtained but little advantage to His doctrine and person if He should have offered to prove His mission by such a miracle. For if Christ had said to the guests, To prove that I am come from God, I will change this water into wine, well might this prove His mission: but if while the guests were wondering at this, He should proceed and say, 'Wonder ye not at this, for I will do a stranger thing than it, for this water shall be changed into wine, and yet I will so order it, that it shall look like water, and taste like it, so that you shall not know one from the other,' certainly this would have made the whole matter very ridiculous. And indeed it is a strange device of these men to suppose God to work so many prodigious miracles as must be in Transubstantiation, if it were at all, and yet that none of these should be seen; for to what purpose is a miracle that cannot be perceived?

VI.99

Transubstantiation impossible

For this conversion is not generation, it is not corruption, it is not creation, because Christ's body already is, and cannot be produced again; it is not after the manner of natural conversion, it differs from the supernatural: there is no change of one form into another, the same first matter does not remain under several forms, first of bread, then of Christ's body. It is turned into the substance of Christ's body, and yet nothing of the bread becomes any thing of the body of Christ. It is turned into Christ, and yet it is turned into nothing, the substance is not annihilated (for then it were not turned into Christ's body) and yet it is annihilated or turned to nothing, for it does not become Christ's body; it is determined upon Christ's body, and yet does not become it, though it be changed into it. For if bread could become Christ's body, then bread could receive a greater honour than any of the servants of Christ; for it could be glorified with the biggest glorification, it would be exalted far above all angels, bread should reign for ever, and be king of all the world, which are honours not communicable to mere man, and by no change can be wrought upon him: and if they may upon bread, then bread is exalted higher than the sons of men; and yet so it is if it be naturally and substantially changed into the body of Christ.

VI.126

The Bread can never 'become' Christ

By this doctrine Christ's body is there where it was not before; and yet not by change of place, for it descends not; nor by production, for it was produced before; not by natural mutation, for Christ himself is wholly immutable, and though the bread be mutable, it can never become Christ. That which is now and was always, begins to be, and yet it cannot begin which was so long before. And by this doctrine is affirmed that which even themselves judge to be simply and absolutely impossible; for if after a thing hath his being, and during the first being, it shall have every day many new beginnings without multiplying the beings, then the same thing is under two times at the same time; it is but a day old and yet was six days ago, and six ages, and sixteen. The body of Christ obtains to be what it was not before, and yet it is wholly the same without becoming what it was not. It obtains to be under the form of bread, and that which it is now and was not before, is neither perfective of his being, nor destructive, nor alterative, nor augmentative, nor diminutive, nor conservative. It is as it were a production, as it were a creation, as a conservation, as an adduction: that is, it is as it were just nothing; for it is not a creation, not a generation, not an adduction not a conservation.

VI.127

Adoration of Sacrament not ancient

And let it be considered, whether if the primitive church had ever done or taught that the divine worship ought to be given to the sacrament, it had not been certain that the heathen would have retorted most of the arguments upon their heads by which the Christians reproved their worshipping of images. The Christians upbraided them with worshipping the works of their hands, to which themselves gave what figure they pleased, and then by certain forms consecrated them, and made by invocation (as they supposed) a divinity to dwell there. They objected to them that they worshipped that which could neither see, nor hear, nor smell, nor taste, nor move, nor understand: that which could grow old and perish, that could be broken and burned, that was subject to the injury of rats and mice, of worms and creeping things, that can be taken by enemies, and carried away, that is kept under lock and key for fear of thieves and sacrilegious persons. Now if the church of those ages had thought and practised as they have done at Rome in these last ages, might not they have said, 'Why may not we as well as you? do not you worship that with divine honours, and call it your God, which can be burnt, and broken, which yourselves form into a round or a square figure, which the oven first hardens, and then your priests consecrate, and by invocation make to be your God, which can see no more, nor hear, nor smell, than the silver and old upon our images?'

VI.167

From Introduction to 'Worthy Communicant' – 'clothed with a mystery'

For as God descended and came into the tabernacle invested with a cloud, so Christ comes to meet us clothed with a mystery: He hath a house below as well as above; here is His dwelling and here are His provisions, here is His fire and here His meat; hither God sends His Son, and here His Son manifests Himself: the church and the holy table of the Lord, the assemblies of saints, and the devotions of His people, the word and the sacrament, the oblation of bread and wine and the offering of ourselves, the consecration and the communion, are the things of God and of Jesus Christ, and he that is employed in these is there where God loves to be, and where Christ is to be found; in the employments in which God delights, in the ministries of His own choice, in the work of the gospel and the methods of grace, in the economy of heaven and the dispensations of eternal happiness.

And now that we may know where to find Him, we must be sure to look after Him: He hath told us where He would be, behind what pillar, and under what cloud, and covered with what veil, and conveyed by what ministry, and present in what sacrament: and we must not look for Him in the highways of ambition and pride, of wealth or sensual pleasures; these things are not found 'in the house of His Father,' neither may they come near His dwelling. But if we seek for Christ, we shall find Him in the methods of virtue and the paths of God's commandments, in the houses of prayer and the offices of religion, in the persons of the poor and the retirements of an afflicted soul: we shall find Him in holy reading and pious meditation, in our penitential sorrows and in the time of trouble, in pulpits and upon altars, in the word and in the sacraments. If we come hither as we ought, we are sure to find our beloved, Him whom our soul longeth after.

VIII.6–7

'To persuade, not dispute'

My purpose is not to dispute, but to persuade; not to confute any one, but to instruct those that need; not to make a noise, but to excite devotion; not to enter into curious, but material enquiries; and to gather together into an union all those several portions of truth, and differing apprehensions of mysteriousness, and various methods and rules of preparation, and seemingly opposed doctrines, by which even good men stand at distance and are afraid of each other. For since all societies of Christians pretend to the greatest esteem of this above all the rites or external parts and ministries of religion, it cannot be otherwise but that they will all speak honourable things of it, and suppose holy things to be in it, and great blessings one way or other to come by it; and it is contemptible only among the profane and the atheistical; all the innumerable differences which are in the discourses and consequent practices relating to it, proceed from some common truths and universal notions and mysterious or inexplicable words, and tend all to reverential thoughts and pious treatment of these rites and holy offices; and therefore it will not be impossible to find honey or wholesome dews upon all this variety of plants; and the differing opinions and several understandings of this mystery, which (it may be) no human understanding can comprehend, will serve to excellent purposes of the spirit, if, like men of differing interest, they can be reconciled in one communion; at least the ends and designs of them all can be conjoined in the design and ligatures of the same reverence and piety and devotion.

My purpose therefore is to discourse of the nature, excellencies, uses and intention of the holy sacrament of the Lord's supper, the blessings and fruits of the sacrament; all the advantages of a worthy communion, the public and the private, the personal and the ecclesiastical, that we may understand what it is that we go about, and how it is to be treated: I shall account also concerning all the duties of preparation, ordinary and extraordinary, more and less solemn; of the rules and manners of deportment in the receiving; the gesture and the offering, the measures and instances of our duty, our comport and conversation in and after it; together with the cases of conscience that shall occur under these titles respectively, relating to the particular matters.

It matters not where we begin: for if I describe the excellencies of this sacrament, I find it engages us upon matters of duty and enquiries practical: if I describe our duty, it plainly signifies the greatness and excellency of the mystery: the very notion is practical, and the practice is information; we cannot discourse of the secret, but by describing our duty: and we cannot draw all the lines of duty, but so much duty must needs open a cabinet of mysteries. If we understand what we are about, we cannot choose but be invested with fear and reverence: and if we look in with fear and reverence, it cannot be but we shall understand many secrets. But because the natural order of theology is by faith to build up good life, by a rectified understanding to regulate the will and the affections; I shall use no other method, but first discourse of the excellent mystery, and then of the duty of the communicant, direct and collateral.

VIII.9–10

What we receive in the Sacrament

It is strange that Christians should pertinaciously insist upon carnal significations and natural effects in sacraments and mysteries, when our blessed Lord hath given us a sufficient light to conduct and secure us from such misapprehensions. "The flesh profiteth nothing; the words which I speak unto you, they are spirit and they are life;" that is, the flesh is corruption, and its senses are ministers of death: and this one word alone was perpetually sufficient for Christ's disciples. For when upon occasion of the gross understanding of their Master's words by the men of Capernaum, they had been once clearly taught that the meaning of all these words was wholly spiritual, they rested there and enquired no further: insomuch that when Christ at the institution of the supper affirmed of the bread and wine that they were His body and His blood, they were not at all offended, as being sufficiently before instructed in the nature of that mystery. And besides this, they saw enough to tell them that what they eat was not the natural body of their Lord: this was the body which Himself did or might eat with His body: one body did eat, and the other was eaten; both of them were His body, but after a diverse manner.—For the case is briefly this;—

We have two lives, a natural and a spiritual, and both must have bread for their support and maintenance in proportion to their needs and to their capacities: and as it would be an intolerable charity to give nothing but spiritual nutriment to a hungry body, and pour diagrams and wise propositions into an empty stomach; so it would be as useless and impertinent to feed the soul with wheat or flesh, unless that were the conveyance of a spiritual delicacy.

In the holy sacrament of the eucharist the body of Christ, according to the proper signification of a human body, is not at all, but in a sense differing from the proper and natural body, that is, in a sense more agreeing to sacraments.

VIII.14–15

Spiritual presence

Christ being the food of our souls, He is pleased to signify this food to us by such symbols and similitudes as His present state could furnish us withal. He had nothing about him but flesh and blood which are like to meat and drink; and therefore what He calls 'Himself,' saying, "I am the bread of life," He afterwards calls 'His flesh and His blood,' saying, "My flesh is meat indeed, and My blood is drink indeed;" that is, that you may perceive Me to be indeed the food of your souls, see, here is meat and drink for you, My flesh, and My blood: so to represent Himself in a way that was nearest to our capacity, and in a more intelligible manner; not further from a mystery, but nearer to our manner of understanding; and yet so involved in figure, that it is never to be drawn nearer than a mystery, till it comes to experience, and spiritual relish and perception. But because we are not in darkness, but within the fringes and circles of a bright cloud, let us search as far into it as we are guided by the light of God, and where we are forbidden by the thicker part of the cloud, step back and worship.

For we have yet one further degree of charity and manifestation of this mystery. The 'flesh' of Christ is His word: the 'blood' of Christ is His spirit; and by believing in His word, and being assisted and conducted by His spirit, we are nourished up to life; and so Christ is our food, so He becomes life unto our souls.

VIII.18

Mystery not obscure

Thus are sensible things the sacrament and representation of the spiritual and eternal; and spiritual things are the fulfillings of the sensible. But the consequent of these things is this; that since Christ always was, is, and shall be the food of the faithful, and is that bread which came down from heaven; since we eat Him here and shall, eat Him there, our eating both here and there is spiritual; only, the word of teaching shall be changed into the word of glorification and our faith into charity; and all the way our souls live a new life by Christ: of which eating and drinking is the symbol and the sacrament. And this is not done to make this mystery obscure, but intelligible and easy. For so the pains of hell are expressed by fire, which to our flesh is most painful; and the joys of God by that which brings us greatest pleasure, by meat and drink; and the growth in grace by the natural instruments of nutrition; and the work of the soul by the ministries of the body, and the graces of God by the blessings of nature; for these we know, and we know nothing else; and but by phantasms and ideas of what we see and feel we understand nothing at all.

Now this is so far from being a diminution of the glorious mystery of our communion, that the changing all into spirituality is the great increase of blessing in the world. And when He gives us His body and His blood, He does not fill our stomachs with good things; for of whatsoever goes in thither, it is affirmed by the apostle that 'God will destroy both it and them;' but our hearts are to be replenished; and by receiving His spirit we receive the best thing that God gives; not His lifeless body, but His flesh with life in it; that is, His doctrine and His spirit to imprint it, so to beget a living faith and a lively hope that we may live and live for ever.

VIII.21

Sacrament as 'visible word' (Augustine)

And in the same divine method the Word and the Spirit are ministered to us in the sacrament of the Lord's supper. For as in baptism so here also there is a word proper to the ministry. "So often as we eat this bread and drink this cup, ye declare the Lord's death till He come." This indeed is a word of comfort. "Christ died for our sins;" that is, our repentance which was consigned in baptism shall be to purpose; we shall be washed white and clean in the blood of the sacrificed Lamb. This is *verbum visibile* the same word read to the eye and to the ear. Here the word of God is made our food in a manner so near to our understanding, that our tongues and palates feel the metaphor and the sacramental signification; here faith is in triumph and exaltation: but as in all the other ministries evangelical, we eat Christ by faith, here we have faith also by eating Christ. Thus eating and drinking is faith; it is faith in mystery and faith in ceremony; it is faith in act and faith in habit; it is exercised and it is advanced; and therefore it is certain that here we eat the flesh and drink the blood of Christ with much eminency and advantage.

The sum is this. —Christ's body, His flesh and His blood, are therefore called our meat and our drink, because by His incarnation and manifestation in the flesh He became life unto us: so that it is mysterious indeed in the expression, but very proper and intelligible in the event, to say that we eat His flesh and drink His blood, since by these it is that we have and preserve life. But because what Christ begun in His incarnation He finished in His body on the cross, and the whole progression of mysteries in His body was still an operatory of life and spiritual being to us; the sacrament of the Lord's supper being a commemoration and exhibition of this death which was the consummation of our redemption by His body and blood, does contain in it a 'visible word,' the word in symbol and visibility, and special manifestation: Consonant to which doctrine; the fathers by an elegant expression called the blessed sacrament 'the extension of the incarnation.'

VIII.23

Baptism and Eucharist 'do something in the hand of God'

I shall not enter into so useless a discourse as to enquire whether the sacraments confer grace by their own excellency and power with which they are endued from above; because they who affirm they do, require so much duty on our parts as they also do who attribute the effect to our moral dispositions: but neither one nor the other say true; for neither the external act nor the internal grace and morality does effect our pardon and salvation; but the Spirit of God who blesses the symbols, and assists the duty; makes them holy, and this acceptable. Only they that attribute the efficacy to the ministration of the sacrament, choose to magnify the immediate work of man rather than the immediate work of God, and prefer the external, at least in glorious appellations, before the internal: and they that deny efficacy to the external work, and wholly attribute the blessing and grace to the moral co-operation, make too open a way for despisers to neglect the divine institution, and to lay aside or lightly esteem the sacraments of the church. It is in the sacraments as it is in the word preached; in which not the sound, or the letters and syllables, that is, not the material part, but the formal, the sense and the signification, prepare the mind of the hearer to receive the impresses of the holy Spirit of God; without which all preaching and all sacraments are ineffectual: so does the internal and formal part, the signification and sense of the sacrament, dispose the spirit of the receiver the rather to admit and entertain the grace of the Spirit of God there consigned and there exhibited and there collated; but neither the outward nor the inward part does effect it; neither the sacrament, nor the moral disposition; only the Spirit operates by the sacrament and the communicant receives it by his moral dispositions, by the hand of faith. And what have we to do to enquire into the philosophy of sacraments? These things do not work by the methods of nature. But here the effect is imputed to this cause, and yet can be produced without this cause; because this cause is but a sign in the hand of God, by which He tells the soul when He is willing to work.

Thus baptism was the instrument and sign in the hands of God to confer the holy Spirit upon believers: but the holy Ghost sometimes comes like lightning, and will not stay the period of usual expectation; for when Cornelius had heard S. Peter preach, he received the holy Ghost; and as sometimes the holy Ghost was given because they had been baptized, now he and his company were to be baptized because they had received the holy Ghost. And it is no good argument to say, The graces of God are given to believers out of the sacrament, *ergo* not by or in the sacrament; but rather thus, If God's grace overflows sometimes and goes without His own instruments, much more shall He give it in the use of them. If God gives pardon without the sacrament, then rather also with the sacrament: for supposing the sacraments in their design and institution to be nothing but signs and ceremonies, yet they cannot hinder the work of God, and therefore holiness in the reception of them will do more than holiness alone. For God does nothing in vain; the sacraments do something in the hand of God; eat least they are God's proper and accustomed times of grace; they are His seasons, and our opportunity; when the angel stirs the pool, when the Spirit moves upon the waters, then there is a ministry of healing.

VIII.27–8

Justification and Sanctification continuous

For justification and sanctification are continued acts; they are like the issues of a fountain into its receptacles; God is always giving; and we are always receiving; and the signal effects of God's holy spirit sometimes give great indications, but most commonly come without observation. And therefore in these things we must not discourse as in the conduct of other causes and operations natural: for although in natural effects we can argue from the cause to the event: yet in spiritual things we are to reckon only from the sign in the event. And the signs of grace we are to place instead of natural causes: because a sacrament in the hand of God is a proclamation of His graces; He then gives us notice that the springs of heaven are opened, and then is the time to draw living waters from the fountains of salvation.

VIII.31

The heavenly altar – and the role of the priest

It is the greatest solemnity of prayer, the most powerful liturgy and means of impetration in this world. For when Christ was consecrated on the cross and became our high-priest, having reconciled us to God by the death of the cross, He became infinitely gracious in the eyes of God, and was admitted to the celestial and eternal priesthood in heaven; where in the virtue of the cross He intercedes for us, and represents an eternal sacrifice in the heavens on our behalf. That He is a priest in heaven, appears in the large discourses and direct affirmatives of S. Paul; that there is no other sacrifice to be offered but that on the cross, it is evident, because 'He hath but once appeared in the end of the world to put away sin by the sacrifice of Himself;' and therefore since it is necessary that He hath something to offer so long as He is a priest; and there is no other sacrifice but that of Himself offered upon the cross, it follows that Christ in heaven perpetually offers and represents that sacrifice to His heavenly Father, and in virtue of that obtains all good things for His church.

Now what Christ does in heaven, He hath commanded, us to do on earth, that is, to represent His death, to commemorate this sacrifice, by humble prayer and thankful record; and by faithful manifestation and joyful eucharist to lay it before the eyes of our heavenly Father, so ministering in His priesthood, and doing according to His commandment and His example; the church being the image of heaven, the priest the minister of Christ; the holy table being a copy of the celestial altar, and the eternal sacrifice of the lamb slain from the beginning of the world being always the same; it bleeds no more after the finishing of it on the cross; but it is wonderfully represented in heaven, and graciously represented here; by Christ's action there, by His commandment here. And the event of it is plainly this; that as Christ in virtue of His sacrifice on the cross intercedes for us with His Father, so does the minister of Christ's priesthood here, that the virtue of the eternal sacrifice may be salutary and effectual to all the needs of the church both for things temporal and eternal. And therefore it was not without great mystery and clear signification that our blessed Lord was pleased to command the representation of His death and sacrifice on the cross should be made by breaking bread and effusion of wine; to signify to us the nature and sacredness of the liturgy we are about; and that we minister in the priesthood of Christ, who is "a priest for ever after the order of Melchisedec;" that is, we are ministers in that unchangeable priesthood, imitating in the external ministry the prototype Melchisedec, of whom it was said, "he brought forth bread and wine, and was the priest of the most high God;" arid in the internal, imitating the antitype or the substance, Christ himself; who offered up His body and blood for atonement for us, and by the sacraments of bread and wine, and the prayers of oblation and intercession commands us to officiate in His priesthood, in the external ministering like Melchisedec; in the internal after the manner of Christ himself.

VIII.37–8

Eucharist and Resurrection

By the means of this sacrament, our bodies are made capable of the resurrection to life and eternal glory. For when we are externally and symbolically in the sacrament, and by faith and the Spirit of God internally united to Christ and made partakers of His body and His blood, we are joined and made one with Him who did rise again; and when the head is risen, the members shall not see corruption for ever, but rise again after the pattern of our Lord. If by the sacrament we are really united and made one with Christ, then it shall be to us in our proportion as it was to Him; we shall rise again, and we shall enter into glory. But it is certain we are united to Christ by it; we eat His body and drink His blood sacramentally by our mouths, and therefore really and spiritually, by our spirits and by spiritual actions co-operating. For what good will it do us to partake of His body, if we do not also partake of His spirit?

VIII.40

Communicating infants lawful but not necessary

[T]he refusing to communicate infants entered into the church upon an unwarrantable ground; for though it was confessed that the communion would do them benefit, yet it was denied to them then when the doctrine of transubstantiation entered, upon pretence lest by puking up the holy symbols the sacrament should be dishonoured: which indeed though that doctrine were true, were infinitely unreasonable; as supposing that Christ who suffered His body to be broken upon the cross that He might convey grace to them and us, would refuse to expose the symbols to the accidents of a child's stomach, and rather deny them that grace than endure that sight; who yet does daily suffer mice and mouldiness to do worse unto it.

But on the other side, they that without interest and partiality deny to communicate infants, can consider,—That infants being in baptism admitted to the promises of the gospel, and their portion in the kingdom of Christ, can have upon them no necessity to be communicated; for by their first sacrament they are drawn from their mere natural state and lifted up to the adoption of sons, and by the second sacrament alone they can go no further;—that although the first grace which is given in baptism be given them as their first being, yet the second graces are given to us upon other accounts, even for well using the first free grace;—that in baptism there were promises made which are to be personally accepted and verified before any new grace can be sacramentally imparted;—that it was necessity which gave them baptism before their reason, and that necessity being served, there can he no profit in proceeding upon the same method without the same reason;—that baptism is the sacrament of the new-born, the beginning, the gate of the church, the entry of the kingdom, the birth of a Christian; but the holy eucharist is the sacrament of them that grow in grace, of them that are perfect in Christ Jesus;—and lastly, to him that lists to be contentious we are to say as S. Paul did, "we have no such custom, nor the churches of God."

Now these probabilities on both sides may both of them be heard, and both of them prevail in the sense of the former determination: for by the first it may appear that to communicate infants is lawful; but the second proves that it is not necessary: for having in baptism received sufficient title to the kingdom of heaven, they who before the use of reason cannot sin and cannot fall from the grace they have received, cannot be obliged to the use of that sacrament which is for their reparation and security: and therefore in this case the present practice of the church is to be our rule and measure of peace.

VIII.94

Frequency of Communion

But let every one do what according to his faith he piously believes ought to be done. For neither of them dishonours the body and blood of the Lord, if they in their several ways contend who shall most honour the most holy sacrament. For Zaccheus and the centurion did not prefer themselves before one another, when the one received Christ into his house, and the other said he was not worthy to receive Him under his roof; both of them honouring our blessed Saviour by a divers, and almost a contrary way; both of them were miserable by sins and both of them obtained mercy.

VIII.185

At the Consecration

When the holy man reaches forth his hands upon the symbols and prays over them, and intercedes for the sins of the people, and breaks the holy bread and pours forth the sacred calico, place thyself by faith and meditation in heaven; and see Christ doing in His glorious manner this very thing which thou seest ministered and imitated upon the table of the Lord; and then remember that it is impossible thou shouldest miss of eternal blessings which are so powerfully procured for thee by the Lord himself; unless thou wilt despise all this, and neglect so great salvation, and choosest to eat with swine the dirty pleasures of the earth, rather than thus to feast with saints and angels, and to eat the body of thy Lord with a clean heart and humble affections.

VIII.224

Ordination

Baptism by the ordained only

[T]he ordinary minister of baptism is a person consecrated; the apostles and their successors in the office apostolical, and all those that partake of that power; and it needs no other proof, but the plain production of the commission; they who are teachers by ordinary power and authority, they also had command to baptize all nations: and baptism being the solemn rite of initiating disciples, and making the first public profession of the institution, it is in reason and analogy of the mystery to bc ministered by those who were appointed to collect the church, and make disciples.

I.24

Priesthood and intercession

This is not to lessen the power, but to understand it: for the priest's ministry is certainly the instrument of conveying all the blessings of the people, which are annexed to the ordinary administration of the Spirit. But when all the office of Christ's priesthood in heaven is called 'intercession for us,' and Himself makes the sacrifice of the cross effectual to the salvation and graces of His church by His prayer, since we are ministers of the same priesthood, can there be a greater glory than to have our ministry like to that of Jesus? not operating by virtue of a certain number of syllables, but by a holy, solemn, determined, and religious prayer, in the several manners and instances of intercession: according to the analogy of all the religions in the world, whose most solemn mystery was their most solemn prayer: I mean it in the matter of sacrificing; which also is true in the most mysterious solemnity of christianity, in the holy sacrament of the Lord's supper, which is hallowed and lifted up from the common bread and wine by mystical prayers and solemn invocations of God.

I.45

Solemnity of Ordination in the primitive Church

The holy Ghost was the first consecrator, that is made evident; and the persons first consecrated were the apostles, who received the several parts of the priestly order at several times; the power of consecration of the eucharist, at the institution of it; the power of remitting and retaining sins in the octaves of Easter; the power of baptizing and preaching, together with universal jurisdiction, immediately before the Ascension, when they were commanded to 'go into all the world, preaching and baptizing.' This is the whole office of the priesthood; and nothing of this was given in Pentecost when the holy Spirit descended and rested upon all of them; the apostles, the brethren, the women: for then they received those great assistances which enabled them who had been designed for embassadors to the world, to do their great work: and others of a lower capacity had their proportion, as the effect of the promise of the Father, and a mighty verification of the truth of christianity.

Now all these powers which Christ hath given to His apostles were by some means or other to be transmitted to succeeding persons, because the several ministries were to abide for ever. All nations were to be converted, a church to be gathered and continued, the new converts to be made confessors, and consigned with baptism, sins to be remitted, flocks to be fed and guided, and the Lord's death declared, represented, exhibited, and commemorated until His second coming. And since the powers of doing these offices are acts of free and gracious concession, emanations of the holy Spirit, and admissions to a vicinity with God, it is not only impudence and sacrilege in the person, falsely to pretend (that is, to belie) the holy Ghost, and thrust into these offices, but there is an impossibility in the thing, it is null in the very deed doing, to handle these mysteries without some appointment by God; unless He calls and points out the person either by an extraordinary or by an ordinary vocation.

I.54

The life of a priest

Let not the name of the church be made a pretence for personal covetousness, by saying, 'you are willing to remit many things, but you must not wrong the church:' for though it be true that you are not to do prejudice to succession, yet many things may be forgiven upon just occasions, from which the church shall receive no incommodity; but be sure that there are but few things which thou art bound to do in thy personal capacity, but the same also, and more, thou art obliged to perform as thou art a public person.

Never exact the offerings, or customary wages, and such as are allowed by law, in the ministration of the sacraments, nor condition for them, nor secure them beforehand; but first do your office, and minister the sacraments purely, readily, and for Christ's sake; and when that is done, receive what is your due.

Avoid all pride, as you would flee from the most frightful apparition, or the most cruel enemy; and remember that you can never truly teach humility, or tell what it is, unless you practise it yourselves.

Take no measures of humility but such as are material and tangible; such which consist not in humble words, and lowly gestures; but what is first truly radicated in your souls, in low opinion of yourselves, and in real preferring others before yourselves; and in such significations which can neither deceive yourselves nor others.

Let every curate of souls strive to understand himself best; and then to understand others. Let him spare himself least; but most severely judge, censure, and condemn himself. If he be learned, let him shew it by wise teaching, and humble manners: if he be not learned, let him be sure to get so much knowledge as to know that, and so much humility, as not to grow insolent, and puffed up by his emptiness. For many will pardon a good man that is less learned; but if he be proud no man will forgive him.

Let every minister be careful to live a life as abstracted from the affairs of the world as his necessity will permit him; but at no hand to be immerged and principally employed in the affairs of the world. What cannot be avoided, and what is of good report, and what he is obliged to by any personal or collateral duty, that he may do, but no more; ever remembering the saying of our blessed Lord, "In the world ye shall have trouble, but in Me ye shall have peace:" and consider this also, which is a great truth,—that every degree of love to the world is so much taken from the love of God.

I.102

From the Dedication in 'Episcopacy Asserted'

My Lord,

When we make books and publish them, and by dedications implore the patronage of some worthy person, I find by experience that we cannot acquire that end which is pretended to by such addresses; for neither friendship nor power, interest or favour, can give those defences to a book which it needs: because the evil fortune of books comes from causes discernible indeed, but irremediable; and the breath of the people is like the voice of an exterminating angel, not so killing but so secret. But that's not; it is also as contingent as the smiles of an infant, or the fall of a die, which is determined by every part of motion which can be in any part of the hand or arm. For when I consider that the infinite variety of understandings is greater than that of faces, not only because the lines that make our faces are finite, but the things that integrate and actuate the understanding are not; but also because every man hath a face, but every man hath not understanding; and men with their understandings, or with their no understandings, give their sentence upon books, not only before they understand all, not only before they read all, but before they read three pages, receiving their information from humour or interest, from chance or mistake, from him that reads in malice, or from him that reads after dinner; I find it necessary that he that writes should secure himself and his own reputation by all the ways of prudence and religion; that God, who takes care of fame as certainly as of lives, may do that which is best in this instance; for no other patron can defend him that writes from him that reads, and understands either too much or too little. And therefore, my lord, I could not choose you to be the patron of my book upon hopes you can by greatness or interest secure it against the stings of insects and imperfect creatures; nothing but Domitian's style can make them harmless; but I can from your wisdom and your learning, the great reputation you have abroad and the honour you have at home, hope that for the relation-sake some will be civil to it, at least until they read it, and then I give them leave to do what they please, for I am secure enough in all this; because my writings are not intended as a stratagem for noises; I intend to do not only what is good, but what is best; and therefore I am not troubled at any event, so I may but justly hope that God is glorified in the ministration: but he that seeks any thing but God's service, shall have such a reward as will do him no good.

V.1–2

Imposition of hands – a bishop's ministry

The sum is this: Imposition of hands is a duty and office necessary for the perpetuating of a church, *ne gens sit unius ætatis,* 'lest it expire in one age.' This power of imposition of hands for ordination was fixed upon the apostles and apostolic men, and not communicated to the seventy-two disciples or presbyters; for the apostles and apostolic men did so *de facto,* and were commanded to do so, and the seventy-two never did so. Therefore this office and ministry of the apostolate is distinct and superior to that of presbyters; and this distinction must be so continued to all ages of the church; for the thing was not temporary, but productive of issue and succession, and therefore as perpetual as the clergy, as the church itself.

V.27

Episcopacy, jurisdiction as 'angel of the church'

If superiority of jurisdiction was necessary in the ages apostolical for the regiment of the church, there is no imaginable reason why it should not be necessary in succession, since upon the emergency of schisms and heresies, which were foretold should multiply in descending ages, government and superiority of jurisdiction, unity of supremacy, and coercion, was more necessary than at first, when extraordinary gifts might supply what now we expect to be performed by an ordinary authority.

Whatsoever was the regiment of the church in the apostles' times, that must be perpetual, (not so as to have all that which was personal and temporary, but so as to have no other;) for that and that only is of divine institution which Christ committed to the apostles; and if the church be not now governed as then, we can shew no divine authority for our government; which we must contend to do, and do it too, or be called usurpers. For either the apostles did govern the church as Christ commanded them, or not. If not, then they failed in the founding of the church, and the church is not built upon a rock. If they did, as most certainly they did, then either the same disparity of jurisdiction must be retained, or else we must be governed with an unlawful and unwarranted equality, because not by that which only is of immediate divine institution; and then it must needs be a fine government, where there is no authority, and where no man is superior.

We see a disparity in the regiment of churches warranted by Christ himself, and confirmed by the Holy Ghost, in fairest intimation. I mean the seven angel-presidents of the seven Asian churches. If these seven angels were seven bishops, that is, prelates or governors of these seven churches, in which it is evident and confessed of all sides there were many presbyters, then it is certain that a superiority of jurisdiction was intended by Christ himself, and given by Him, insomuch as He is the fountain of all power derived to the church; for Christ writes to these seven churches, and directs His epistles to the seven governors of these churches, calling them angels; which it will hardly be supposed He would have done if the function had not been a ray of the Sun of righteousness; they had not else been angels of light, nor stars held in Christ's own right hand.

This is certain, that the function of these angels, whatsoever it be, is a divine institution; let us then see what is meant by these stars and angels. "The seven stars are the angels of the seven churches, and the seven candlesticks are the seven churches."

First then it is evident, that although the epistles were sent with a final intention for the edification and confirmation of the whole churches or people of the diocese, with an *Attendite quid Spiritus dicit ecclesiis;* yet the personal direction was not to the whole church, for the whole church is called the candlestick, and the superscription of the epistles is not to the seven 'candlesticks,' but to the seven 'stars,' which are the angels of the seven churches, viz., the lights shining in the candlesticks. By the angel therefore is not, cannot be meant, the 'whole church.'

VI. 35–6

Episcopacy not of dominical institution, but necessary

Although we had not proved the immediate divine institution of episcopal power over presbyters and the whole flock, yet episcopacy is not less than an apostolical ordinance, and delivered to us by the same authority that the observation of the Lord's day is. For that in the New testament we have no precept, and nothing but the example of the primitive disciples meeting in their *synaxes* upon that day, and so also they did on the Saturday in the Jewish synagogues, but yet (however that at Geneva they were once in meditation to have changed it into a Thursday meeting, to have shown their christian liberty) we should think strangely of those men that called the Sunday festival less than an apostolical ordinance, and necessary now to be kept holy with such observances as the church hath appointed.

Baptism of infants is most certainly a holy and charitable ordinance, and of ordinary necessity to all that ever cried, and yet the church hath founded this rite upon the tradition of the apostles; and wise men do easily observe that the anabaptists can by the same probability of scripture enforce a necessity of communicating infants upon us, as we do of baptizing infants upon them, if we speak of immediate divine institution, or of practice apostolical recorded in scripture; and therefore a great master of Geneva, in a book he writ against the anabaptists, was forced to fly to apostolical traditive ordination: and therefore the institution of bishops must be served first, as having fairer plea and clearer evidence in scripture than the baptizing of infants, and yet they that deny this are by the just *anathema* of the catholic church confidently condemned for heretics.

VI.68–9

Two dominical Sacraments – and others – the role of the Bishop

The sacraments and mysteries of christianity if compared among themselves, are greater and lesser in several respects. For since they are all in order to several ends, that is, productive of several effects, and they all are excellent, every rite and sacrament in respect of its own effect is more excellent than the other not ordained to that effect. For example; matrimony is ordained for a means to preserve chastity, and to represent the mystical union of Christ and His church, and therefore in these respects is greater than baptism, which does neither; but baptism is for 'remission of sins,' and in that is more excellent than matrimony. The same may be said for ordination and consecration, the one being in order to Christ's natural body, as the schools speak, the other in order to His mystical body, and so have their several excellencies respectively; but for an absolute pre-eminence of one above the other, I said there was no basis to fix that upon, and I believe all men will find it so that please to try; but in a relative or respective excellency they go both before and after one another. Thus wool and a jewel are better than each. other; for wool is better for warmth, and a jewel for ornament. A frog hath more sense in it than the sun, and yet the sun shines brighter.

Suppose consecration of the eucharist were greater than ordaining priests, yet that cannot hinder but that the power of ordaining may make a higher and distinct order; because the power of ordaining hath in it the power of consecrating and something more; it is all that which makes the priest, and it is something more besides which makes the bishop. Indeed if the bishop had it not and the priest had it, then supposing consecration to be greater than ordination the priest would not only equal but excel the bishop; but because the bishop hath that and ordination besides, therefore he is higher both in order and dignity.

VI.108

The Apostolic Succession (from a sermon at his own consecration)

Who are these rulers of Christ's family? For though Christ knew it, and therefore needed not to ask; yet we have disputed it so much and obeyed so little, that we have changed the plain hypothesis into an entangled question. The answer yet is easy as to some part of the enquiry: the apostles are the first meaning of the text; for they were our fathers in Christ, they begat sons and daughters unto God; and where a spiritual paternity is evident, we need look no further for spiritual government, because in the paternal rule all power is founded; they begat the family by the power of the word and the life of the Spirit, and they fed this family, and ruled it by the word of their proper ministry; they had the keys of this house, the steward's ensign; and they had the rulers' place, for they sat on twelve thrones and judged the twelve tribes of Israel. But of this there is no question.

And as little of another proposition, that this stewardship was to last for ever; for the power of ministering in this office and the office itself were to be perpetual: for the issues and powers of government are more necessary for the perpetuating the church, than for the first planting; and if it was necessary that the apostle should have a rod and a staff at first, it would be more necessary afterwards, when the family was more numerous, and their first zeal abated, and their native simplicity perverted into arts of hypocrisy and forms of godliness, when 'heresies should arise,' and 'the love of many should wax cold.' The apostles had also a power of ordination; and that the very power itself does denote, for it makes perpetuity, that could not expire in the days of the apostles; for by it they themselves propagated a succession. And Christ having promised His spirit to abide with His church for ever, and made His apostles the channels, the ministers and conveyances of it, that it might descend as the inheritance and eternal portion of the family; it cannot be imagined that when the first ministers were gone, there should not others rise up in the same places, some like to the first, in the same office and ministry of the Spirit.

VIII. 310–11

Bishops get an extra guardian angel

Consider therefore what is your great duty. Consider what is your great danger. The lines of duty I have already described; only remember how dear and precious souls are to God, since for their salvation Christ gave His blood, and therefore will not easily lose them whom, though they had sinned against Him, yet He so highly valued; remember that you are Christ's deputies in the care of souls, and that you succeed in the place of the apostles. *Non est facile stare loco Pauli, et tenere gradum Petri,* you have undertaken 'the work of S. Paul, and the office of S. Peter,' and what think you upon this account will be required of us? . . . The ancient fathers had a pious opinion, that besides the angel guardian which is appointed to the guard of every man, there is to every bishop a second angel appointed to him at the consecration; and to this Origen alludes, saying that every bishopric hath two angels, the one visible and the other invisible. This is a great matter, and shews what a precious thing that order and those persons are in the eyes of God; but then this also means, that we should live angelic lives.

VIII.326

Confirmation

Confirmation originally separate hand-laying by bishop

Concerning the subject of this discourse, the Rite of Confirmation, it were easy to recount many great and glorious expressions which we find in the sermons of the holy fathers of the primitive ages: so certain it is that in this thing we ought to be zealous, as being desirous to persuade our people to give us leave to do them great good. But the following pages will do it I hope competently: only we shall remark, that when they had gotten a custom anciently that in cases of necessity they did permit deacons and laymen sometimes to baptize, yet they never did confide in it much, but with much caution and curiosity commanded that such persons should, when that necessity was over, be carried to the bishop to be confirmed, so to supply all precedent defects relating to the past imperfect ministry, and future necessity and danger.

V.612

Baptism and Confirmation considered – Confirmation defended

By baptism we are heirs, and are adopted to the inheritance of sons, admitted to the covenant of repentance, and engaged to live a good life; yet this is but the solemnity of the covenant, which must pass into after-acts by other influences of the same divine principle. Until we receive the spirit of obsignation or confirmation, we are but 'babes in Christ' in the meanest sense, infants that can do nothing, that cannot speak, that cannot resist any violence, exposed to every rudeness and perishing by every temptation.

But therefore as God at first appointed us a ministry of a new birth, so also hath He given to His church the consequent ministry of a new strength. The Spirit moved a little upon the waters of baptism, and gave us the principles of life, but in confirmation He makes us able to move ourselves. In the first He is the spirit of life, but in this He is the spirit of strength and motion . . . that as we are baptized into the death and resurrection of Christ, so in confirmation we may be renewed in the inner man, and strengthened in all our holy vows and purposes by the Holy Ghost ministered according to God's ordinance.

The holy rite of confirmation is a divine ordinance, and it produces divine effects and is ministered by divine persons, that is, by those whom God hath sanctified and separated to this ministration. At first all that were baptized were also confirmed, and ever since all good people that have understood it have been very zealous for it; and time was in England, even since the first beginnings of the Reformation, when confirmation had been less carefully ministered for about six years, when the people had their first opportunities of it restored, they ran to it in so great numbers that churches and churchyards would not hold them; insomuch that I have read that the bishop of Chester was forced to impose hands on the people in the fields, and was so oppressed with multitudes that he had almost been trod to death by the people, and had died with the throng if he had not been rescued by the civil power.

But men have too much neglected all the ministries of grace, and this most especially, and have not given themselves to a right understanding of it, and so neglected it yet more. But because the prejudice which these parts of the christian church have suffered for want of it is very great (as will appear by enumeration of the many and great blessings consequent to it) I am not without hope that it may be a service acceptable to God, and an useful ministry to the souls of my charges, if by instructing them that know not, and exhorting them that know, I set forward the practice of this holy rite, and give reason why the people ought to love it and to desire it, and how they are to understand and practise it, and consequently with what duteous affections they are to relate to those persons whom God hath in so special and signal manner made to be, for their good and eternal benefit, the ministers of the Spirit and salvation.

V.616–17

Confirmation not a sacrament like Baptism and Eucharist, but 'of great use and holiness'

Whether confirmation be a sacrament or no, is of no use to dispute; and if it be disputed, it can never be proved to be so as baptism and the Lord's supper, that is, 'as generally necessary to salvation;' but though it be no sacrament, it cannot follow that it is not of very great use and holiness: and as a man is never the less tied to repentance, though it be no sacrament; so neither is he ever the less obliged to receive confirmation, though it be (as it ought) acknowledged to be of an use and nature inferior to the two sacraments of divine, direct and immediate institution. It is certain that the fathers in a large symbolical and general sense call it a sacrament, but mean not the same thing by that word when they apply it to confirmation as they do when they apply it to baptism and the Lord's supper. That it is an excellent and divine ordinance to purposes spiritual, that it comes from God and ministers in our way to God, that is all we are concerned to enquire after: and this I shall endeavour to prove not only against the Jesuits, but against all opponents of what side soever.

V.618–19

Form of Confirmation distinct from other rites of hand-laying in New Testament

We have seen the original from Christ, the practice and exercise of it in the apostles and the first converts in christianity; that which I shall now remark is, that this is established and passed into a christian doctrine. The warranty for what I say is the words of S. Paul, where the holy rite of confirmation, so called from the effect of this ministration, and expressed by the ritual part of it, imposition of hands, is reckoned a fundamental point . . . "Not laying again the foundation of repentance from dead works and of faith towards God, of the doctrine of baptisms, and of laying on of hands, of resurrection from the dead, and eternal judgment." Here are six fundamental points of S. Paul's catechism, which he laid as the foundation or the beginning of the institution of the christian church; and among these imposition of hands is reckoned as a part of the foundation, and therefore they who deny it dig up foundations. Now that this imposition of hands is that which the apostles used in confirming the baptized, and invocating the Holy Ghost upon them, remains to be proved.

For it is true that imposition of hands signifies all christian rites except baptism and the Lord's supper; not the sacraments, but all the sacramentals of the church: it signifies confirmation, ordination, absolution, visitation of the sick, blessing single persons (as Christ did the children brought to Him) and blessing marriages; all these were usually ministered by imposition of hands. Now the three last are not pretended to be any part of this foundation; neither reason, authority, nor the nature of the thing suffer any such pretension: the question then is between the first three.

V.630–1

Liturgy

Consecration by prayer

Now whether this consecration by prayer did mean to reduce the words of institution to the sense and signification of a prayer, or that they mean the consecration was made by the other prayers annexed to the narrative of the institution, according to the several senses of the Greek and Latin church, yet still the ministry of the priest, whether in the words of consecration or in the annexed prayers, is still by way of prayer.

I.47

The Prayer Book extolled

But I delight not to observe the correspondencies of such sad accidents, which as they may happen upon divers causes, or may be forced violently by the strength of fancy, or driven on by jealousy and the too fond openings of troubled hearts and afflicted spirits; so they do but help to vex the offending part, and relieve the afflicted but with a fantastic and groundless comfort: I will therefore deny leave to my own affections to ease themselves by complaining of others; I shall only crave leave that I may remember Jerusalem, and call to mind the pleasures of the temple, the order of her services, the beauty of her buildings, the sweetness of her songs, the decency of her ministrations, the assiduity and economy of her priests and Levites, the daily sacrifice, and that eternal fire of devotion that went not out by day nor by night; these were the pleasures of our peace, and there is a remanent felicity in the very memory of those spiritual delights which we then enjoyed, as antepasts of heaven and consignations to an immortality of joys. And it may be so again, when it shall please God who lath the hearts of all princes in His hand, and turneth them as the rivers of waters; and when men will consider the invaluable loss that is consequent, and the danger of sin that is appendent, to the destroying such forms of discipline and devotion in which God was purely worshipped, and the church was edified, and the people instructed to great degrees of piety, knowledge, and devotion.

And such is the liturgy of the church of England. I shall not need to enumerate the advantages of liturgy in general, though it be certain, that some liturgy or other is most necessary in public addresses, 1) that so we may imitate the perpetual practice of all settled churches since christianity, or ever since Moses' law or the Jewish church came to have a settled foot, and any rest in the land of Canaan; 2) that we may follow the example and obey the precept of our blessed Saviour, who appointed a set form of devotion; and certainly they that profess enmity against all liturgy can in no sense obey the precept given by Him who gave command, "When ye pray, say, Our Father;" '3) that all that come may know the condition of public communion, their religion, and manner of address to God almighty; 4) that the truth of the proposition, the piety of the desires and the honesty of the petitions, the simplicity of our purposes and the justice of our designs, may be secured beforehand; because 'whatsoever is not of faith is sin,' and it is impossible that we should pray to God in the *ex tempore* prayers of the priest by any faith but unreasonable, unwarranted, insecure, and implicit; 5) that there may be union of hearts, and spirits, and tongues; 6) that there may be a public symbol of communion in our prayers, which are the best instruments of endearing us to God and to one another; . . . 'private prayer, not assisted with the concord and unity of a public spirit, is weaker and less effectual,' saith S. Basil; 7) that the ministers less learned may have provisions of devotions made for them; 8) that the more learned may have no occasion of ostentation ministered to them, lest their best actions, their prayers, be turned into sin; 9) that extravagant levities, and secret impieties, be prevented; 10) that the offices ecclesiastical may the better secure the articles of religion; 11) that they may edify the people, by being repositories of holy and necessary truths ready formed out of their needs, and described in their books of daily use; for that was one of the advices of the apostle, "teaching and admonishing one another in psalms and hymns, and spiritual songs;" 12) that men by the intervening of authority may be engaged to certain devotions; 13) that not only the duty, but the very form of its ministration may be honoured by the countenance of authority, and not be exposed to contempt by reason of the insufficiency of its external warrant; 14) that the assignation of such offices, and appropriating them to the ministry of certain persons, may be a cancel to secure the enclosures of the clerical orders from the usurpings and invasions of pretending and unhallowed spirits; 15) that indetermination of the office may not introduce indifferency, nor indifferency lead in a freer liberty, or liberty degenerate into licentiousness, or licentiousness into folly and vanity; and these come sometimes attended with secular designs, lest these be cursed with the immission of a peevish spirit upon our priests, and that spirit be a teacher of lies, and these lies become the basis of impious theorems, which are certainly attended with ungodly lives; and then either atheism or antichristianism may come, according as shall happen in the conjunction of time and other circumstances; for this would be a sad. climax, a ladder upon which are no angels ascending or descending, because the degrees lead to darkness and misery.

VI. 232–3

. . . and defended

Certain it is that there is no part of religion, as it is a distinct virtue, and is to be exercised by interior acts and forms of worship, but is in the offices of the church of England. For if the soul desires to be humbled, she hath provided forms of confession to God before His church; if she will rejoice and give God thanks for particular blessings, there are forms of thanksgiving described and added by the king's authority upon the conference at Hampton-court, which are all the public, solemn, and foreseen occasions for which by law and order provision could be made. If she will commend to God the public and private necessities of the church and single persons, the whole body of collects and devotions supplies that abundantly: if her devotion be high and pregnant and prepared to fervency and importunity of congress with God, the litanies are an admirable pattern of devotion, full of circumstances proportionable for a quick and an earnest spirit: when the revolution of the anniversary calls on us to perform our duty of special meditation and thankfulness to God for the glorious benefits of Christ's incarnation, nativity, passion, resurrection, and ascension (blessings which do as well deserve a day of thanksgiving as any other temporal advantage, though it be the pleasure of a victory), then we have the offices of Christmas, the Annunciation, Easter, and Ascension: if we delight to remember those holy persons whose bodies rest in the bed of peace and whose souls are deposited in the hands of Christ till the day of restitution of all things, we may by the collects and days of anniversary festivity not only remember but also imitate them too in our lives, if we will make that use of the proportions of scripture allotted for the festival which the church intends: to which if we add the advantages of the whole psalter, which is an entire body of devotion by itself, and hath in it forms to exercise all graces by way of internal act and spiritual intention, there is not any ghostly advantage which the most religious can either need or fancy but the English liturgy in its entire constitution will furnish us withal. And certainly it was a very great wisdom and a very prudent and religious constitution, so to order that part of the liturgy which the ancients called the *Lectionarium* that the psalter should be read over twelve times in the year, the Old testament once, and the New testament thrice, besides the epistles and gospels, which renew with a more frequent repetition such choice places as represent the entire body of faith and good life.

VI.247

'The Westminster Directory' condemned

I have read over this book which the Assembly of Divines is pleased to call 'The Directory for Prayer.' I confess I came to it with much expectation, and was in some measure confident I should have found it an exact and unblamable model of devotion, free from all those objections which men of their own persuasion had obtruded against the public liturgy of the church of England; or at least it should have been composed with so much artifice and fineness that it might have been to all the world an argument of their learning and excellency of spirit, if not of the goodness and integrity of their religion and purposes. I shall give no other character of the whole but that the public disrelish which I find amongst persons of great piety of all qualities, not only of great but even of ordinary understandings, is to me some argument that it lies so open to the objections even of common spirits, that the compilers of it did intend more to prevail by the success of their armies than the strength of reason and the proper grounds of persuasion, which yet most wise and good men believe to be the more christian way of the two. But because the judgment I made of it from an argument so extrinsical to the nature of the thing could not reasonably enable me to satisfy those many persons who in their behalf desired me to consider it, I resolve to look upon it nearer, and to take its account from something that was ingredient to its constitution, 'that I might be able both to exhort and convince the gainsayers,' who refuse to hold fast . . . that 'faithful word which they had been taught' by their mother the church of England.

VI. 259

Set forms necessary – and better

But now then this distinction evacuates all the former discourse, and since it is permitted that every man in private use what forms he please, the Spirit hath all that liberty that is necessary, and so much as can be convenient; the church may be edified by every man's gifts the affections of all men may be complied withal, words may be fitted to their fancies, their devotions quickened, their weariness helped and supported, and whatsoever benefit can be fancied by variety and liberty, all that may be enjoyed, and every reasonable desire or weaker fancy be fully satisfied.

But since these advantages to devotion are accidental, and do consult with weakness and infirmity, and depend upon irregular variety, for which no antecedent rule can make particular provision; it is not to be expected the public constitution and prescribed forms, which are regular, orderly, and determined, can make provision for particulars, for chances, and for infinite varieties. And if this were any objection against public forms, it would also conclude against all human laws, that they did not make provision for all particular accidents and circumstances that might possibly occur; all public sanctions must be of a public spirit and design, and secure all those excellent things which have influence upon societies, communities of men, and public obligations.

Thus if public forms of prayer be described whose matter is pious and holy, whose design is of universal extent, and provisionary for all public, probable, feared, or foreseen events, whose frame and composure is prudent, and by authority competent and high, and whose use and exercise is instrumental to peace and public charity, and all these hallowed by intention and care of doing glory to God and advantages to religion, expressed in observation of all such rules and precedents as are most likely to teach us best and guide us surest, such as are scriptures, apostolical tradition, primitive practice, and precedents of saints and holy persons, the public can do no more; all the duty is performed, and all the care is taken.

Now after all this there are personal necessities and private conveniences or inconveniences, which if men are not so wise as themselves to provide for by casting off all prejudice and endeavouring to grow strong in christianity, men in Christ, and not for ever to be babes in religion, but frame themselves to a capacity of receiving the benefit of the public, without needing other provisions than what will fit the church in her public capacity; the Spirit of God, and the church taught by Him, hath permitted us to comply with our own infirmities, while they are innocent, and to pray in private in any form of words which shall be most instrumental to our devotion in the present capacity.

V.280

Collective authorization means some limitations

But now if the church in her united capacity makes prayers for he people, they cannot be supposed to be other than limited and determined forms; for it is not practicable, or indeed imaginable, that a synod of church governors, be they who they will, so they be of Christ's appointment, should meet in every church and pray as every man list; their counsels are united, and their results are conclusions and final determinations, which like general propositions are applicable to particular instances; so that first, since the Spirit being the great dictator of holy prayers; and secondly, the Spirit is promised to the church in her united capacity; and thirdly, in proportion to the assembled, *cæteris paribus,* so are measures of the Spirit poured out; and fourthly, when the church is assembled, the prayers which they teach the people are limited and prescribed forms; it follows that limited and prescribed forms are in all reason emanations from the greatest portion of the Spirit, warranted by special promises, which are made to every man there present that does his duty as a private member of the christian church, and are due to him as a ruler of the church, and yet more especially and in a further degree to all them met together; where, if ever, the Holy Spirit gives such helps and graces which relate to the public government, and have influence upon the communities of Christians, that is, will bless their meeting, and give them such assistances as will enable them to do the work for which they convene.

V.286

Ministers should use common prayer, not make up their own, as praying on behalf of Church

For why are not the ministers to be left as well to their liberty in making their prayers, as their sermons? I answer, The church may if she will, but whether she doth well or no, let her consider: this I am sure, there is not the same reason, and I fear the experience the world hath already had of it will make demonstration enough of the inconvenience. But however, the differences are many.

First, Our prayers offered up by the minister are in behalf and in the name of the people, and therefore great reason they should know beforehand what is to be presented, that if they like not the message they may refuse to communicate; especially since people are so divided in their opinions, in their hopes, and in their faiths, it being a duty to refuse communion with those prayers which they think to have in them the matter of sin or doubting. Which reason on the other part ceases; for the minister being to speak from God to the people, if he speaks what he ought not, God can right Himself, however is not a partner of the sin, as in the other case the people possibly may be.

V.308–9

Preaching rightly restricted by clergy of the Westminster Assembly

But indeed, if I may freely declare my opinion, I think it were not amiss if the liberty of making sermons were something more restrained than it is, and that either such persons only were intrusted with the liberty for whom the church herself may safely be responsive, that is, to men learned and pious, and that the other part, the *vulgus cleri,* should instruct the people out of the fountains of the church and the public stock, till by so long exercise and discipline in the schools of the prophets they may also be intrusted to minister of their own unto the people. This I am sure was the practice of the primitive church, when preaching was as ably and religiously performed as now it is; but in this I prescribe nothing. But truly I think the reverend divines of the Assembly are many of them of my mind in this particular, and that they observe a liberty indulged to some persons to preach, which I think they had rather should hold their peace, and yet think the church better edified in their silence than their sermons.

V.310

Golden Grove introduction – depth of feeling against the Commonwealth

But now instead of this excellency of condition and constitution of religion, the people are fallen under the harrows and saws of impertinent and ignorant preachers, who think all religion is a sermon, and all sermons ought to be libels against truth and old governors, and expound chapters that the meaning may never be understood, and pray, that they may be thought able to talk, but not to hold their peace, they casting not to obtain any thing but wealth and victory, power and plunder. And the people have reaped the fruits apt to grow upon such crabstocks: they grow idle and false, hypocrites and careless, they deny themselves nothing that is pleasant, they despise religion, forget government; and some never think of heaven; and they that do, think to go thither in such paths which all the ages of the church did give men warning of, lest they should that way go to the devil.

But when men have tried all that they can, it is to be supposed they will return to the excellency and advantages of the christian religion, as it is taught by the church of England; for by destroying it, no end can be served but of sin and folly, faction, and death eternal. For besides that no church that is enemy to this, does worship God in that truth of propositions, in that unblamable and pious liturgy, and in preaching the necessities of holy life, so much as the church of England does; besides this (I say) it cannot be persecuted by any governor that understands his own interest, unless he be first abused by false preachers, and then prefers his secret opinion before his public advantage. For no church in the world is so great a friend to loyalty and obedience, as she and her sisters of the same persuasion. They that hate bishops have destroyed monarchy, and they that would erect an ecclesiastical monarchy, must consequently subject the temporal to it. And both one and the other would be supreme in consciences; and they that govern there, with an opinion that in all things they ought to be attended to, will let their prince govern others, so long as he will be ruled by them. And certainly, for a prince to persecute the protestant religion, is as if a physician should endeavour to destroy all medicaments, and fathers kill their sons, and the master of ceremonies destroy all formalities and courtships; and as if the pope should root out all the ecclesiastic state. Nothing so combines with government, if it be of God's appointment, as the religion of the church of England, because nothing does more adhere to the word of God, and disregard the crafty advantages of the world. If any man shall not decline to try his title by the word of God, it is certain there is not in the world a better guard for it, than the true protestant religion, as it is taught in our church.

VII.590

From the preface to 'Collection of Offices'

AN ADVERTISEMENT
TO THEM THAT SHALL USE THESE PRAYERS

Because no prayers are the more pleasing to God for being long, and they are oftentimes displeasing even to good men if they be very long; and yet on the other side if the devotion be long it is the better, and if that be lasting, it ought to be supplied with materials, like gums to the altar of incense, and fuel for the holy fires: he that collected these devotions did design to serve the advantages both of length and shortness, that the most devout may be fitted, and the most secular and employed may not be wearied.

Therefore, although every thing is set down at length, that the trouble of references and turnings back might be avoided, and therefore seem longer than they are; and the hymns are sometimes double, that the variety might be more apt to please and to instruct, and the offices are made full, that upon the more solemn days, when people come with a greater and more active devotion and greater leisure, their time and their piety might be employed; yet on other days there is but one lesson appointed, and one hymn to follow it.

The prayers arc divided into smaller portions, that with ease any of them may be omitted by persons whose occasions force them from their attendance on longer offices; besides that there are two forms of morning and evening prayer, the one shorter, the other longer.

In the beginning of morning and evening prayer, some of the devotions which are set down are desired and intended to be used but seldom; not only to avoid tediousness, but for other reasons very obvious, that the minister's more solemn power and office might not be less regarded, by being daily (and consequently very often without just dispositions) offered: I mean it concerning the form of absolution. The confession may be shortened as there is cause, by making use only of some of the sections, and leaving out the other.

If upon communion days the morning prayer and the communion office be not read at one time, but the morning prayer be read at seven or eight of the clock in the morning, and the communion office at the time of celebration,—or if it be convenient that they be both together, if then the sermon be in the afternoon,—the length will be very tolerable.

These prayers being intended only as a charitable ministry to them who are not permitted to use those which were appointed formerly, there is no necessity upon any one, and he may use as much or as little as he please, and therefore no man will have cause to complain of length or shortness.

VIII, 574–5

Taylor's Communion Rite – central section

N.B. Note the Eastern features: the hymn better known now as 'Let all mortal flesh keep silence', from the Liturgy of St James; a proper invocation of the Holy Spirit; and a lengthy 'anamnesis' ('remembrance' prayer), but – like many some of the Syriac prayers – addressed to Christ.

Let all corruptible flesh be silent, and stand with fear and trembling, and think within itself nothing that is earthly, nothing that is unholy. The King of kings and the Lord of lords, Christ our God comes down from heaven unto us, and gives Himself to be meat for the souls of all faithful people. All the glorious companies of angels behold this and wonder, and love and worship Jesus. Every throne and dominion, the cherubims with many eyes, and the seraphims with many wings cover their faces before the majesty of His glory, and sing a perpetual song for ever,—

Alleluiah, Alleluiah!
Glory be to God on high,
and in earth peace, good will towards men.
Alleluiah.

Then shall follow this prayer of consecration, to be said by the minister standing.

I

Have mercy upon us, O heavenly Father, according to Thy glorious mercies and promises, send Thy holy Ghost upon our hearts, and let Him also descend upon these gifts, that by His good, His holy, His glorious presence, He may sanctify and enlighten our hearts, and He may bless and sanctify these gifts.

That this bread may become the holy body of Christ.
Amen.

And this chalice may become the life-giving blood of Christ.
Amen.

That it may become unto us all that partake of it this day, a blessed instrument of union with Christ, of pardon and peace, of health and blessing, of holiness and life eternal, through Jesus Christ our Lord.
Amen.

II

Holy and blessed art Thou, O king of eternal ages, fountain and giver of all righteousness.

Holy art Thou, the eternal and only-begotten Son of God, our Lord Jesus Christ, Redeemer of the world.

Holy art Thou, O blessed Spirit, that searchest all things, even the depths and hidden things of God.

Thou, O God, art almighty: Thou art good and gracious, dreadful and venerable, holy and merciful to the work of Thine own hands.

Thou didst make man according to Thine image; Thou gavest him the riches and the rest of paradise: when he fell and broke Thy easy commandment, Thou didst not despise his folly, nor leave him in his sin, but didst chastise him with Thy rod, and restrain him by Thy law, and instruct him by Thy prophets, and at last didst send Thy holy Son into the world, that He might renew and repair Thy broken image.

The people shall answer, Blessed be God!

He coming from heaven, and taking our flesh, by the power of the holy Ghost, of the virgin Mary, conversed with men, and taught us the way of God, and the dispensation of eternal life.

People. Holy Jesus! blessed be God.

But when for the redemption of us sinners He would suffer death upon the cross, without sin, for us who were nothing but sin and misery, in the night in which He was betrayed, He took bread, He looked up to heaven, He gave thanks, He sanctified it, He brake it, and gave it to His apostles, saying, Take, eat, this is My body which is broken for you; do this in remembrance of Me.

Likewise after supper He took the cup, and when He had given thanks and blessed it, He gave it to them, saying, Drink ye all of this, for this is My blood of the New testament, which is shed for you and for many for the remission of sins; do this in remembrance of Me.

For as often as ye shall eat this bread, and drink this cup, ye shall shew forth the Lord's death till He come.

The people shall answer, Amen.
Minister. We believe, and we confess.
People. We declare Thy death, and confess Thy resurrection.
Then the minister kneeling shall say this prayer of oblation.

I

We sinners, Thy unworthy servants, in remembrance of Thy life-giving passion, Thy cross and Thy pains, Thy death and Thy burial, Thy resurrection from the dead and Thy ascension into heaven, Thy sitting at the right hand of God, making intercession for us; and expecting with fear and trembling Thy formidable and glorious return to judge the quick and dead, when Thou shalt render to every man according to his works; do humbly present to Thee, O Lord, this present sacrifice of remembrance and thanksgiving, humbly and passionately praying Thee not to deal with us according to our sins, nor recompense us after our transgressions; but according to Thy abundant mercy and infinite goodness to blot out and take away the hand-writing that is against us in the book of remembrances which Thou hast written: and that Thou wilt give unto us spiritual, celestial and eternal gifts, which neither eye hath seen nor ear hath heard, neither hath it entered into the heart of man to understand, which God hath prepared for them that love Him, through Jesus Christ our Lord. *Amen.*

Then shall follow the reception and distribution, of the holy sacrament.

The minister first receiving, and privately saying this short prayer.

O blessed Jesus, my Lord and my God, Thou art the celestial food and the life of every man that cometh unto Thee. I have sinned against heaven and before Thee, and am not worthy to partake of these holy mysteries: but Thou art my merciful Saviour; grant that I may religiously, thankfully, and without reproof partake of Thy blessed body and blood, for the remission of my sins, and unto life eternal. Amen.

Then reverently taking in his hand the consecrated bread that he means to eat, let him say,

The body of our Lord Jesus which was broken for me, preserve my body and soul into everlasting life. Amen.

Then praying awhile privately, let him receive the chalice, saying,

The blood of our Lord Jesus Christ which was shed for the remission of my sins, cleanse my soul, and preserve it to into everlasting life. Amen.

Then let him pray awhile privately, and recommend to God his own personal necessities spiritual and temporal, and the needs of all his relatives, &c.

After that, let him distribute it first to the clergy that helps to officiate, and after that, to the whole congregation that offers themselves, saying the same words, changing the person.

While the minister of the mysteries is praying privately, the people may secretly pray thus, or to this purpose;

I believe, O God, and confess that Thou art Christ the Son of the living God, who came into the world to save sinners, whereof I am chief. Lord, make me this day partaker of Thy heavenly table; for Thou dost not give Thy secrets to Thy enemies, but to the sons of Thine own house. Let me never give Thee a Judas kiss; I confess Thee and Thy glories, I invocate Thee and Thy mercies, I trust upon Thee and Thy goodness, like the thief upon the cross; Lord, remember me in Thy kingdom, with the remembrances of an everlasting love.

Lord, I am not worthy that Thou shouldest come under my roof; but as Thou didst vouchsafe to lie in a manger with beasts, and to enter into the house of Simon the leper, nor didst despise the repenting harlot when she kissed Thy feet; so vouchsafe to lodge in my soul, though it be a place of beastly affections and unreasonable passions; throw them out and dwell there for ever; purify my soul, accept the sinner, cleanse the leper, so shall I be worthy to partake of this divine banquet. Amen.

VIII.624–7

From Taylor's Baptism Rite – after the Baptism

N.B. Note the very Trinitarian prayer for the newly baptised; the prayer for the guardian angel; and the judicious redrafting of the Prayer Book exhortation to the godparents.

O God, be Thou his father for ever, Christ his elder brother and his Lord, the church his mother; let the body of Christ be his food, the blood of Christ his drink, and the Spirit the earnest of his inheritance. Let faith be his learning, religion his employment, his whole life be spiritual, heaven the object of his hopes and the end of his labours; let him be Thy servant in the kingdom of grace, and Thy son in the kingdom of glory, through Jesus Christ our Lord. *Amen.*

Then shall the priest add this blessing.

Our blessed Lord God, the Father of men and angels, who hath sent forth His angels ministers, appointing them to minister to the good of them who shall be heirs of salvation: He of His mercy and goodness send His holy angel to be the guardian of this child, and keep him from the danger and violence of fire and water, of falls and sad accidents, from evil tongues and evil eyes, from witchcraft and all impressions of the spirits of darkness, from convulsions and rickets, from madness and stupidity, from folly and evil principles, from bad examples and from evil teachers, from crookedness and deformity, from the mutilation of a member or the loss of sense, from being useless and unprofitable, from being impious, harsh-natured, and unreasonable; and make him a wise, useful, and a holy person, beloved of men and beloved of God, through Jesus Christ our Lord. Amen. Amen.

You the godfathers and godmothers of the child, as you have done this charity to the infant to bring him to holy baptism, so you must be sure to continue your care over him till he be instructed in his duty, taught what vow he hath made by you, and how he shall perform it. To this purpose you shall take care that he may learn the Lord's prayer, the apostles' creed, and the commandments of our Lord; that he may know how to pray, what to believe, and what to practise: and when he is in all these things competently instructed, neglect not any opportunity of bringing him to the bishop, that he, by imposition of hands and invocation of the holy Spirit of God, may procure blessing and spiritual strength to this child. Which duty when you have done, you are discharged of this trust, and from the mercies of God may humbly hope for the reward of your charity.

VIII.638

A widow's prayer

Great God of mercy, heal all the breaches of this family, preserve and increase the remaining comforts and advantages of it, support the estate, renew Thy favour to it, and perpetually pour down Thy blessings upon it; for the light of Thy countenance and Thy gracious influence cloth preserve and bless, support and nourish, honour and advance, persons, families, and kingdoms. Bless my eldest son; give him an obedient and a loving spirit, a provident and a wise heart, a worthy and a pious comportment, a blessed [and an honourable] posterity: to my younger sons give health and holiness, wisdom and fair fortunes, the love of God and good men: to my daughters give Thy perpetual grace and favour, that they may live in honour and a severe chastity, free from sin and shame, from temptation and a snare, and let their portion be in the blessing, in the love and service of God. Let them live in the favour of God and man, useful to others, an honour to their family, a comfort to all their relatives and friends, and servants to Thy divine majesty.

VIII.651

From Taylor's rite for Visitation of the Sick – a prayer for repentance by a lay person

O Almighty God, and most merciful Father, who delightest not in the death of a sinner, but that he be converted from his sin, and Thou be turned from Thine anger; give unto Thy servant a deep contrition for his [her] sins, a perfect hatred of them, a timely and an entire dereliction of them; grace to fear Thee, and grace to love Thee; powers to serve Thee, and time and grace to finish all the work of God which Thy servant ought to do; that the soul of Thy servant being washed white in the blood of Jesus, may be justified by Thy mercy, sanctified by Thy spirit, blessed by Thy providence, saved by Thy infinite and eternal goodness, through Jesus Christ our Lord.

VIII.677

4

Sermons, Friendship, Toleration, Popery, Original Sin

Sermons

Rules and advices concerning preaching

Let every minister be diligent in preaching the word of God, according to the ability that God gives him: ever remembering, that to minister God's word unto the people is the one half of his great office and employment.

Let every minister be careful that what he delivers be indeed the word of God: that his sermon be answerable to the text; for this is God's word, the other ought to be according to it; that although in itself it be but the word of man, yet by the purpose, truth, and signification of it, it may in a secondary sense be the word of God.

Do not spend your sermons in general and indefinite things, as in exhortations to the people to get Christ, to be united to Christ, and things of the like unlimited signification; but tell them in every duty what are the measures, what circumstances, what instruments, and what is the particular minute meaning of every general advice. For generals not explicated do but fill the people's heads with empty notions, and their mouths with perpetual unintelligible talk: but their hearts remain empty, and themselves are not edified.

Let not the humours and inclinations of the people be the measures of your doctrines, but let your doctrines be the measure of their persuasions. Let them know from you what they ought to do; but if you learn from them what you ought to teach, you will give but a very ill account at the day of judgment of the souls committed to you. He that receives from the people what he shall teach them, is like a nurse that asks of her child what physic she shall give him.

I.107

Sermon on Christ's advent: a scheme of salvation

I shall draw a short scheme, which although it must needs be infinitely short of what God hath done for us, yet it will be enough to shame us. God did not only give His Son for an example, and the Son gave Himself for a price for us, but both gave the Holy Spirit to assist us in mighty graces, for the verifications of faith, and the entertainments of hope, and the increase and perseverance of charity;—God gave to us a new nature, He put another principle into us, a third part, a perfective constitution; we have the Spirit put into us to be a part of us, as properly to produce actions of holy life as the soul of man in the body does produce the natural;—God hath exalted human nature, and made it in the person of Jesus Christ to sit above the highest seat of angels, and the angels are made ministering spirits, ever since their Lord became our brother;—Christ hath by a miraculous sacrament given us His body to eat and His blood to drink; He made ways that we may become all one with Him; He hath given us an easy religion, and hath established our future felicity upon natural and pleasant conditions, and we are to be happy hereafter if we suffer God to make us happy here; and things are so ordered, that a man must take more pains to perish than to be happy;—God hath found out rare ways to make our prayers acceptable, our weak petitions, the desires of our imperfect souls, to prevail mightily with God, and to lay a holy violence and an undeniable necessity upon Himself: and God will deny us nothing but when we ask of Him to do us ill offices, to give us poisons and dangers, and evil nourishment, and temptations; and He that hath given such mighty power to the prayers of His servants, yet will not be moved by those potent and mighty prayers to do any good man an evil turn, or to grant him one mischief; in that only God can deny us;—but in all things else, God hath made all the excellent things in heaven and earth to join towards holy and fortunate effects; for He hath appointed an angel to present the prayers of saints, and Christ makes intercession for us, and the Holy Spirit makes intercession for us with groans unutterable.

IV.28

Sermon on 'The Return of Prayers': sluggishness in prayer

Henceforth therefore never any more wonder that men pray so seldom; there are few that feel the relish, and are enticed with the deliciousness, and refreshed with the comforts, and instructed with the sanctity, and acquainted with the secrets of a holy prayer: but cease also to wonder, that of those few that say many prayers, so few find any return of any at all. To make up a good and a lawful prayer, there must be charity, with all its daughters, "alms," "forgiveness," not judging uncharitably; there must be purity of spirit, that is, purity of intention; and there must be purity of the body and soul, that is, the cleanness of chastity; and there must be no vice remaining, no affection to sin: for he that brings his body to God, and hath left his will in the power of any sin, offers to God the calves of his lips, but not a whole burnt-offering; a lame oblation but not a "reasonable sacrifice;" and therefore their portion shall be amongst them whose prayers were never recorded in the book of life, whose tears God never put into His bottle, whose desires shall remain ineffectual to eternal ages. Take heed you do not lose your prayers, "for by them ye hope to have eternal life;" and let any of you whose conscience is most religious and tender, consider what condition that man is in that hath not said his prayers in thirty or forty years together; and that is the true state of him who hath lived so long in the course of an unsanctiticd life; in all that while he never said one prayer that did him any good; but they ought to be reckoned to him upon the account of his sins. He that is in the affection, or in the habit, or in the state, of any one sin whatsoever, is at such distance from and contrariety to God, that he provokes God to anger in every prayer he makes: and then add but this consideration; that prayer is the great sum of our religion, it is the effect, and the exercise, and the beginning, and the promoter, of all graces, and the consummation and perfection of many; and all those persons who pretend towards heaven, and yet are not experienced in the secrets of religion, they reckon their piety, and account their hopes, only upon the stock of a few prayers. It may be they pray twice every day, it may be thrice, and blessed be God for it; so far is very well but if it shall be remembered and considered that this course of piety is so far from warranting any one course of sin, that any one habitual and cherished sin destroys the effect of all that piety, we shall see there is reason to account this to be one of those great arguments, with which God hath so bound the duty of holy living upon us, that without a holy life we cannot in any sense be happy, or have the effect of one prayer. But if we be returning and repenting sinners, God delights to hear, because He delights to save us . . .

When a man is holy, then God is gracious, and a holy life is the best, and it is a continual prayer; and repentance is the best argument to move God to mercy, because it is the instrument to unite our prayers to the intercession of the holy Jesus.

IV.57–8

Attitude and prayer

[E]very man that is in the state of grace, every man that can pray without a sinful prayer, may also intercede for others; and it is a duty for all men to do it; all men, I say, who can pray at all acceptably: "I will therefore that prayers, and supplications, and intercessions, and giving of thanks, be made for all men;" and this is a duty that is prescribed to all them that are concerned in the duty and in the blessings of prayer; but this is it which I say, if their piety be but ordinary, their prayer can be effectual but in easy purposes and to smaller degrees; but he that would work effectually towards a great deliverance, or in great degrees towards the benefit or ease of any of his relatives, can be confident of his success but in the same degree in which his person is gracious. "There are strange things in heaven:" judgments there are made of things and persons by the measures of religion; and a plain promise produces effects of wonder and miracle; and the changes that are there made, are not effected by passions, and interests, and corporal changes; and the love that is there, is not the same thing that is here; it is more beneficial, more reasonable, more holy, of other designs and strange productions; and upon, that stock it is that a holy poor man, that possesses no more (it may be) than a ewe-lamb, that eats of his bread, and drinks of his cup, and is a daughter to him, and is all his temporal portion,—this poor man is ministered to by angels, and attended to by God, and the Holy Spirit makes intercession for him, and Christ joins the man's prayer to His own advocation, and the man by prayer shall save the city, and destroy the fortune of a tyrant army, even then when God sees it good it should be so: for He will no longer deny him any thing, but when it is no blessing; and when it is otherwise, his prayer is most heard when it is most denied.

IV.75

Sermon on godly fear: 'No fear displeasing to God'

For we must know, that no fear is displeasing to God; no fear of itself, whether it be fear of punishment, or fear to offend; the "fear of servants," or the "fear of sons:" but the effects of fear do distinguish the man, and are to be entertained or rejected accordingly. If a servile fear makes us to remove our sins, and so passes us towards our pardon, and the receiving such graces which may endear our duty and oblige our affection; that fear is imperfect, but not criminal; it is "the beginning of wisdom," and the first introduction to it; but if that fear sits still, or rests in a servile mind, or a hatred of God, or speaking evil things concerning Him, or unwillingness to do our duty, that which at first was indifferent, or at the worst imperfect, proves miserable and malicious. So we do our duty, it is no matter upon what principles we do it; it is no matter where we begin, so from that beginning we pass on to duties and perfection. If we fear God as an enemy, an enemy of our sins, and of our persons for their sakes, as yet this fear is but a servile fear; it cannot be a filial fear, since we ourselves are not sons; but if this servile fear makes us to desire to be reconciled to God, that He may no longer stay at enmity with us, from this fear we shall soon pass to carefulness, from carefulness to love, from love to diligence, from diligence to perfection; and the enemies shall become servants, and the servants shall become adopted sons, and pass into the society and the participation of the inheritance of Jesus: for this fear is also reverence, and then our God, instead of being" a consuming fire," shall become to us the circle of a glorious crown, and a globe of eternal light.

IV.106

Dreams

To this may be reduced the observation of dreams, and fears commenced from the fancies of the night. For the superstitious man does not rest even when he sleeps; neither is he safe because dreams usually are false, but he is afflicted for fear they should tell true. Living and waking men have one world in common, they use the same air and fire, and discourse by the same principles of logic and reason; but men that are asleep have every one a world to himself, and strange perceptions; and the superstitious hath none at all: his reason sleeps, and his fears are waking; and all his rest, and his very securities, to the fearful man turn into affrights and insecure expectation of evils that never shall happen; they make their rest uneasy and chargeable, and they still vex their weary soul, not considering there is no other sleep, for sleep to rest in: and therefore if the sleep be troublesome, the man's cares be without remedy, till they be quite destroyed. Dreams follow the temper of the body, and commonly proceed from trouble or disease, business or care, an active head and a restless mind, from fear or hope, from wine or passion, from fulness or emptiness, from fantastic remembrances, or from some demon, good or bad: they are without rule and without reason, they are as contingent, as if a man should study to make a prophecy, and by saying ten thousand things may hit upon one true, which was therefore not foreknown, though it was forespoken; and they have no certainty, because they have no natural causality nor proportion to those effects which many times they are said to foresignify.

IV.113

Sermon on flesh and spirit: knowing one's weaknesses

Some men are wise and know their weaknesses, and to prevent their startings back, will make fierce and strong resolutions, and bind up their gaps with thorns, and make a new hedge about their spirits; and what then? This shews indeed that "the spirit is willing;" but the storm arises, and winds blow, and rain descends, and presently the earth trembles, and the whole fabric falls into ruin and disorder. A resolution such as we usually make is nothing but a little trench which every child can step over; and there is no civil man that commits a willing sin but he does it against his resolution; and what Christian lives that will not say and think that he hath repented in some degree; and yet still they commit sin, that is, they break all their holy purposes as readily as they lose a dream; and so great is our weakness, that to most men the strength of a resolution is just such a restraint as he suffers who is imprisoned in a curtain, and secured with doors and bars of the finest linen: for though "the spirit be strong" to resolve, "the flesh is weak" to keep it.

IV.127

The importance of reason

Men at first think themselves wise, and are always most confident when they have the least reason; and to-morrow they begin to perceive yesterday's folly, and yet they are not wise; but as the little embryo, in the natural sheet and lap of its mother, first distinguishes into a little knot, and that in time will be the heart, and then into a bigger bundle, which after some days' abode grows into two little spots, and they, if cherished by nature, will become eyes, and each part by order commences into weak principles, and is preserved with nature's greatest curiosity; that it may assist first to distinction, then to order, next to usefulness, and from thence to strength, till it arrive at beauty and a perfect creature;

so are the necessities, and so are the discourses of men; we first learn the principles of reason, which breaks obscurely through a cloud, and brings a little light, and then we discern a folly, and by little and little leave it, till that enlightens the next corner of the soul: and then there is a new discovery; but the soul is still in infancy and childish follies; and every day does but the work of one day; but therefore art and use, experience and reason, although they do something, yet they cannot do enough, there must be something else: but this is to be wrought by a new principle, that is, by the Spirit of grace: nature and reason alone cannot do it, and therefore the proper cure is to be wrought by those general means of inviting and cherishing, of getting and entertaining God's spirit, which when we have observed, we may account ourselves sufficiently instructed towards the repair of our breaches, and reformation of our evil nature.

IV.132

Sermon on lukewarmness: setting the scene

JER. xlviii. verse 10, first part.
Cursed be he that doth the work of the Lord deceitfully.

Christ's kingdom, being in order to the kingdom of His Father which shall be manifest at the day of judgment, must therefore be spiritual; because then it is that all things must become spiritual; not only by way of eminency, but by entire constitution and perfect change of natures. Men shall be like angels, and angels shall be comprehended in the lap of spiritual and eternal felicities; the soul shall not understand by material phantasms, neither be served by the provisions of the body, but the body itself shall become spiritual, and the eye shall see intellectual objects, and the mouth shall feed upon hymns and glorifications of God; the belly shall be then satisfied by the fulness of righteousness, and the tongue shall speak nothing but praises and the propositions of a celestial wisdom; the motion shall be the swiftness of an angel, and it shall be clothed with white as with a garment: holiness is the sun, and righteousness is the moon in that region; our society shall be choirs of singers, and our conversation wonder; contemplation shall be our food, and love shall be 'the wine of elect souls.' And as to every natural appetite there is now proportioned an object, crass, material, unsatisfying, and allayed with sorrow and uneasiness: so there be new capacities and equal objects, the desires shall be fruition, and the appetite shall not suppose want, but a faculty of delight, and an unmeasurable complacency: the will and the understanding, love and wonder, joys every day and the same for ever: this shall be their state who shall be accounted worthy of the resurrection to this life; where the body shall be a partner, but no servant; where it shall have no work of its own, but it shall rejoice with the soul; where the soul shall rule without resistance or an enemy; and we shall be fitted to enjoy God who is the Lord and Father of spirits. In this world we see it is quite contrary; we long for perishing meat, and fill our stomachs with corruption; we look after white and red, and the weaker beauties of the night; we are passionate after rings and seals, and enraged at the breaking of a crystal; we delight in the society of fools and weak persons; we laugh at sin and contrive mischiefs; and the body rebels against the soul and carries the cause against all its just pretences; and our soul itself is, above half of it, earth and stone, in its affections and distempers; our hearts are hard and inflexible to the softer whispers of mercy and compassion, having no loves for any thing but strange flesh, and heaps of money, and popular noises, for misery and folly; and therefore we are a huge way off from the kingdom of God, whose excellencies, whose designs, whose ends, whose constitution, is spiritual and holy, and separate, and sublime, and perfect. Now between these two states of natural flesh and heavenly spirit, that is, the powers of darkness and the regions of light, the miseries of man and the perfections of God; the imperfection of nature where we stand by our creation and supervening follies, and that state of felicities whither we are designed by the mercies of God; there is a middle state, 'the kingdom of grace,' wrought for us by our Mediator, the man Christ Jesus, who came to perfect the virtue of religion and the designs of God, and to reform our nature, and to make it possible for us to come to that spiritual state where all felicity does dwell. The religion that Christ taught is a spiritual religion; it designs, so far as this state can permit, to make us spiritual; that is, so as the Spirit be the prevailing ingredient. God must now be worshipped in spirit, and not only so but with a fervent spirit; and though God in all religions did seize upon the spirit, and even under Moses' law did by the shadow of the ceremony require the substantial worship, by cutting off the flesh intended the circumcision of the heart; yet because they were to mind the outward action, it took off much from the intention and activity of the spirit; man could not do both busily. And then they failed also in the other part of a spiritual religion; for the nature of a spiritual religion is, that in it we serve God with our hearts and affections; and because while the spirit prevails, we do not to evil purposes of abatement converse with flesh and blood, this service is also fervent, intense, active, wise, and busy, according to the nature of things spiritual. Now because God always perfectly intended it, yet because He less perfectly required it in the law of Moses, I say they fell short in both.

IV.143–4

Faith and intention

Faith is the remedy of all our evils, but then it is never of force, but when we either have endeavoured or undertaken to do all good; this in baptism, that after; faith and repentance at first, and faith and charity at last; and because we fail often by infirmity and sometimes by inadvertency, sometimes by a surprise and often by omission, and all this even in the midst of a sincere endeavour to live justly and perfectly; therefore the passion of our Lord pays for this, and faith lays hold upon that. But without a hearty and sincere intent, and vigorous protection of all parts of our duty, faith is but a word, not so much as a cover to the naked bosom, nor a pretence big enough to deceive persons that are not willing to be cozened.

IV.151

Sermon on 'House of Feasting': moderation

Though reason be so strictly to be preserved at our tables as well as at our prayers, and we can never have leave to do any violence to it; yet the measures of nature may be enlarged beyond the bounds of prime and common necessity. For besides hunger and thirst, there are some labours of the body, and others of the mind, and there are sorrows and loads upon the spirit by its communications with the indispositions of the body; and as the labouring man may be supplied with bigger quantities, so the student and contemplative man with more delicious and spriteful nutriment: for as the tender and more delicate easily-digested meats will not help to carry burdens upon the neck, and hold the plough in society and yokes of the laborious oxen; so neither will the pulse and the leeks, Lavinian sausages, and the Cisalpine suckets or gobbets of condited bull's flesh minister such delicate spirits to the thinking man; but his notion will be as flat as the noise of the Arcadian porter, and thick as the first juice of his country lard, unless he makes his body a fit, servant to the soul, and both fitted for the employment.

But in these cases necessity and prudence and experience are to make the measures and the rule; and so long as the just end is fairly designed and aptly ministered to, there ought to be no scruple concerning the quantity or quality of the provision: and he that would stint a swain by the commons of a student, and give Philotas the Candian the leavings of Plato, does but ill serve the ends of temperance, but worse of prudence and necessity.

IV.200

On Drink

Methinks it were but reason, that if to give life to uphold a cause be not too much, they should not think too much to be hungry and suffer thirst for the reputation of that cause; and therefore much rather that they would think it but duty to be temperate for its honour, and eat and drink in civil and fair measures, that themselves might not lose the reward of so much suffering; and of so good a relation, nor that which they value most be destroyed by drink.

There are in the world a generation of men that are engaged in a cause which they glory in, and pride themselves in its relation and appellative: but yet for that cause they will do nothing but talk and drink; they are valiant in wine, and witty in healths, and full of stratagem to promote debauchery; but such persons are not considerable in wise accounts. That which I deplore is, that some men prefer a cause before their life, and yet prefer wine before that cause, and by one drunken meeting set it more backward in its hopes and blessings than it can be set forward by the counsels and arms of a whole year. God hath ways enough to reward a truth without crowning it with success in the hands of such men. In the meantime they dishonour religion, and make truth be evil spoken of; and innocent persons to suffer by their very relation, and the cause of God to be reproached in the sentences of erring and abusing people; and themselves lose their health and their reason, their honour and their peace, the rewards of sober counsels, and the wholesome effects of wisdom. . . .

Wine discovers more than the rack, and he that will be drunk is not a person fit to be trusted: and though it cannot he expected men should be kinder to their friend or their prince or their honour, than to God and to their own souls and to their own bodies; yet when men are not moved by what is sensible and material, by that which smarts and shames presently, they are beyond the cure of religion and the hopes of reason; and therefore they must "lie in hell like sheep, death gnawing upon them, and the righteous shall have dominion over them in the morning" of the resurrection. . . .

Much safer it is to go to the severities of a watchful and a sober life: for all that time of life is lost, when wine, and rage, and pleasure, and folly, steal away the heart of a man, and make him go singing to his grave.

IV.206

Sermon on the marriage ring: definition

Marriage was ordained by God, instituted in paradise, was the relief of a natural necessity and the first blessing from the Lord; He gave to man not a friend, but a wife, that is, a friend and a wife too; for a good woman is in her soul the same that a man is, and she is a woman only in her body; that she may have the excellency of the one, and the usefulness of the other, and become amiable in both. It is the seminary of the church, and daily brings forth sons and daughters unto God; it was ministered to by angels, and Raphael waited upon a young man that he might have a blessed marriage, and that that marriage might repair two sad families, and bless all their relatives. Our blessed Lord though He was born of a maiden, yet she was veiled under the cover of marriage; and she was married to a widower: for Joseph the supposed father of our Lord had children by a former wife. The first miracle that ever Jesus did was to do honour to a wedding. Marriage was in the world before sin, and is in all ages of the world the greatest and most effective antidote against sin, in which all the world had perished if God had not made a remedy: and although sin hath soured marriage, and stuck the man's head with cares, and the woman's bed with sorrows in the production of children; yet these are but throes of life and glory, and "she shall be saved in child-bearing, if she be found in faith and righteousness." Marriage is a school and exercise of virtue; and though marriage hath cares, yet the single life hath desires which are more troublesome and more dangerous, and often end in sin, while the cares are but instances of duty and exercises of piety; and therefore if single life hath more privacy of devotion, yet marriage hath more necessities and more variety of it, and is an exercise of more graces. In two virtues celibate or single life may have the advantage of degrees ordinarily and commonly, that is, in chastity and devotion; but as in some persons this may fail, and it does in very many, and a married man may spend as much time in devotion as any virgins or widows do; yet as in marriage even those virtues of chastity and devotion are exercised, so in other instances this state hath proper exercises and trials for those graces for which single life can never be crowned. Here is the proper scene of piety and patience, of the duty of parents and the charity of relatives; here kindness is spread abroad, and love is united and made firm as a centre: marriage is the nursery of heaven; the virgin sends prayers to God, but she carries but one soul to Him; but the state of marriage fills up the numbers of the elect; and hath in it the labour of love, and the delicacies of friendship, the blessing of society, and the union of hands and hearts; it hath in it less of beauty, but more of safety, than the single life; it hath more care, but less danger; it is more merry, and more sad; is fuller of sorrows, and fuller of joys; it lies under more burdens, but it is supported by all the strengths of love and charity, and those burdens are delightful. Marriage is the mother of the world, and preserves kingdoms, and fills cities, and churches, and heaven itself. Celibate, like the fly in the heart of an apple, dwells in a perpetual sweetness, but sits alone, and is confined and dies in singularity; but marriage, like the useful bee, builds a house and gathers sweetness from every flower, and labours and unites into societies and republics, and sends out colonies, and feeds the world with delicacies, and obeys their king, and keeps order, and exercises many virtues, and promotes the interest of mankind, and is that state of good things to which God hath designed the present constitution of the world.

IV.210–11

Mutual tolerance

Let man and wife be careful to stifle little things, that as fast as they spring they be cut down and trod upon; for if they be suffered to grow by numbers, they make the spirit peevish, and the society troublesome, and the affections loose and easy by an habitual aversation. Some men are more vexed with a fly than with a wound; and when the gnats disturb our sleep, and the reason is disquieted but not perfectly awakened, it is often seen that he is fuller of trouble than if in the daylight of his reason he were to contest with a potent enemy. In the frequent little accidents of a family a man's reason cannot always be awake; and when his discourses are imperfect, and a trifling trouble makes him yet more restless, he is soon betrayed to the violence of passion. It is certain that the man or woman are in a state of weakness and folly then when they can be troubled with a trifling accident, and therefore it is not good to tempt their affections when they are in that state of danger. In this case the caution is to subtract fuel from the sudden flame; for stubble though it be quickly kindled, yet it is as soon extinguished if it be not blown by a pertinacious breath, or fed with new materials. Add no new provocations to the accident, and do not inflame this, and peace will soon return, and the discontent will pass away soon as the sparks from the collision of a flint: ever remembering that discontents proceeding from daily little things, do breed a secret undiscernible disease which is more dangerous than a fever proceeding from a discerned notorious surfeit.

IV.217

Sermon on good and evil tongue: the beginning

EPHES. iv.29

Let no corrupt communication proceed out of your mouth, but that which is good to the use of edifying, that it may minister grace unto the hearers.

He that had an ill memory did wisely comfort himself by reckoning the advantages he had by his forgetfulness. For by this means he was hugely secured against malice, and ambition: for his anger went off with the short notice and observation of the injury; and he saw himself unlit for the businesses of other men, or to make records in his head, and undertake to conduct the intrigues of affairs of a multitude, who was apt to forget the little accounts of his own seldom reading. He also remembered this, that his pleasures in reading books were more frequent, while he remembered but little of yesterday's study, and to-morrow the book is news, and with its novelties gives him fresh entertainment, while the retaining brain lays the book aside, and is full already: every book is new to an ill memory, and one long book is a library, and its parts return fresh as the morning, which becomes a new day though by the revolution of the same sun. Besides these, it brought him to tell truth for fear of shame, and in mere necessity made his speech little and his discourses short; because the web drawn from his brain was soon spun out, and his fountain grew quickly dry, and left running through forgetfulness.

IV.273

'Stultiloquy': the words of weaker people

[C]oncerning stultiloquy it is to be observed that the masters of spiritual life mean not the talk and useless babble of weak and ignorant persons; because in their proportions they may serve their little mistaken ends of civility and humanity as seemingly to them, as the strictest and most observed words of the wiser; if it be their best, their folly may be pitied. but not reproved; and to them there is no caution to be added, but that it were well if they would put the bridle into the hands of another, who may give them check when themselves cannot; and no wisdom can be required or useful to them but to suspect themselves and choose to be conducted by another. For so the little birds and laborious bees, who having no art and power of contrivance, no distinction of time or foresight of new necessities, yet being guided by the hand and counselled by the wisdom of the supreme Power, their Lord and ours, do things with greater niceness and exactness of art, and regularity of time, and certainty of effect, than the wise counsellor, who, standing at the back of the prince's chair, guesses imperfectly, and counsels timorously, and thinks by interest, and determines extrinsical events by inward and unconcerning principles; because these have understanding, but it is less than the infinity of accidents and contingences without; but the other having none, are wholly guided by Him that knows and determines all things: so it is in the imperfect designs and actions and discourses of weaker people; if they can be ruled by an understanding without when they have none within, they shall receive this advantage, that their own passions shall not transport their minds, and the divisions and weakness of their own sense and notices shall not make them uncertain and indeterminate; and the measures they shall walk by shall be disinterest, and even, and dispassionate, and full of observation.

IV.287

Custody of the tongue

These are the vanities and evil fruits of the easy talker, the instances of a trifling impertinent conversation. And yet it is observable that although the instances in the beginning be only vain, yet in the issue and effects they are troublesome and full of mischief; and that we may perceive that even all effusion and multitude of language and vainer talk cannot be innocent, we may observe that there are many good things which are wholly spoiled if they do but touch the tongue; they are spoiled with speaking: such as is, the sweetest of all christian graces, humility; and the noblest actions of humanity, the doing favours and acts of kindness. If you speak of them, you pay yourself, and lose your kindness; humility is by talking changed into pride and hypocrisy, and patience passes into peevishness, and secret trust into perfidiousness, and modesty into dissolution, and judgment into censure; but by silence and a restrained tongue, all the first mischiefs are avoided, and all these graces preserved.

IV.297

Sermon on spirit of grace: the workings of the Spirit

But beyond this is the reason which is the consummation of all the faithful. The gospel is called the Spirit, because by and in the gospel God hath given to us not only 'the Spirit of manifestation,' that is, of instruction and of catechism, of faith and confident assent; but the 'Spirit of confirmation,' or 'obsignation,' to all them that believe and obey the gospel of Christ: that is, the power of God is come upon our hearts, by which in an admirable manner we are made sure of a glorious inheritance; made sure, I say, in the nature of the thing; and our own persuasions also are confirmed with an excellent, a comfortable, a discerning, and a reasonable hope; in the strength of which, and by whose aid, as we do not doubt of the performance of the promise, so we vigorously pursue all the parts of the condition, and are enabled to work all the work of God, so as not to be affrighted with fear, or seduced by vanity, or oppressed by lust, or drawn oft by evil example, or abused by riches, or imprisoned by ambition and secular designs. This the Spirit of God does work in all His servants; and is called 'the Spirit of obsignation'; or 'the confirming Spirit,' because it confirms our hope, and assures our title to life eternal; and by means of it, and other its collateral assistances, it also confirms us in our duty, that we may not only profess in word, but live lives according to the gospel. And this is the sense of 'the Spirit' mentioned in the text; "Ye are not in the flesh but in the Spirit, if so be that the Spirit of God dwell in you:" that is, if ye be made partakers of the gospel, or of 'the Spirit of manifestation;' if ye be truly entitled to God, and have received the promise of the Father, then are ye not carnal men; ye are 'spiritual,' ye are 'in the Spirit:' if ye have the Spirit in one sense to any purpose, ye have it also in another: if the Spirit be in you, you are in it; if it hath given you hope, it hath also enabled and ascertained your duty. For 'the Spirit of manifestation' will but upbraid you in the shame and horrors of a sad eternity if you have not 'the Spirit of obsignation:' if the Holy Ghost be not come upon you to great purposes of holiness, all other pretences are vain, ye are still in the flesh, which shall never inherit the kingdom of God.

IV.334–5

Invalidity of late or deathbed repentance: denial of God

For he that hath dishonoured God by sins, that is, hath denied by a moral instrument of duty and subordination to confess the glories of His power and the goodness of His laws, and hath dishonoured and despised His mercy which God intended as an instrument of our piety, hath no better way to glorify God than by returning to his duty to advance the honour of the divine attributes, in which He is pleased to communicate Himself, and to have entercourse with man. He that repents, confesses his own error and the righteousness of God's laws; and by judging himself confesses that he deserves punishment, and therefore that God is righteous if He punishes him; and by returning confesses God to be the fountain of felicity, and the foundation of true, solid, and permanent joys, saying in the sense and passion of the disciples, "Whither shall we go? for Thou hast the words of eternal life:" and by humbling himself exalts God, by making the proportions of distance more immense and vast. And as repentance does contain in it all the parts of holy life which can be performed by a returning sinner, all the acts and habits of virtue being but parts, or instances, or effects of repentance; so all the actions of a holy life do constitute the mass and body of all those instruments whereby God is pleased to glorify Himself. For if God is glorified in the sun and moon, in the rare fabric of the honeycombs, in the discipline of bees, in the economy of pismires, in the little houses of birds, in the curiosity of an eye, God being pleased to delight in those little images and reflexes of Himself from those pretty mirrors, which, like a crevice in a wall, through a narrow perspective transmit the species of a vast excellency: much rather shall God be pleased to behold Himself in the glasses of our obedience, in the emissions of our will and understanding; these being rational and apt instruments to express Him, far better than the natural, as being nearer communications of Himself.

IV.382

The convenience of such confessions

Well, let us suppose our penitent advanced thus far as that he decrees against all sin, and in has hearty purposes resolves to decline it, as in a severe sentence he hath condemned it as his betrayer and his murderer; yet we must be curious,—for now only the repentance properly begins,—that it be not only like the springings of the thorny or the high-way ground, soon up and soon down; for some men, when a sadness or an unhandsome accident surprises them, then they resolve against their sin; but like the goats in Aristotle, they give their milk no longer than they are stung; as soon as the thorns are removed, these men return to their first hardness, and resolve then to act their first temptation. Others there are who never resolve against a sin but either when they have no temptation to it, or when their appetites are newly satisfied with it; like those who immediately after a full dinner resolve to fast at supper, and they keep it till their appetite returns, and then their resolution unties like the cords of vanity, or the gossamer against the violence of the northern wind. Thus a lustful person fills all the capacity of his lust; and when he is wearied, and the sin goes off with unquietness and regret, and the appetite falls down like a horse-leech when it is ready to burst with putrefaction and an unwholesome plethory, then he resolves to be a good man, and could almost vow to be a hermit; and hates his lust as Amnon hated his sister Tamar just when he had newly acted his unworthy rape: but the next spring-tide that comes, every wave of the temptation makes an inroad upon the resolution, and gets ground, and prevails against it more than his resolution prevailed against his sin. How many drunken persons, how many swearers, resolve daily and hourly against their sin, and yet act them not once the less for all their infinite heap of shamefully retreating purposes! That resolution that begins upon just grounds of sorrow and severe judgment, upon fear and love, that is made in the midst of a temptation, that is inquisitive into all the means and instruments of the cure, that prays perpetually against a sin, that, watches continually against a surprise, and never sinks into it by deliberation; that fights earnestly and carries on the war prudently and prevails by a never ceasing diligence against the temptation; that only is a pious and well begun repentance. They that have their fits of a quartan, well and ill for ever, and think themselves in perfect health when the ague is retired till its period returns, are dangerously mistaken. Those intervals of imperfect and fallacious resolution are nothing but states of death: and if a man should depart this world in one of those godly fits, as he thinks them, he is no nearer to obtain his blessed hope than a man in the stone-colic is to health when his pain is eased for the present, his disease still remaining, and threatening an unwelcome return. That resolution only is the beginning of a holy repentance which goes forth into act, and whose acts enlarge into habits, and whose habits are productive of the fruits of a holy life.

IV.387–8

Sermon on the deceitfulness of the heart: opening

JEREMY XVII.9

The heart is deceitful above all things, and desperately wicked; who can know it?

Folly and subtilty divide the greatest part of mankind, and there is no other difference but this, that some are crafty enough to deceive, others foolish enough to be cozened and abused; and yet the scales also turn, for they that are the most crafty to cozen others are the veriest fools, and most of all abused themselves. They rob their neighbour of his money, and lose their own innocency; they disturb his rest, and vex their own conscience; they throw him into prison, and themselves into hell; they make poverty to be their brother's portion, and damnation to be their own. Man entered into the world first alone; but as soon as he met with one companion, he met with three to cozen him: the serpent, and Eve, and himself, all joined, first to make him a fool and to deceive him, and then to make him miserable. But he first cozened himself, giving himself up to believe a lie; and being desirous to listen to the whispers of a tempting spirit, he sinned before he fell; that is, he had within him a false understanding, and a depraved will: and these were the parents of his disobedience, and this was the parent of his infelicity, and a great occasion of ours. And then it was that he entered, for himself and his posterity, into the condition of an ignorant, credulous, easy, wilful, passionate, and impotent person; apt to be abused, and so loving to have it so that if nobody else will abuse him he will be sure to abuse himself; by ignorance and evil principles being open to an enemy, and by wilfulness and sensuality doing to himself the most unpardonable injuries in the whole world. So that the condition of man in the rudenesses and first lines of its visage seems very miserable, deformed, and accursed.

IV.414

Sermon on growth in grace: not always discernible

The growth of grace is to be estimated as other moral things are, not according to the growth of things natural. Grace does not grow by observation, and a continual efflux, and a constant proportion; and a man cannot call himself to an account for the growth of every day, or week, or month; but in the greater portions of our life, in which we have had many occasions and instances to exercise and improve our virtues, we may call ourselves to account; but it is a snare to our consciences to be examined in the growth of grace in every short revolution of solemn duty, as against every communion or great festival.

Growth in grace is not always to be discerned, either in single instances or in single graces. Not in single instances: for every time we are to exercise a virtue we are not in the same natural dispositions, nor do we meet with the same circumstances: and it is not always necessary that the next act should be more earnest and intense than the former, all single acts are to be done after the manner of men, and therefore are not always capable of increasing, and they have their terms beyond which they cannot easily swell; and therefore if it be a good act and zealous, it may proceed from a well grown grace, and yet a younger and weaker person may do some acts as great and as religious as it. But neither do single graces always afford a regular and certain judgment in this affair. For some persons at the first had rather die than be unchaste or perjured; and "greater love than this no man hath, that he lay down his life" for God: he cannot easily grow in the substance of that act; and if other persons, or himself, in process of time, do it more cheerfully or with fewer fears, it is not always a sign of a greater grace, but sometimes of greater collateral assistances, or a better habit of body, or more fortunate circumstances: for he that goes to the block tremblingly for Christ, and yet endures his death certainly, and endures his trembling too, and runs through all his infirmities and the bigger temptations, looks not so well many times in the eyes of men, but suffers more for God than those confident martyrs that courted death in the primitive church, and therefore may be much dearer in the eyes of God. But that which I say in this particular is, that a smallness in one is not an argument of the imperfection of the whole estate: because God does not always give to every man occasions to exercise, and therefore not to improve, every grace; and the passive virtues of a Christian are not to be expected to grow so fast in prosperous as in suffering Christians. But in this case we are to take accounts of ourselves by the improvement of those graces which God makes to happen often in our lives; such as are charity and temperance in young men, liberality and religion in aged persons, ingenuity and humility in scholars, justice in merchants and artificers, forgiveness of injuries in great men and persons tempted by law-suits: for since virtues grow like other moral habits, by use, diligence, and assiduity, there where God hath appointed our work and our instances, there we must consider concerning our growth in grace; in other things we are but beginners. But it is not likely that God will try us concerning degrees hereafter, in such things of which in this world He was sparing to give us opportunities.

Be careful to observe that these rules are not all to be understood negatively, but positively and affirmatively: that is, that a man may conclude that he is grown in grace if he observes these characters in himself which I have here discoursed of; but he must not conclude negatively, that he is not grown in grace if he cannot observe such signal testimonies: for sometimes God covers the graces of His servants, and hides the beauty of his tabernacle with goat's hair and the skins of beasts, that he may rather suffer them to want present comfort than the grace of humility. For it is not necessary to preserve the gaieties and their spiritual pleasures; but if their humility fails (which may easily be under the sunshine of conspicuous and illustrious graces,) their virtues and themselves perish in a sad declension. But sometimes men have not skill to make a judgment; and all this discourse seems too artificial to be tried by, in the hearty purposes of religion. Sometimes they let pass much of their life, even of their better days, without observance of particulars; sometimes their cases of conscience are intricate, or allayed with unavoidable infirmities; sometimes they are so uninstructed in the more secret parts of religion, and there are so many illusions and accidental miscarriages, that if we shall conclude negatively in the present question we may produce scruples infinite, but understand nothing more of our estate, and do much less of our duty.

IV.516–17

Sermon on 'The Foolish Exchange'

He that enjoys a great portion of this world hath most commonly the allay of some great cross, which although sometimes God designs in mercy, to wean his affections from the world, and for the abstracting them from sordid adherencies and cohabitation, to make his eyes like stars, to fix them in the orbs of heaven and the regions of felicity, yet they are an inseparable appendant and condition of humanity. Solomon observed the vanity of some persons, that heaped up great riches for their heirs, and yet 'knew not whether a wise man or a fool should possess them; this is a great evil under the sun.' And if we observed the great crosses many times God permits in great families, as discontent in marriages, artificial or natural bastardies, a society of man and wife like the conjunction of two politics, full of state and ceremony and design, but empty of those sweet caresses and natural hearty complications and endearments usual in meaner and innocent persons; the perpetual sickness, fulness of diet, fear of dying, the abuse of flatterers, the trouble and noise of company, the tedious officiousness of impertinent and ceremonious visits, the declension of estate, the sadness of spirit, the notoriousness of those dishonours which the meanness of lower persons conceals, but their eminency makes as visible as the spots in the moon's face; we shall find him to be most happy that hath most of wisdom and least of the world, because he only hath the least danger and the most security.

And lastly, his soul so gets nothing that wins all this world if he loses his soul, that it is ten to one but he that gets the one therefore shall lose the other; for to a great and opulent fortune sin is so adherent and insinuating, that it comes to him in the nature of civility. It is a sad sight to see a great personage undertake an action passionately and upon great interest; and let him manage it as indiscreetly, let the whole design be unjust, let it be acted with all the malice and impotency in the world, he shall have enough to tell him that he proceeds wisely enough, to be servants of his interest and promoters of his sin, instruments of his malice and actors of revenge; but which of all his relatives shall dare to tell him of his indiscretion, of his rage, and of his folly? He had need be a bold man and a severe person that shall tell him of his danger, and that he is in a direct progress towards hell. And indeed such personages have been so long nourished up in softness, flattery, and effeminacy, that too often themselves are impatient of a monitor, and think the charity and duty of a modest reprehension to be a rudeness and incivility. That prince is a wise man that loves to have it otherwise; and certainly it is a strange civility and dutifulness in friends and relatives to suffer him to go to hell uncontrolled, rather than to seem unmannerly towards a great sinner. But certainly this is none of the least infelicities of them who are lords of the world, and masters of great possessions.

IV.557

Sermon on Christian prudence

It is the office of christian prudence so to order the affairs of our life, as that in all the offices of our souls and conversation we do honour and reputation to the religion we profess; for the follies and vices of the professors give great advantages to the adversary to speak reproachfully, and do aliene the hearts and hinder the compliance of those undetermined persons, who are apt to be persuaded if their understandings be not prejudiced.

But as our necessary duty is bound upon us by one ligament more in order to the honour of the cause of God, so it particularly binds us to many circumstances, adjuncts, and parts of duty, which have no other commandment but the law of prudence. There are some sects of Christians which have some one constant indisposition which as a character divides them from all others, and makes them reproved on all hands. Some are so suspicious and ill-natured that if a person of a facile nature and gentle disposition fall into their hands, he is presently soured, and made morose, unpleasant, and uneasy in his conversation. Others there are that do things so like to what themselves condemn, that they are forced to take sanctuary and labour in the mine of unsignificant distinctions, to make themselves believe they are innocent; and in the mean time they offend all men else, and open the mouths of their adversaries to speak reproachful things, true or false as it happens. And it requires a great wit to understand all the distinctions and devices thought of for legitimating the worshipping of images; and those people that are liberal in their excommunications, make men think they have reason to say, their judges are proud, or self-willed, or covetous, or ill-natured people. These that are the faults of governors, and continued, are quickly derived upon the sect, and cause a disreputation to the whole society and institution. And who can think that congregation to be a true branch of the christian, which makes it their profession to kill men to save their souls against their will and against their understanding; who calling themselves disciples of so meek a Master, do live like bears upon prey, and spoil, and blood? It is a huge dishonour to the sincerity of a man's purposes to be too busy in fingering money in the matters of religion; and they that are zealous for their rights and tame in their devotion, furious against sacrilege and companions of drunkards, implacable against breakers of a canon and careless and patient enough with them that break the fifth or sixth commandments of the decalogue, tell all the world their private sense is to preserve their own interest with scruple and curiosity, and leave God to take care for His.

IV.583–4

Sermon on Christian simplicity

But in this part of simplicity we Christians have a most especial obligation; for our religion being ennobled by the most and the greatest promises, and our faith made confident by the veracity of our Lord, and His word made certain by miracles and prophecies, and voices from heaven, and all the testimony of God himself; and that truth itself is bound upon us by the efficacy of great endearments and so many precepts; if we shall suffer the faith of a Christian to be an instrument to deceive our brother, and that he must either be incredulous or deceived, uncharitable or deluded like a fool, we dishonour the sacredness of the institution, and become strangers to the Spirit of truth and to the eternal word of God. Our blessed Lord would not have His disciples to swear at all, no, not in public judicature, if the necessities of the world would permit Him to be obeyed. If Christians will live according to the religion, the word of a Christian were a sufficient instrument to give testimony, and to make promises, to secure a faith; and upon that supposition oaths were useless, and therefore forbidden, because there could be no necessity to invoke God's name in promises or affirmations if men were indeed Christians, and therefore in that case would be a taking it in vain: but because many are not, and they that are in name, oftentimes are so in nothing else, it became necessary that men should swear in judgment and in public courts. But consider who it was that invented and made the necessity of oaths, of bonds, of securities, of statutes, extents, judgments, and all the artifices of human diffidence and dishonesty. These things were indeed found out by men; but the necessity of these was from him that is the father of lies, from him that hath made many fair promises, but never kept any; or if he did, it was to do a bigger mischief, to cozen the more. For so does the devil: he promises rich harvests, and blasts the corn in the spring; he tells his servants they shall be rich, and fills them with beggarly qualities, makes them base and indigent, greedy and penurious; and they that serve him entirely, as witches and such miserable persons, never can be rich: if he promises health, then men grow confident and intemperate, and do such things whereby they shall die the sooner, and die longer; they shall die eternally. He deceives men in their trust, and frustrates their hopes, and eludes their expectations; and his promises have a period set beyond which they cannot be true; for wicked men shall enjoy a fair fortune but till their appointed time, and then it ends in perfect and most accomplished misery: and therefore even in this performance, he deceives them most of all, promising jewels, and performing coloured stones and glass-gems, that he may cozen them of their glorious inheritance. All fraudulent breakers of promises dress themselves by his glass, whose best imagery is deformity and lies.

IV.619–20

Sermon on divine mercy: God stands with the poor and marginalized

They that love to talk of the mercies of the Lord and to recount His good things, cannot but have observed that God delights to be called by such appellatives which relate to miserable and afflicted persons: he is 'the father of the fatherless' and 'an avenger of the widow's cause'; He 'standeth at the right hand of the poor to save his soul from unrighteous judges;' and He is 'with us in tribulation.' And upon this ground let us account whether mercy be not the greater ingredient in that death and deprivation, when I lose a man, and get God to be my Father: and when my weak arm of flesh is cut from my shoulder, and God makes me to lean upon Him, and becomes my Patron and my Guide, my Advocate and Defender. And if in our greatest misery God's mercy is so conspicuous, what can we suppose Him to be in the endearment of His loving kindness? if His veil be so transparent, well may we know that upon His face dwells glory, and from His eyes light and perpetual comforts run in channels larger than the returns of the sea when it is driven and forced faster into its natural course by the violence of a tempest from the north.—The sum is this: God intends every accident should minister to virtue, and every virtue is the mother and the nurse of joy, and both of them daughters of the divine goodness; and therefore if our sorrows do not pass into comforts, it is besides God's intention; it is because we will not comply with the act of that mercy which would save us by all means and all varieties, by health and by sickness, by the life and by the death of our dearest friends, by what we choose and by what we fear; that as God's providence rules over all chances of things and all designs of men, so His mercy may rule over all His providence.

IV.645

Mercy to be shown – and lived — to others

The whole religion of a Christian, as it relates to others, is nothing but justice and mercy, certain parents of peace and benefit; and upon this supposition, what evil can come to a just and a merciful, to a necessary and useful person? For the first permission of evil was upon the stock of injustice. He that kills may be killed, and he that does injury may be mischieved; he that invades another man's right must venture the loss of his own; and when I put my brother to his defence, he may chance drive the evil so far from himself that it may reach me. Laws and judges, private and public judicatures, wars and tribunals, axes and wheels were made not for the righteous but for the unjust; and all that whole order of things and persons would be useless, if men did do as they would willingly suffer.

And because there is no evil that can befall a just man unless it comes by injury and violence, our religion hath also made as good provisions against that too as the nature of the thing will suffer. For by patience we are reconciled to the sufferance, and by hope and faith we see a certain consequent reward; and by praying for the persecuting man we are cured of all the evil of the mind, the envy and the fretfulness that uses to gall the troubled and resisting man: and when we turn all the passion into charity, and God turns all the suffering into reward, there remains nothing that is very formidable. So that our religion obliges us to such duties which prevent all evils that happen justly to men; and in our religion no man can suffer as a malefactor, if he follows the religion truly; and for the evils that are unavoidable and come by violence, the graces of this discipline turn them into virtues and rewards, and make them that in their event they are desirable, and in the suffering they are very tolerable.

IV.649–50

Do not be 'hardened against kindness'

The result of this consideration is, that as we fear the divine judgments, so that we adore and love His goodness, and let the golden chains of the divine mercy tie us to a noble prosecution of our duty and the interests of religion. For he is the worst of men whom kindness cannot soften nor endearments oblige, whom gratitude cannot tie faster than the bands of life and death. He is an ill-natured sinner, if he will not comply with the sweetnesses of heaven, and be civil to his angel-guardian, or observant of his 'Patron God,' who made him, and feeds him, and keeps all his faculties, and takes care of him, and endures his follies, and waits on him more tenderly than a nurse, more diligently than a client, who hath greater care of him than his father, and whose bowels yearn over him with more compassion than a mother; who is bountiful beyond our needs, and merciful beyond our hopes, and makes capacities in us to receive more. Fear is stronger than death, and love is more prevalent than fear, and kindness is the greatest endearment of love; and yet to an ingenuous person gratitude is greater than all these, and obliges to a solemn duty when love fails, and fear is dull and unactive, and death itself is despised. But the man who is hardened against kindness, and whose duty is not made alive with gratitude, must be used like a slave, and driven like an ox, and enticed with goads and whips, but must never enter into the inheritance of sons. Let us take heed; for mercy is like a rainbow, which God set in the clouds to remember mankind: it shines here as long as it is not hindered; but we must never look for it after it is night, and it shines not in the other world. If we refuse mercy here, we shall have justice to eternity.

IV.672

Sermon at opening of Parliament, Dublin, May 1661: obedience

You have no other way of peace, no better way to appease and quiet the quarrels in religion which have been too long among us, but by reducing all men to obedience, and all questions to the measures of the laws: for they on both sides pretend scripture, but one side only can pretend to the laws: and they that do admit no authority above their own to expound scripture, cannot deny but kings and parliaments are the makers and proper expounders of our laws; and if ever you mean to have 'truth and peace kiss each other,' let no man dispute against your laws. For did not our blessed Saviour say that an oath is the end of all questions, and after depositions are taken, all judges go to sentence? What oaths are to private questions, that laws are to public. And if it be said that laws may be mistaken; it is true, but may not an oath also be a perjury? And yet because in human affairs we have no greater certainty, and greater than God gives we may not look for, let the laws be the last determination; and in wise and religious governments no disputation is to go beyond them.

VIII.349–50

Bad laws and passive obedience are no good

To conclude this point; let us consider whether it were not an intolerable mischief if the judges should give sentence in causes of instance by the measures of their own fancy, and not by the laws; who would endure them? and yet why may they not do that as well as any ecclesiastic person preach religion, not which the laws allow, but what is taught him by his own private opinion? But he that hath the laws on his side, hath ever something of true religion to warrant him, and can never want a great measure of justification: 'the laws and the customs of the country' are the results of wise counsels or long experience; they ever comply with peace and public benefit: and nothing of this can be said of private religions; for they break the peace, and trouble the conscience, and undo government, and despise the laws, and offend princes, and dishonour the wisdom of parliaments, and destroy obedience.

Well, but in the last place, 'But if we cannot do what the laws command, we will suffer what they impose; and then all is well again.' But first, who ever did so that could help it? And secondly, this talking of passive obedience is but a mockery; for what man did ever say the laws were not good, but he also said the punishment was unjust? And thirdly, which of all the recusants did not endeavour to get ground upon the laws, and secretly or openly asperse the authority that put him to pain for doing that which he calls his duty? and can any man boast of his passive obedience that calls it persecution? He may think to please himself, but he neither does or says any thing that is for the reputation of the laws. Such men are like them that sail in a storm; they may possibly be thrown into a harbour, but they are very sick all the way.

But after all this I have one thing to observe to such persons, that such a passive obedience as this does not acquit a man before God; and he that suffers what the law inflicts is not discharged in the court of conscience, but there is still a sinner and a debtor: for "the law is not made for the righteous, but for sinners;" that is, the punishment appointed by the law falls on him only that hath sinned: but an offending subject cannot 'with the fruit of his body pay for the sin of his soul:' when he does evil he must suffer evil; but if he does not repent besides, a worse thing will happen to him; for we are not tied to obey only for wrath, but also for conscience. Passive obedience is only the correspondent of wrath, but it is the active obedience that is required by conscience; and whatever the subject suffers for his own fault, it matters nothing as to his duty, but this also God will exact at the hands of every man that is placed under authority.

VIII.352–3

Justice and religion

The best way to make men to be good subjects to the king, is to make them good servants of God. Suffer not drunkenness to pass with impunity; let lust find a public shame: let the sons of the nobility and gentry no more dare to dishonour God than the meanest of the people shall: let baseness be basely esteemed; that is, put such characters of shame upon dishonourable crimes, that it be esteemed more against the honour of a gentleman to be drunk than to be kicked, more shame to fornicate than to be caned: and for honour's sake and the reputation of christianity, take some course that the most unworthy sins of the world have not reputation added to them by being the practice of gentlemen and persons of good birth and fortunes; lest it be said that in Ireland it is not lawful for any man to sin, unless he be a person of quality . . .

And God is thus to be obeyed, and you are to take care that He be, so God also must be honoured, by paying that reverence and religious obedience which is due to those persons whom He hath been pleased to honour by admitting them to the dispensation of His blessings, and the ministries of your religion. For certain it is, this is a right way of giving honour and obedience to God. The church is in some very peculiar manner the portion and the called and the care of God: and it will concern you in pursuance of your obedience to God, to take care that they in whose hands religion is to be ministered and conducted, be not discouraged. For what your judges are to the ministry of laws, that your bishops are in the ministries of religion; and it concerns you that the hands of neither of them be made weak: and so long as you make religion your care, and holiness your measure, you will not think that authority is the more to be despised because it is in the hands of the church; or that it is a sin to 'speak evil of dignities,' unless they be ecclesiastical, but that they may be reviled; and that though nothing is baser than for a man to be a thief, yet sacrilege is no dishonour; and indeed to be an oppressor is a great and crying sin, yet to oppress the church, to diminish her rents, to make her beggarly and contemptible, that's no offence; and that though it is not lawful 'to despise government,' yet if it be church-government, that then the case is altered. Take heed of that, for then God is dishonoured, when any thing is the more despised by how much it relates nearer unto God.

VIII.354–5

Sermon on the faith and patience of the saints: the arrival of Christianity

And now began to work the greatest glory of the divine providence; here was the case of christianity at stake. The world was rich and prosperous, learned and full of wise men; the gospel was preached with poverty and persecution, in simplicity of discourse, and in demonstration of the Spirit: God was on one side, and the devil on the other; they each of them dressed up their city; Babylon upon earth, Jerusalem from above. The devil's city was full of pleasure, triumphs, victories, and cruelty; good news, and great wealth; conquest over kings, and making nations tributary: they bound kings in chains, and the nobles with links of irons; and the inheritance of the earth was theirs: the Romans were lords over the greatest part of the world; and God permitted to the devil the firmament and increase, the wars and the success of that people giving to him an entire power of disposing the great changes of the world, so as might best increase their greatness and power: and he therefore did it, because all the power of the Roman greatness was a professed enemy to christianity. And on the other side God was to build up Jerusalem and the kingdom of the gospel; and He chose to build it of hewn stone, cut and broken: the apostles He chose for preachers, and they had no learning; women and mean people were the first disciples, and they had no power; the devil was to lose his kingdom, and he wanted no malice: and therefore he stirred up, and as well as he could he made active all the power of Rome, and all the learning of the Greeks, and all the malice of barbarous people, and all the prejudice and the obstinacy of the Jews, against this doctrine and institution, which preached and promised, and brought persecution along with it. On the one side there was *scandalum crucis*, on the other *patientia sanctorum*; and what was the event? They that had overcome the world could not strangle christianity.

VIII.349

Sermon to the University of Dublin: the good life and wisdom

He therefore who so understands the words of God: that he not only believes but loves the proposition; he who consents with all his heart, and being convinced of the truth does also apprehend the necessity, and obeys the precept, and delights in the discovery, and lays his hand upon his heart, and reduces the notices of things to the practice of duty; he who dares trust his proposition, and drives it on to the utmost issue, resolving to go after it whithersoever it can invite him; this man walks in the Spirit; at least thus far he is gone towards it; his understanding is brought . . . into the obedience of Christ. This is a 'loving God with all our mind;' and whatever goes less than this, is but memory, and not understanding; or else such notice of things by which a man is neither the wiser nor the better.

Sometimes God gives to His choicest, His most elect and precious servants, a knowledge even of secret things, which He communicates not to others. We find it greatly remarked in the case of Abraham, Gen. xviii. 17. "And the Lord said, Shall I hide from Abraham that thing that I do?" Why not from Abraham? God tells us, ver. 19. "For I know him, that he will command his children and his household after him, and they shall keep the way of the Lord, to do justice and judgment." And though this be irregular and infrequent, yet it is a reward of their piety, and the proper increase also of the spiritual man. We find this spoken by God to Daniel, and promised to be the lot of the righteous man in the days of the Messias; Dan. xii. 10, "Many shall be purified, and made white, and tried; but the wicked shall do wickedly:" and what then? "None of the wicked shall understand, but the wise shall understand." Where besides that the wise man and the wicked are opposed, plainly signifying that the wicked man is a fool and an ignorant; it is plainly said that 'none of the wicked shall understand' the wisdom and mysteriousness of the kingdom of the Messias.

A good life is the best way to understand wisdom and religion, because by the experiences and relishes of religion there is conveyed to them such a sweetness, to which all wicked men are strangers: there is in the things of God to them which practise them a deliciousness that makes us love them, and that love admits us into God's cabinet, and strangely clarifies the understanding by the purification of the heart. For when our reason is raised up by the Spirit of Christ, it is turned quickly into experience; when our faith relies upon the principles of Christ, it is changed into vision; and so long as we know God only in the ways of man, by contentious learning, by arguing and dispute, we see nothing but the shadow of Him, and in that shadow we meet with many dark appearances, little certainty, and much conjecture: but when we know Him . . . with the eyes of holiness, and the intuition of gracious experiences, with a quiet spirit and the peace of enjoyment; then we shall hear what we never heard, and see what our eyes never saw; then the mysteries of godliness shall be opened unto us, and clear as the windows of the morning: and this is rarely well expressed by the apostle, 'If we stand up from the dead and awake from sleep, then Christ shall give us light.'

VIII.378–9

Holiness

Holiness is not only an advantage to the learning all wisdom an holiness, but for the discerning that which is wise and holy from what is trifling and useless and contentious; and to one of these heads all questions will return: and therefore in all, from holiness we have the best instructions. And this brings me to the next particle of the general consideration. For that which we are taught by the holy Spirit of God, this new nature, this vital principle within us, it is that which is worth our learning; not vain and empty, idle and insignificant notions, in which when you have laboured till your eyes are fixed in their orbs, and your flesh unfixed from its bones, you are no better and no wiser. If the Spirit of God be your teacher, He will teach you such truths as will make you know and love God, and become like to Him, and enjoy Him for ever, by passing from similitude to union and eternal fruition. But what are you the better if any man should pretend to teach you whether every angel makes a species, and what is the individuation of the soul in the state of separation? what are you the wiser if you should study and find out what place Adam should for ever have lived in if he had not fallen? and what is any man the more learned if he hears the disputes, whether Adam should have multiplied children in the state of innocence, and what would have been the event of things if one child had been born before his father's sin?

Too many scholars have lived upon air and empty notions for many ages past, and troubled themselves with tying and untying knots, like hypochondriacs in a fit of melancholy, thinking of nothing, and troubling themselves with nothing, and falling out about nothings, and being very wise and very learned in things that are not and work not, and were never planted in paradise by the finger of God. Men's notions are too often like the mules, begotten by equivocal and unnatural generations; but they make no species: they are begotten, but they can beget nothing; they are the effects of long study, but they can do no good when they are produced: they are not that which Solomon calls *via intelligentiæ,* 'the way of understanding.' If the Spirit of God be our teacher, we shall learn to avoid evil, and to do good, to be wise and to be holy, to be profitable and careful: and they that walk in this way shall find more peace in their consciences, more skill in the scriptures, more satisfaction in their doubts, than can be obtained by all the polemical and impertinent disputations of the world. And if the holy Spirit can teach us how vain a thing it is to do foolish things, He also will teach us how vain a thing it is to trouble the world with foolish questions, to disturb the church for interest or pride, to resist government in things indifferent, to spend the people's zeal in things unprofitable, to make religion to consist in outsides, and opposition to circumstances and trifling regards. No, no; the man that is wise, he that is conducted by the Spirit of God, knows better in what Christ's kingdom does consist, than to throw away his time and interest, and peace and safety,—for what? for religion? no: for the body of religion? not so much: for the garment of the body of religion? no, not for so much; but for the fringes of the garment of the body of religion; for such and no better are the disputes that trouble our discontented brethren; they are things, or rather circumstances and manners of things, in which the soul and spirit is not at all concerned.

VIII.383–4

Funeral sermon for Lady Carbery: God's work with the departed

If in the state of blessedness there are some actions of the soul which do not pass through the body, such as contemplation of God, and conversing with spirits, and receiving those influences and rare immissions which coming from the holy and mysterious Trinity make up the crown of glory; it follows, that the necessity of the body's ministry is but during the state of this life, and as long as it converses with fire and water, and lives with corn and flesh, and is fed by the satisfaction of material appetites; which necessity and manner of conversation when it ceases, it can be no longer necessary for the soul to be served by phantasms and material representations.

And therefore when the body shall be re-united, it shall be so ordered that then the body shall confess it gives not any thing, but receives all its being and operation, its manner and abode from the soul; and that then it comes not to serve a necessity, but to partake a glory. For as the operations of the soul in this life begin in the body, and by it the object is transmitted to the soul; so then they shall begin in the soul, and pass to the body: and as the operations of the soul by reason of its dependence on the body are animal, natural, arid material; so in the resurrection the body shall be spiritual by reason of the pre-eminence, influence, and prime operation of the soul. Now between these two states stands the state of separation, in which the operations of the soul are of a middle nature, that is, not so spiritual as in the resurrection, and not so animal and natural as in the state of conjunction.

To all which I add this consideration, that our souls have the same condition that Christ's soul had in the state of separation, because He took on Him all our nature, and all our condition; and it is certain Christ's soul in the three days of His separation did exercise acts of life, of joy and triumph, and did not sleep, but visited the souls of the fathers, trampled upon the pride of devils, and satisfied those longing souls which were "prisoners of hope:" and from all this we may conclude that the souls of all the servants of Christ are alive, and therefore do the actions of life, and proper to their state; and therefore it is highly probable that the soul works clearer, and understands brighter, and discourses wiser, and rejoices louder, and loves noblier, and desires purer, and hopes stronger than it can do here.

VIII.440–1

The qualities of Lady Carbery

She was a very constant person at her prayers, and spent all her time which nature did permit to her choice, in her devotions, and reading and meditating, and the necessary offices of household government; every one of which is an action of religion, some by nature, some by adoption. To these also God gave her a very great love to hear the word of God preached; in which because I had sometimes the honour to minister to her, I can give this certain testimony, that she was a diligent, watchful, and attentive hearer: and to this had so excellent a judgment, that if ever I saw a woman whose judgment was to be revered, it was hers alone: and I have sometimes thought that the eminency of her discerning faculties did reward a pious discourse, and placed it in the regions of honour and usefulness, and gathered it up from the ground, where commonly such homilies are spilt, or scattered in neglect and inconsideration. But her appetite was not soon satisfied with what was useful to her soul: she was also a constant reader of sermons, and seldom missed to read one every day; and that she might be full of instruction and holy principles, she had lately designed to have a large book, in which she purposed to have a stock of religion transcribed in such assistances as she would choose, that she might be readily furnished and instructed to every good work. But God prevented that, and hath filled her desires, not out of cisterns and little aqueducts, but hath carried her to the fountain, where she 'drinks of the pleasures of the river,' and is full of God.

She always lived a life of much innocence, free from the violences of great sins: her person, her breeding, her modesty, her honour, her religion, her early marriage, the guide of her soul, and the guide of her youth, were as so many fountains of restraining grace to her, to keep her from the dishonours of a crime. . . . 'it is good to bear the yoke of the Lord from our youth;' and though she did so, being guarded by a mighty providence, and a great favour and grace of God from staining her fair soul with the spots of hell, yet she had strange fears and early cares upon her, but these were not only for herself, but in order to others, to her nearest relatives. For she was so great a lover of this honourable family of which now she was a mother, that she desired to become a channel of great blessings to it unto future ages, and was extremely jealous lest any thing should be done, or lest any thing had been done, though an age or two since, which should entail a curse upon the innocent posterity; and therefore (although I do not know that ever she was tempted with an offer of the crime) yet she did infinitely remove all sacrilege from her thoughts, and delighted to see her estate of a clear and disentangled interest: she would have no mingled rights with it; she would not receive any thing from the church, but religion and a blessing: and she never thought a curse and a sin far enough off, but would desire it to be infinitely distant; and that as to this family God had given much honour and a wise head to govern it, so He would also for ever give many more blessings: and because she knew the sins of parents descend upon children, she endeavoured by justice and religion, by charity and honour to secure that her channel should convey nothing but health, and a fair example and a blessing.

VIII.445–6

Discourse on Friendship

The nature of friendship

So that to your question, how far a dear and perfect friendship is authorized by the principles of christianity? the answer is ready and easy. It is warranted to extend to all mankind; and the more we love, the better we are, and the greater our friendships are, the dearer we are to God; let them be as dear, and let them be as perfect, and let them be as many as you can; there is no danger in it; only where the restraint begins, there begins our imperfection; it is not ill that you entertain brave friendships and worthy societies: it were well if you could love, and if you could benefit all mankind; for I conceive that is the sum of all friendship.

I.73

Friendship necessarily limited

There must be in friendship something to distinguish it from a companion, and a countryman, from a school-fellow or a gossip, from a sweet-heart or a fellow-traveller: friendship may look in at any one of these doors, but it stays not any where till it come to be the best thing in the world: and when we consider that one man is not better than another, neither towards God nor towards many, but by doing better and braver things, we shall also see that that which is most beneficent is also most excellent; and therefore those friendships must needs be most perfect, where the friends can be most useful. For men cannot be useful but by worthinesses in the several instances: a fool cannot be relied upon for counsel, nor a vicious person for the advantages of virtue, nor a beggar for relief, nor a stranger for conduct, nor a tattler to keep a secret, nor a pitiless person trusted with my complaint, nor a covetous man with my child's fortune, nor a false person without a witness, nor a suspicious person with a private design; nor him that I fear with the treasures of my love: but he that is wise and virtuous, rich and at hand, close and merciful, free of his money and tenacious of a secret, open and ingenuous, true and honest, is of himself an excellent man; and therefore fit to be loved; and he can do good to me in all capacities where I can need him, and therefore is fit to be a friend.

I.78

Physical attraction not enough

Among all the pleasures and profits, the sensual pleasure, and the matter of money, are the lowest and the least; and therefore although they may sometimes be used in friendship, and so not wholly excluded from the consideration of him that is to choose, yet of all things they are to be the least regarded.

I.79

Fancy and love – and the special love between Jesus and John, and Jesus and Lazarus

But if you yet enquire further, whether fancy may be an ingredient in your choice? I answer, that fancy may minister to this as to all other actions in which there is a liberty and variety; and we shall find that there may be peculiarities and little partialities, a friendship, improperly so called, entering upon accounts of an innocent passion and a pleased fancy; even our blessed Saviour himself loved S. John and Lazarus by a special love, which was signified by special treatments; and of the young man that spake well and wisely to Christ, it is affirmed, 'Jesus loved him:' that is, He fancied the man, and His soul had a certain cognation and similitude of temper and inclination. For in all things where there is a latitude, every faculty will endeavour to be pleased, and sometimes the meanest persons in a house have a festival; even sympathies and natural inclinations to some persons, and a conformity of humours, and proportionable loves and the beauty of the face, and a witty answer may first strike the flint and kindle a spark, which if it falls upon tender and compliant natures may grow into a flame; but this will never be maintained at the rate of friendship, unless it be fed by pure materials, by worthinesses which are the food of friendship: where these are not, men and women may be pleased with one another's company, and lie under the same roof, and make themselves companions of equal prosperities, and humour their friend; but if you call this friendship, you give a sacred name to humour or fancy; for there is a Platonic friendship as well as a Platonic love; but they being but the images of more noble bodies are but tinsel dressings, which will shew bravely by candle-light, and do excellently in a mask, but are not fit for conversation, and the material entercourses of our life. These are the prettinesses of prosperity and good-natured wit; but when we speak of friendship, which is the best thing in the world (for it is love and beneficence; it is charity that is fitted for society) we cannot suppose a brave pile should be built up with nothing; and they that build castles in the air, and look upon friendship as upon a fine romance, a thing that pleases the fancy, but is good for nothing else, will do well when they are asleep, or when they are come to Elysium.

I.81–2

David and Jonathan

But suppose it, and add this also, that I am equally his brother as he is mine, and then he also must love me whether I love him or no; and if he does not, he says, I must love him though he be my enemy; and so I must; but I must not love my enemy though he be my brother more than I love my friend: and at last if he does love me for being his brother, I confess that this love deserves love again; but then I consider, that he loves me upon an incompetent reason: for he that loves me only because I am his brother, loves me for that which is no worthiness, and I must love him as much as that comes to, and for as little reason; unless this be added, that he loves me first: but whether choice and union of souls, and worthiness of manners, and greatness of understanding, and usefulness of conversation, and the benefits of counsel, and all those endearments which make our lives pleasant and our persons dear, are not better and greater reasons of love and dearness than to be born of the same flesh, I think amongst wise persons needs no great enquiry. For fraternity is but a cognation of bodies, but friendship is an union of souls which are confederated by more noble ligatures. My brother, if he be no more, shall have my hand to help him, but unless he be my friend too, he cannot challenge my heart: and if his being my friend be the greater nearness, then friend is more than brother, and I suppose no man doubts but that David loved Jonathan far more than he loved his brother Eliab.

I.90

Marriage 'the queen of friendships'

One enquiry more there may be in this affair, and that is, whether a friend may be more than a husband or wife; to which I answer, that it can never be reasonable or just, prudent or lawful: but the reason is, because marriage is the queen of friendships, in which there is a communication of all that can be communicated by friendship: and it being made sacred by vows and love, by bodies and souls, by interest and custom, by religion and by laws, by common counsels, and common fortunes; it is the principal in the kind of friendship, and the measure of all the rest. And there is no abatement to this consideration, but that there may be some allay in this as in other lesser friendships, by the incapacity of the persons: if I have not chosen my friend wisely or fortunately, he cannot be the correlative in the best union; but then the friend lives as the soul does after death, it is in the state of separation, in which the soul strangely loves the body and longs to be re-united, but the body is an useless trunk and can do no ministries to the soul; which therefore prays to have the body reformed and restored and made a brave and a fit companion: so must these best friends, when one is useless or unapt to the braveries of the princely friendship, they must love ever and pray ever, and long till the other be perfected and made fit; in this case there wants only the body, but the soul is still a relative and must be so forever.

I.90

Female friendship

But by the way, madam, you may see how much I differ from the morosity of those cynics who would not admit your sex into the communities of a noble friendship. I believe some wives have been the best friends in the world; and few stories can out-do the nobleness and piety of that lady that sucked the poisonous purulent matter from the wound of our brave prince in the holy land, when an assassin had pierced him with a venomed arrow. And if it be told that women cannot retain counsel, and therefore can be no brave friends; I can best confute them by the story of Porcia, who being fearful of the weakness of her sex, stabbed herself into the thigh to try how she could bear pain; and finding herself constant enough to that sufferance, gently chid her Brutus for not daring to trust her, since now she perceived that no torment could wrest that secret from her, which she hoped might be intrusted to her. If there were not more things to be said for your satisfaction, I could have made it disputable whether have been more illustrious in their friendships, men or women.

I cannot say that women are capable of all those excellencies by which men can oblige the world; and therefore a female friend in some cases is not so good a counsellor as a wise man, and cannot so well defend my honour, nor dispose of reliefs and assistances if she be under the power of another: but a woman can love as passionately, and converse as pleasantly, and retain a secret as faithfully, and be useful in her proper ministries.

I.94

Toleration

The Papacy refuted

[I]f the words were never so appropriate to Peter, or also communicated to his successors, yet of what value will the consequent be? what prerogative is entailed upon the chair of Rome? For that S. Peter was the ministerial head of the church is the most that is desired to be proved by those and all other words brought for the same purposes and interests of that see; now let the ministerial head have what dignity can be imagined, let him be the first (and in all communities that are regular and orderly there must be something that is first, upon certain occasions where an equal power cannot be exercised, and made pompous or ceremonial) but will this ministerial headship infer an infallibility? will it infer more than the headship of the Jewish synagogue, where clearly the high priest was supreme in many senses, yet in no sense infallible; will it infer more to us than it did amongst the apostles, amongst whom if for order's sake S. Peter was the first, yet he had no compulsory power over the apostles? there was no such thing spoke of, nor any such thing put in practice. And that the other apostles were by a personal privilege as infallible as himself, is no reason to hinder the exercise of jurisdiction, or any compulsory power over them; for though in faith they were infallible, yet in manners and matter of fact as likely to err as S. Peter himself was: and certainly there might have something happened in the whole college that might have been a record of his authority, by transmitting an example of the exercise of some judicial power over some one of them. If he had but withstood any of them to their faces, as S. Paul did him, it had been more than yet is said in his behalf. Will the ministerial headship infer any more than that when the church in a community or a public capacity should do any act of ministry ecclesiastical, he shall be first in order? Suppose this to be a dignity to preside in councils, which yet was not always granted him; suppose it to be a power of taking cognizance of the major causes of bishops when councils cannot be called; suppose it a double voice, or the last decisive, or the negative in the causes exterior: suppose it to be what you will of dignity or external regiment, which, when all churches were united in communion, and neither the interest of states nor the engagement of opinions had made disunion, might better have been acted than now it can: yet this will fall infinitely short of a power to determine controversies infallibly, and to prescribe to all men's faith and consciences. A ministerial headship, or the prime minister, cannot in any capacity become the foundation of the church to any such purpose. And therefore men are causelessly amused with such premises, and are afraid of such conclusions which will never follow from the admission of any sense of these words that can with any probability be pretended.

V.470–1

Toleration cuts both ways

But now I know beforehand that those men who will endure none but their own sect will make all manner of attempts against these purposes of charity and compliance, and, say I or do I what I can, will tell all their proselytes that I preach indifferency of religion; that I say it is no matter how we believe nor what they profess, but that they may comply with all sects and do violence to their own consciences; that they may be saved in all religions; and so make way for a *colluvies* of heresies, and by consequence destroy all religion. Nay, they will say worse than all this; and, but that I am not used to their phrases and forms of declamation, I am persuaded I might represent fine tragedies beforehand. And this will be such an objection, that although I am most confident I shall make it apparent to be as false and scandalous as the objectors themselves are zealous and impatient; yet besides that I believe the objection will come where my answers will not come, or not be understood, I am also confident that in defiance and incuriousness of all that I shall say, some men will persist pertinaciously in the accusation, and deny my conclusion in despite of me. Well, but however I will try; and,

First I answer, that whatsoever is against the foundation of faith, or contrary to good life and the laws of obedience, or destructive to human society and the public and just interests of bodies politic, is out of the limits of my question, and does not pretend to compliance or toleration: so that I allow no indifferency, nor any countenance to those religions whose principles destroy government, nor to those religions (if there be any such) that teach ill life; nor do I think that any thing will now excuse from belief of a fundamental article, except stupidity or sottishness and natural inability. This alone is sufficient answer to this vanity; but I have much more to say.

Secondly, the intendment of my discourse is, that permissions should be in questions speculative, indeterminable, curious, and unnecessary; and that men would not make more necessities than God made, which indeed are not many. The fault I find, and seek to remedy, is that men are so dogmatical and resolute in their opinions, and impatient of others' disagreeings, in those things wherein is no sufficient means of union and determination; but that men should let opinions and problems keep their own forms and not be obtruded as axioms, nor questions in the vast collection of the system of divinity be adopted into the family of faith.

V.346–7

Liberty and Christian example

But now if men would a little turn the tables, and be as zealous for a good life and all the strictest precepts of christianity (which is a religion the most holy, the most reasonable, and the most consummate that ever was taught to man), as they are for such propositions in which neither the life nor the ornament of christianity is concerned, we should find that as a consequent of this piety men would be as careful as they could to find out all truths, and the sense of all revelations, which may concern their duty; and where men were miserable and could not, yet others that lived good lives too would also be so charitable as not to add affliction to this misery: and both of them are parts of good life. To be compassionate, and to help to bear one another's burdens, not to destroy the weak but to entertain him meekly, that's a precept of charity; and to endeavour to find out the whole will of God, that also is a part of the obedience, the choice and the excellency of faith: and he lives not a good life that does not do both these.

V.360

Liberty and Christian orthodoxy

The sum of this discourse is this; if we take an estimate of the nature of faith from the dictates and promises evangelical and from the practice apostolical, the nature of faith and its integrity consists in such propositions which make the foundation of hope and charity, that which is sufficient to make us to do honour to Christ, and to obey Him, and to encourage us in both; and this is completed in the apostles' creed. And since contraries are of the same extent, heresy is to be judged by its proportion and analogy to faith, and that is heresy only which is against faith. Now because faith is not only a precept of doctrines but of manners and holy life, whatsoever is either opposite to an article of creed, or teaches ill life, that's heresy; but all those propositions which are extrinsical to these two considerations, be they true or be they false, make not heresy, nor the man a heretic; and therefore however he may be an erring person, yet he is to be used accordingly, pitied and instructed, not condemned or excommunicated.

V.409

Conserving riches

There are very many traditions which are lost, and yet they are concerning matters of as great consequence as most of those questions for the determination whereof traditions are pretended: it is more than probable that as in baptism and the eucharist the very forms of ministration are transmitted to us, so also in confirmation and ordination; and that there were special directions for visitation of the sick, and explicit interpretations of those difficult places of S. Paul which S. Peter affirmed to be so difficult that the ignorant do wrest them to their own damnation; and yet no church hath conserved these, or those many more which S. Basil affirms to be so many, that . . . 'the day would fail him in the very simple enumeration of all traditions ecclesiastical.' And if the church hath failed in keeping the great variety of traditions, it will hardly be thought a fault in a private person to neglect tradition, which either the whole church hath very much neglected inculpably, or else the whole church is very much to blame. And who can ascertain us, that she hath not entertained some which are no traditions, as well as lost thousands that are? That she did entertain some false traditions I have already proved; but it is also as probable that some of those which these ages did propound for traditions are not so, as it is certain that some which the first ages called traditions were nothing less.

V.432

The authority of the Fathers not absolute: Augustine on Predestination an example

There are some that think they can determine all questions in the world by two or three sayings of the fathers, or by the consent of so many as they will please to call a concurrent testimony: but this consideration will soon be at an end; for if the fathers when they are witnesses of tradition do not always speak truth, as it happened in the case of Papias and his numerous followers for almost three ages together, then is their testimony more improbable when they dispute or write commentaries.

The fathers of the first ages spake unitedly concerning divers questions of secret oncology, and yet were afterwards contradicted by one personage of great reputation, whose credit had so much influence upon the world as to make the contrary opinion become popular: why then may not we have the same liberty, when so plain an uncertainty is in their persuasions, and so great contrariety in their doctrines? But this is evident in the case of absolute predestination, which till S. Austin's time no man preached, but all taught the contrary; and yet the reputation of this one excellent man altered the scene. But if he might dissent from so general a doctrine, why may not we do so too (it being pretended that he is so excellent a precedent to be followed) if we have the same reason?

V.483

Reason an essential guide

Here then I consider, that although no man may be trusted to judge for all others, unless this person were infallible and authorized so to do, which no man nor no company of men is; yet every man may be trusted to judge for himself, I say, every man that can judge at all; as for others, they are to be saved as it pleaseth God: but others that can judge at all must either choose their guides who shall judge for them, and then they oftentimes do the wisest, and always save themselves a labour, but then they choose too; or if they be persons of greater understanding, then they are to choose for themselves in particular what the others do in general, and by choosing their guide: and for this any man may be better trusted for himself than any man can be for another. For in this case his own interest is most concerned; and ability is not so necessary as honesty, which certainly every man will best preserve in his own case, and to himself, and if he does not it is he that must smart for't; and it is not required of us not to be in error, but that we endeavour to avoid it.

V.494–5

Condemn wrong teaching, but don't persecute or put to death

For although every man may be deceived, yet some are right, and may know it too; for every man that may err, does not therefore certainly err; and if he errs because he recedes from his rule, then if he follows it he may do right; and if ever any man upon just grounds did change his opinion, then he was in the right and was sure of it too: and although confidence is mistaken for a just persuasion many times, yet some men are confident, and have reason so to be. Now when this happens, the question is what deportment they are to use towards persons that disagree from them, and by consequence are in error.

First then, no Christian is to be put to death, dismembered, or otherwise directly persecuted for his opinion, which does not teach impiety or blasphemy. If it plainly and apparently brings in a crime, and himself does act it or encourage it, then the matter of fact is punishable according to its proportion or malignity: as if he preaches treason or sedition, his opinion is not his excuse, because it brings in a crime; and a man is never the less traitor because he believes it lawful to commit treason: and a man is a murderer if he kills his brother unjustly, although he thinks he does God good service in it. Matters of fact are equally judicable whether the principle of them be from within or from without: and if a man could pretend to innocence in being seditious, blasphemous, or perjured, by persuading himself it is lawful, there were as great a gate opened to all iniquity as will entertain all the pretences, the designs, the impostures, and disguises, of the world. And therefore God hath taken order that all rules concerning matters of fact and good life shall be so clearly explicated, that without the crime of the man he cannot be ignorant of all his practical duty. And therefore the apostles and primitive doctors made no scruple of condemning such perrsons for heretics that did dogmatize a sin.

V.514–15

Established religion needed to counteract licence – but with toleration

But I consider that in the toleration of a different opinion, religion is not properly and immediately concerned, so as in any degree to be endangered. For it may be safe in diversity of persuasions; and it is also a part of Christian religion, that the liberty of men's consciences should be preserved in all things where God hath not set a limit and made a restraint; that the soul of man should be free, and acknowledge no master but Jesus Christ; that matters spiritual should not be restrained by punishments corporal; that the same meekness and charity should be preserved in the promotion of christianity, that gave it foundation and increment and firmness in its first publication; that conclusions should not be more dogmatical than the virtual resolution and efficacy of the premises; and that the persons should not more certainly be condemned than their opinions confuted; and lastly, that the infirmities of men and difficulties of things should be both put in balance, to make abatement in the definitive sentence against men's persons. But then because toleration of opinions is not properly a question of religion, it may be a question of policy: and although a man may be a good christian though he believe an error not fundamental, and not directly or evidently impious, yet his opinion may accidentally disturb the public peace, through the overactiveness of the persons, and the confidence of their belief, and the opinion of its appendent necessity; and therefore toleration of differing persuasions in these cases is to be considered upon political grounds, and is just so to be admitted or denied as the opinions or toleration of them may consist with the public and necessary ends of government. Only this; as christian princes must look to the interest of their government, so especially must they consider the interests of christianity, and not call every redargution or modest discovery of an established error by the name of disturbance of the peace. For it is very likely that the peevishness and impatience of contradiction in the governors may break the peace. Let them remember but the gentleness of christianity, the liberty of consciences which ought to be preserved, and let them do justice to the persons whoever they are that are peevish, provided no man's person be overborne with prejudice. For if it be necessary for all men to subscribe to the present established religion, by the same reason at another time a man may be bound to subscribe to the contradictory, and so to all religions in the world. And they only who by their too much confidence entitle God to all their fancies, and make them to be questions of religion, and evidences for heaven or consignations to hell, they only think this doctrine unreasonable, and they are the men that first disturb the church's peace, and then think there is no appeasing the tumult by getting the victory.

V.534–5

Arguments for infant baptism – against Anabaptism

For I consider that the baptizing of infants does rush us upon such inconveniences, which in other questions we avoid like rocks: which will appear if we discourse thus;—

Either baptism produces spiritual effects, or it produces them not. If it produces not any, why is such contention about it? what are we the nearer heaven if we are baptized, and if it be neglected what are we the farther off? But if (as without all peradventure all the pædo-baptists will say) baptism does do a work upon the soul, producing spiritual benefits and advantages, these advantages are produced by the external work of the sacrament alone, or by that as it is helped by the co-operation and predispositions of the suscipient.

If by the external work of the sacrament alone, how does this differ from the *opus operatum* of the papists, save that it is worse? For they say the sacrament does not produce its effect but in a suscipient disposed by all requisites and due preparatives of piety, faith, and repentance; though in a subject so disposed they say the sacrament by its own virtue does it: but this opinion says, it does it of itself, without the help, or so much as the coexistence, of any condition but the mere reception.

But if the sacrament does not do its work alone, but *per modum recipientis,* according to the predispositions of the suscipient, then because infants can neither hinder it nor do any thing to further it, it does them no benefit at all. And if any man runs for succour to that exploded κρησφύγετον, that infants have faith, or any other inspired habit of I know not what or how, we desire no more advantage in the world, than that they are constrained to an answer without revelation, against reason, common sense, and all the experience in the world.

V.556

Christianity and social order

For the religion of Jesus Christ is the best establisher of the felicity of private persons and of public communities: it is a religion that is prudent and innocent, humane and reasonable, and brought infinite advantages to mankind, but no inconvenience, nothing that is unnatural, or unsociable, or unjust. And if it be certain that this world cannot be governed without laws, and laws without a compulsory signify nothing; then it is certain that it is no good religion that teaches doctrine whose consequents will destroy all government; and therefore it is as much to be rooted out as any thing that is the greatest pest and nuisance to the public interest.

V.590

Against becoming Roman Catholic

Dedication to Bishop of Rochester (opening)

RIGHT REVEREND FATHER,
I am against my resolution and proper disposition by the overruling power of the divine providence which wisely disposes all things, accidentally engaged in the question of Transubstantiation, which hath already so many times passed by the fire and 'under the saw' of contention, that it might seem nothing could remain which had not been already considered and sifted to the bran. I had been by chance engaged in a conference with a person of another persuasion, the man not unlearned nor unwary, but much more confident than I perceived the strength of his argument could warrant; and yet he had some few of the best which their schools did furnish out and ordinarily minister to their emissaries and ministers of temptation to our people. I then began to consider whether there were not much more in the secret of the question which might not have persuaded him more fiercely than I could then see cause for, or others at least from whom upon the strength of education he might have derived his confidence; and searching into all the secrets of it, I found infinite reason to reprove the boldness of those men who in the sum of affairs and upon examination will be found to think men damned, if they will not speak nonsense, and disbelieve their eyes and ears, and defy their own reason, and recede from antiquity, and believe them in whatsoever they dream, or list to obtrude upon the world, who hath been too long credulous, or it could never have suffered such a proposition to be believed by so many men against all the demonstration in the world. And certainly it is no small matter of wonder that those men of the Roman church should pretend learning, and yet rest their new articles of faith upon propositions against all learning: that they should engage their scholars to read and believe Aristotle, and yet

destroy his philosophy, and reason by their article; that they should think all the world fools but themselves, and yet talk and preach such things which if men had spoken before this new device arose, they would have been thought mad. But if these men had by chance or intuition do force us to understand the sacrament in a sense not natural but spiritual, that is, truly sacramental. And all this is beside the plain demonstrations of sense, which tells us it is bread and it is wine naturally as much after as before consecration. And afer all, the natural sense is such as our blessed Saviour reproved in the men of Capernaum, and called them to a spiritual understanding the natural sense being not only unreasonable and impossible; but also to no purpose of the Spirit, or any ways perfective of the soul as hath been clearly demonstrated by many learned men against the fond hypothesis of the church of Rome in this article.

VI.207–8

From the letter about not becoming Roman Catholic

For surely it is lawful for a man to serve God without images; but that to worship images is lawful is not so sure. It is lawful to pray to God alone, to confess Him to be true, and every man a liar, to call no man master upon earth, but to rely upon God teaching us; but it is at least hugely disputable, and not at all certain, that any man or society of men can be infallible, that we may put our trust in saints, in certain extraordinary images, or burn incense and offer consumptive oblations to the virgin Mary, or make vows to persons of whose state, or place, or capacities, or condition we have no certain revelation: we are sure we do well when in the holy communion we worship God and Jesus Christ our Saviour, but they who also worship what seems to be bread are put to strange shifts to make themselves believe it to be lawful. It is certainty lawful to believe what we see and feel; but it is an unnatural thing upon pretence of faith to disbelieve our eyes, when our sense and our faith can better be reconciled, as it is in the question of the real presence, as it is taught by the church of England.

So that unless you mean to prefer a danger before safety, temptation to unholiness before a severe and a holy religion, unless you mean to lose the benefit of your prayers by praying what you perceive not, and the benefit of the sacrament in great degrees by falling from Christ's institution, and taking half instead of all; unless you desire to provoke

God to jealousy by images, and man to jealousy in professing a religion in which you may in many cases have leave to forfeit your faith and lawful trust, unless you will still continue to give scandal to those good people with whom you have lived in a common religion, and weaken the hearts of God's afflicted ones, unless you will choose a catechism without the second commandment, and a faith that grows bigger or less as men please, and a hope that in many degrees relies on men and vain confidences, and a charity that damns all the world but yourselves, unless you will do all this, that is, suffer an abuse in your prayers, in the sacrament, in the commandments, in faith, in hope, in charity, in the communion of saints, and your duty to your supreme, you must return to the bosom of your mother the church of England from whence you have fallen, rather weakly than maliciously, and I doubt not but you will find the comfort of it all your life, and in the day of your death, and in the day of judgment. If you will not, yet I have freed mine own soul, and done an act of duty and charity, which at least you are bound to take kindly if you will not entertain it obediently.

V.651–2

Repentance and Original Sin

Repentance: a process

Men need not to dissemble tears or sorrow in that case; but as if men were in no danger when they are enemies to God, and as if to lose heaven were no great matter, and to be cast into hell were a very tolerable condition, and such as a man might very well undergo, and laugh heartily for all that; they seem so unconcerned in the actions of religion, and in their obedience to the severe laws of repentance, that it looks as if men had no design in the world but to be suffered to die quietly, to perish tamely, without being troubled with the angry arguments of churchmen, who by all means desire they should live and recover, and dwell with God for ever. Or if they can be forced to the further entertainments of repentance, it is nothing but a calling for mercy, an ineffective prayer, a moist cloud, a resolution for to-day, and a solemn shower at the most . . .

For repentance is thought to be just as other graces, fit for their proper season, like fruits in their own month; but then every thing else must have its day too: we shall sin, and we must repent; but sin will come again, and so may repentance: for 'there is a time for every thing under the sun;' and the time for repentance is when we can sin no more, when every objection is answered, when we can have no more excuse; and they who go upon that principle will never do it till it be too late: for every age hath temptations of its own, and they that have been used to the yoke all their life time, will obey their sin when it comes in any shape in which they can take any pleasure. But men are infinitely abused, and by themselves most of all. For repentance is not like the summer fruits, fit to be taken a little and in their own time; it is like bread, the provisions and support of our life, the entertainment of every day, but it is 'the bread of affliction' to some, and 'the bread of carefulness' to all; and he that preaches this with the greatest zeal and the greatest severity, it may be he takes the liberty of an enemy, but he gives the counsel and the assistance of a friend.

VII.5

Repentance and absolution

I sin indeed in some instances, but I do my duty in many; and every man hath his infirmities; no man can say, My soul is pure from sin; but I hope that because I repent still as I sin, my sins are but as single actions; and since I resist them what I can, I hope they will be reckoned to me but as sins of infirmity, without which no man is or can be in this state of imperfection. For if I pray against a sin, and my spirit does resist it, though the flesh prevails, yet I am in the state of grace. For that I may own publicly what I am publicly taught; a man cannot be soon out of the state of grace, but he may be soon in; God's love is lasting and perpetual when it hath once begun; and when the curtain is drawn over the state of grace by the intervening of a sin, yet as soon as ever we begin to cry for pardon, nay when we do but say we will confess our sins, nay when we do but resolve we will, God meets us with His pardon, and prevents us with some portions of it. And let things be at the worst they can, yet he that confesseth his sins to God shall find mercy at the hands of God; and He hath established a holy ministry in His church to absolve all penitents; and if I go to one of them, and tell the sad story of my infirmity, the good man will presently warrant my pardon, and absolve me.

VII.11

Roman Catholic customs on Confession inadequate

I have other purposes also in the publication of this book. The ministers of the church of Rome (who ever love to fish in troubled waters, and to oppress the miserable and afflicted if they differ from them in a proposition) use all the means they can to persuade our people that the man that is afflicted is not alive, that the church of England now it is a persecuted church, is no church at all; and though (blessed be God) our propositions, and doctrines, and liturgy, and communion are sufficiently vindicated in despite of all their petty oppositions and trifling arrests, yet they will never leave making noises and outcries; which for my part I can easily neglect, as finding them to be nothing but noise. But yet I am willing to try the rights and excellencies of a church with them upon other accounts; by such indications as are the most proper tokens of 'life,' I mean, propositions of holiness, the necessities of a holy life: for certainly that church is most to be followed who brings us nearest to God; and they make our approaches nearest who teach us to be most holy, and whose doctrines command the most excellent and severest lives. But if it shall appear that the prevailing doctrines in the church of Rome do consequently teach, or directly warrant, impiety, or which is all one, are too easy in promising pardon, and for it have no defences but distinctions of their own inventing, I suppose it will be a greater reproof to their confidence and bold pretensions, than a discourse against one of their immaterial propositions that have neither certainty nor usefulness. But I had rather that they would preach severity than be reproved for their careless propositions, and therefore am well pleased that even amongst themselves some are so convinced of the weakness of their usual ministries of repentance, that as much as they dare they call upon the priests to be more deliberate in their absolutions and severe in their impositions of satisfactions, requiring a longer time of repentance before the penitents be reconciled.

VII.14

Original Sin – controversy

I know but one objection which I am likely to meet withal (excepting those of my infirmity and disability, which I cannot answer but by protesting the piety of my purposes) but this only, that in the chapter of 'Original sin,' I speak otherwise than is spoken commonly in the church of England: whose ninth article affirms that 'the natural propensity to evil, and the perpetual lusting of the flesh against the spirit, deserves the anger of God and damnation;' against which I so earnestly seem to dispute in the sixth chapter of my book. To this I answer, that it is one thing to say a thing 'in its own nature deserves damnation,' and another to say 'it is damnable to all those persons in whom it is subjected.'

VII.17

Sin and amendment of Life

When a vicious habit is to be extirpated, and the contrary introduced, it is not necessary that the contrary be acted by the body, but be radicated in the soul; it is necessary that the body do not sin in that instance, but it is not always required that contrary acts be done by the body. Suppose Origen had been a lustful person before his castration, yet he might have been habitually chaste afterwards, by doing spiritual acts of a corporal chastity. And there are many sins whose scene lies in the body, to which the body afterwards cannot oppose a bodily act in the same instance; as he that by intemperate drinking once or oftener, falls into a loathing of wine; he that dismembers himself and many others; for which a repentance is possible and necessary, but yet a contrary specific act cannot be opposed. In these cases it is sufficient that the habit be placed in the soul, and a perfect contrary quality superinduced, which is to be done by a frequent repetition of the acts of repentance proper to the sin.

VII.205

The sin of Adam does not damn us

The sin of Adam neither made us

1. Heirs of damnation, nor
2. Naturally and necessarily vicious.

It could not make us heirs of damnation. This I shall the less need to insist upon, because of itself it seems so horrid to impute to the goodness and justice of God to be author of so great a calamity to innocents, that S. Austin's followers have generally left him in that point, and have descended to this lesser proportion, that original sin damns only to the eternal loss of the sight of God's glorious face. But to this, I say these things.

That there are many divines which believe this alone to be the worm that never dies, and the fire that never goeth out; that is, in effect, this, and the anguish for this, is all the hell of the damned. And unless infants remain infants in the resurrection too (which no man that I know affirms) or unless they be senseless and inapprehensive, it is not to be imagined but that all that know they are by way of punishment deprived of the glorious face of God, must needs have a horrible anguish of soul to eternal ages.

VII.252

Original Sin a condition of nature

That every man is inclined to evil, some more, some less, but all in some instances, is very true: and it is an effect or condition of nature, but no sin properly α) Because that which is unavoidable is not a sin. β) Because it is accidental to nature, not intrinsical and essential. γ) It is superinduced to nature, and is after it, and comes by reason of the laws which God made after He made our nature; He brought us laws to check our nature, to cross and displease, that by so doing we may prefer God before ourselves: this also with some variety; for in some laws there is more liberty than in others, and therefore less natural inclination to disobedience. δ) Because our nature is inclined to good and not to evil in some instances, that is, in those which are according to nature, and there is no greater endearment of virtue than the law and inclination of nature in all the instances of that law. ε) Because that which is intended for the occasion of virtue and reward, is not naturally and essentially the principle of evil. ζ) In the instances in which naturally we incline to evil, the inclination is naturally good, because it is to its proper object; but that it becomes morally evil must be personal, for the law is before our persons; it cannot be natural, because the law by which that desire can become evil is after it.

VII.335

Relapse is real – but so is repentance

Well therefore may it be pitied in a child to choose a bright dagger before a warm coat, but when he hath been refreshed by this and smarted by that, if he chooses again, he will choose better. But men that have tried both states, that have rejoiced for their deliverance from temptation, men that have given thanks to God for their safety and innocence, men that have been wearied and ashamed of the follies of sin, that have weighed both sides and have given wise sentence for God and for religion, if they shall choose again, and choose amiss, it must be by something by which Lucifer did in the face of God choose to defy Him, and desire to turn devil, and be miserable and wicked for ever and ever.

If a man repents of his repentances and returns to his sins, all his intermedial repentance shall stand for nothing: the sins which were marked for pardon shall break out in guilt, and be exacted of him in fearful punishments, as if he never had repented. For if good works crucified by sins are made alive by repentance, by the same reason those sins also will live again, if the repentance dies; it being equally just that if the man repents of his repentance, God also should repent of His pardon.

VII.417

Confession before a priest recommended

But now although this cannot be a necessary duty for the reasons before reckoned, because the priest is not the injured person, and therefore cannot have the power of giving pardon properly and sufficiently and effectively; and confession is not an amends to him, and the duty itself of confession is not an enumeration of particulars, but a condemnation of the sin, which is an humiliation before the offended party; yet confession to a priest, the minister of pardon and reconciliation, the curate of souls, and the guide of consciences is of so great use and benefit to all that are heavy laden with their sins, that they who carelessly and causelessly neglect it are neither lovers of the peace of consciences, nor are careful for the advantages of their souls.

VII.446

Taylor's Self-Defence in Preface to *Deus Justificatus*, dedicated to the Dowager Countess of Devonshire

This, madam, is reason sufficient why I offer so many justifications of my doctrine before any man appears in public against it; but because there are many who do enter into the houses of the rich and the honourable, and whisper secret oppositions and accusations rather than arguments against my doctrine; the good women that are zealous for religion, and make up in the passions of one faculty what is not so visible in the actions and operations of another, are sure to be affrighted before they be instructed, and men enter *caveats* in that court before they try the cause. But that is not all; for I have found that some men, to whom I gave and designed my labours, and for whose sake I was willing to suffer the persecution of a suspected truth, have been so unjust to me, and so unserviceable to yourself, madam, and to some other excellent and rare personages, as to tell stories, and give names to my proposition, and by secret murmurs hinder you from receiving that good which your wisdom and your piety would have discerned there, if they had not affrighted you with telling that a snake lay under the plantane, and that this doctrine, which is as wholesome as the fruits of paradise, was enwrapped with the infoldings of a serpent, subtle and fallacious.

VII.406

Postscript

From the Funeral Sermon by George Rust

This was the spirit of this great man; he weighed men's reasons, and not their names, and was not scared with the ugly visors men usually put upon persons they hate, and opinions they dislike; not affrighted with the anathemas and execrations of an infallible chair, which he looked upon only as bug-bears to terrify weak and childish minds. He considered, that it is not likely any one party should wholly engross truth to themselves; that obedience is the only way to true knowledge; (which is an argument that he has managed rarely well in that excellent sermon of his which he calls *Via intelligentiæ*;) that God always, and only, teaches docible and ingenuous minds, that are willing to hear, and ready to obey according to their light; that it is impossible a pure, humble, resigned, godlike soul, should be kept out of heaven, whatever mistakes it might be subject to in this state of mortality; that the design of heaven is not to fill men's heads, and feed their curiosities, but to better their hearts, and mend their lives. Such considerations as these made him impartial in his disquisitions, and give a due allowance to the reasons of his adversary, and contend for truth and not for victory.

And now you will easily believe that an ordinary diligence would he able to make great improvements upon such a stock of parts and endowments; but to these advantages of nature, and excellency of his spirit, he added an indefatigable industry, and God gave a plentiful benediction: for there were very few kinds of learning but he was a *mystes* and a great master in them. He was a rare humanist, and hugely versed in all the polite parts of learning; and had throughly concocted all the ancient moralists, Greek and Roman, poets and orators; and was not unacquainted with the refined wits of the later ages, whether French or Italian.

But he had not only the accomplishments of a gentleman, but so universal were his parts that they were proportioned to every thing; and though his spirit and humour were made up of smoothness and gentleness, yet he could bear with the harshness and roughness of the schools and was not unseen in their subtilties and spinosities, and upon occasion could make them serve his purpose; and yet I believe he thought many of them very near a-kin to the famous knight of the Mancha, and would make sport sometimes with the romantic sophistry and fantastic adventures of school-errantry. His skill was great, both in the civil and canon law, and casuistical divinity; and he was a rare conductor of souls, and knew how to counsel and to advise; to solve difficulties, and determine cases, and quiet consciences. And he was no novice in. . . controversy; but could manage an argument and repartees with a strange dexterity; he understood what the several parties in christendom have to say for themselves, and could plead their cause to better advantage than any advocate of their tribe: and when he had done, he could confute them too; and shew that better arguments than ever they could produce for themselves, would afford no sufficient ground for their fond opinions.

It would be too great a task to pursue his accomplishments through the various kinds of literature: I shall content myself to add only his great acquaintance with the fathers and ecclesiastical writers, and the doctors of the first and purest ages both of the Greek and Latin church; which he has made use of against the Romanist, to vindicate the church of England from the challenge of innovation, and prove her to be truly ancient, catholic, and apostolical.

But religion and virtue is the crown of all other accomplishments; and it was the glory of this great man to be thought a Christian, and whatever you added to it, he looked upon as a term of diminution: and yet he was a zealous son of the church of England, but that was because he judged her (and with great reason) a church the most purely christian of any in the world. In his younger years he met with some assaults from popery, and the high pretensions of their religious orders were very accommodate to his devotional temper: but he was always so much master of himself that he would never be governed by any thing but reason, and the evidence of truth, which engaged him in the study of those controversies; and to how good purpose, the world is by this time a sufficient witness: but the longer and the more he considered, the worse he liked the Roman cause, and became at last to censure them with some severity; but I confess I have so great an opinion of his judgment, and the charitableness of his spirit, that I am afraid he did not think worse of them than they deserve.

But religion is not a matter of theory and orthodox notions; and it is not enough to believe aright, but we must practise accordingly; and to master our passions, and to make a right use of that α'τεξούσιον and power that God has given us over our own actions, is a greater glory than all other accomplishments that can adorn the mind of man; and therefore I shall close my character of this great personage with a touch upon some of those virtues for which his memory will be precious to all posterity. He was a person of great humility; and notwithstanding his stupendous parts, and learning, and eminency of place, he had nothing in him of pride and humour, but was courteous and affable, and of easy access, and would lend a ready ear to the complaints, yea to the impertinencies, of the meanest persons. His humility was coupled with an extraordinary piety, and I believe he spent the greatest part of his time in heaven.

Select Bibliography

A. M. Allchin, 'Anglican Spirituality', in S. Sykes and J. Booty (eds), *The Study of Anglicanism*, London: SPCK and Minneapolis: Fortress, 1988.

Reginald Askew, *Muskets and Altars: Jeremy Taylor and the Last of the Anglicans*, London: Mowbrays, 1997.

A. Bartlett, *A Passionate Balance: The Anglican Tradition*, London: Darton, Longman, and Todd and New York: Orbis, 2001.

F. R. Bolton, *The Caroline Tradition of the Church of Ireland with Particular Reference to Jeremy Taylor*, London: Longmans, 1958.

Thomas K. Carroll, *Jeremy Taylor: Selected Writings*, Classics of Western Spirituality Series, New York: Paulist Press, 1990.

Thomas Carroll, *Wisdom and Waterland: Jeremy Taylor in his Prose and Preaching Today*, Dublin: Four Courts Press, 2001.

Thomas K. Carroll, 'Jeremy Taylor: Liturgist and Ecumenist: a study of Taylor's sacramental theology and its ecumenical implications', doctoral dissertation, Angelicum University, Rome, 1970.

Robert Gathorne-Hardy and William Proctor Williams, *A Bibliography of the Writings of Jeremy Taylor*, Dakelib IL: Northern Illinois University Press, 1971.

H. E. L. Huntley, *Jeremy Taylor and the Great Rebellion: A Study of His Mind and Temper*, Ann Arbor: University of Michigan Press, 1970.

Denise Inge (ed.), *Happiness and Holiness: Thomas Traherne and His Writings*, Canterbury Studies in Spiritual Theology, Norwich: Canterbury Press, 2008.

Denise Inge, *Wanting Like a God: Desire and Freedom in Thomas Traherne*, London: SCM Press, 2009.

D. M. Loades, *Politics and The Nation, 1450–1660*, London: Collins, 1974.

H. R. McAdoo, *The Spirit of Anglicanism*, London: A&C Black, 1965.

H. R. McAdoo, *The Eucharistic Theology of Jeremy Taylor Today*, Norwich: Canterbury Press, 1988.

H. R. McAdoo, *Anglican Heritage: Spirituality and Theology*, Norwich: Canterbury Press, 1991.

H. R. McAdoo, *First of Its Kind: Jeremy Taylor's Life of Christ*, Norwich: Canterbury Press, 1994.

H. Boone Porter, *Jeremy Taylor – Liturgist*, Alcuin Club Collections 61, London: SPCK, 1979.

Geoffrey Rowell, Kenneth Stevenson and Rowan Williams (eds), *Love's Redeeming Work: The Anglican Quest for Holiness*, Oxford: University Press, 2001.

John Spurr, *The Restoration Church of England, 1646–1690*, New Haven and London: Yale University Press, 1991.

P. G. Stanwood (ed.), *Jeremy Taylor: Holy Living and Holy Dying*, vol. I: *Holy Living*, Oxford: Clarendon Press, 1989.

P. G. Stanwood (ed.), *Jeremy Taylor: Holy Living and Holy Dying*, vol. II: *Holy Dying*, Oxford: Clarendon Press, 1989.

Kenneth W. Stevenson, *Covenant of Grace Renewed: A Vision of the Eucharist in the Seventeenth Century*, London: Dalton, Longman and Todd, 1994.

Kenneth W. Stevenson, *The Mystery of Baptism in the Anglican Tradition*, Norwich: Canterbury Press, 1998.

C. J. Stranks, *The Life and Writings of Jeremy Taylor*, Church Historical Society, London: SPCK, 1952.

Charles Taliaferro and Alison J. Teply (eds), *Cambridge Platonist Spirituality*, Classics of Western Spirituality, New York: Paulist Press, 2004.

Hugh Ross Williamson, *Jeremy Taylor*, London: Dobson, 1951.

Lightning Source UK Ltd.
Milton Keynes UK
176319UK00004B/2/P

9 781853 119828